Mediating War and Identity

Mediating War and Identity

Figures of Transgression in 20th and 21st Century War Representation

Edited by Lisa Purse and Ute Wölfel

EDINBURGH
University Press

Edinburgh University Press is one of the leading university presses in the UK. We publish academic books and journals in our selected subject areas across the humanities and social sciences, combining cutting-edge scholarship with high editorial and production values to produce academic works of lasting importance. For more information visit our website: edinburghuniversitypress.com

© editorial matter and organisation Lisa Purse and Ute Wölfel, 2020, 2022
© the chapters their several authors, 2020, 2022

Edinburgh University Press Ltd
The Tun – Holyrood Road
12 (2f) Jackson's Entry
Edinburgh EH8 8PJ

First published in hardback by Edinburgh University Press 2020

Typeset in 11/13 Monotype Ehrhardt by
IDSUK (DataConnection) Ltd

A CIP record for this book is available from the British Library

ISBN 978 1 4744 4626 6 (hardback)
ISBN 978 1 4744 4627 3 (paperback)
ISBN 978 1 4744 4628 0 (webready PDF)
ISBN 978 1 4744 4629 7 (epub)

The right of Lisa Purse and Ute Wölfel to be identified as the editors of this work has been asserted in accordance with the Copyright, Designs and Patents Act 1988, and the Copyright and Related Rights Regulations 2003 (SI No. 2498).

Contents

List of Figures		vii
Acknowledgements		ix
Notes on the Contributors		x
1	Introduction Lisa Purse and Ute Wölfel	1
2	Momentary Rupture? *Dawn* (1928) and the Transgressive Potential of the Edith Cavell Case Claudia Sternberg	14
3	'An act of wilful defiance': Objection, Protest and Rebellion in the Imperial War Museum's First World War Galleries Rebecca Clare Dolgoy	37
4	Figures of Transgression in Representations of the First World War on British Television Emma Hanna	54
5	The End of Transgression: Fritz Bauer as Traitor on the German Screen Ute Wölfel	75
6	'Just another Kraut'? The Wehrmacht Traitor as 'Good German' in Hollywood's *Decision before Dawn* (1951) Patrick Major	97
7	Religious Pacifism and the Hollywood War Film: From *Sergeant York* (1941) to *Hacksaw Ridge* (2017) Guy Westwell	117
8	Military Masculinity and the Deserting Soldier in *Stop-Loss* (2008) Thomas Ærvold Bjerre	135

9	Activist, Mother, Filmmaker: Competing Transgressions in the Syrian War Documentary *Lisa Purse*	152
10	Marie Colvin – The War Hero and the 'Nasty Woman' *Agnieszka Piotrowska*	171

Index 192

Figures

2.1 'Woman and the War Machine': a proto-feminist peace politics? Still from *Dawn* (1928). (Source: Cinémathèque Royale de Belgique.) 23

2.2 'We killed': Mars and the fugitive boy soldier. Still from *Dawn*. (Source: Cinémathèque Royale de Belgique.) 24

2.3 At eye level: Cavell's residual agency before death. Still from *Dawn* (1928). (Source: Cinémathèque Royale de Belgique.) 29

4.1 Percy Toplis (Paul McGann) impersonating a dead officer. Still from *The Monocled Mutineer* (BBC, 1986). 59

4.2 A scene from the deserters' camp. Still from *The Monocled Mutineer*. 60

4.3 Tommy Shelby (Cillian Murphy, right) comforts Danny 'Whiz Bang' (Samuel Edward-Cook). Still from series one of *Peaky Blinders* (BBC, 2014). 70

5.1 Karl Angermann as an outsider in his wife's conservative family. Still from *Der Staat gegen Fritz Bauer* (2015). 88

5.2 Bauer and Hell with the 'salon' in the background: 'A reckoning with the past is necessary not because the old Germany deserves it, but because the new Germany needs it.' Still from *Die Akte General* (2016). 90

5.3 Angermann and Bauer in Bauer's modernist flat with a Feininger painting. Still from *Der Staat gegen Fritz Bauer* (2015). 91

6.1 Karl Maurer/Happy (Oskar Werner) sacrificing himself to save the mission. Still from *Decision before Dawn* (1951). 102

6.2 'So die all TRAITORS TO THE FATHERLAND!' Wehrmacht drumhead justice. Still from *Decision before Dawn*. 106

6.3 Hilde (Hildegard Knef): 'there are thousands and thousands like me'. Still from *Decision before Dawn*. 107

6.4	Hitler Youth Kurt (Adi Lödel). Still from *Decision before Dawn*.	108
6.5	Lt Rennick (Richard Basehart). Still from *Decision before Dawn*.	108
7.1	York joins the religious community and embraces pacifism. Still from *Sergeant York* (1941).	123
7.2	York determines to reconcile his pacifism with the need to defend his country. Still from *Sergeant York*.	126
7.3	Doss's pacifism sanctifies military violence. Still from *Hacksaw Ridge* (2016).	130
8.1	Ryan Phillippe as Staff Sergeant Brandon King in charge of roadblock duty in Tikrit, Iraq. Still from *Stop-Loss* (2008).	142
8.2	Staff Sergeant Brandon King and Channing Tatum as Sgt Steve Shriver. Still from *Stop-Loss*.	145
8.3	Staff Sergeant Brandon King and Sgt Steve Shriver on their way back to Iraq. Still from *Stop-Loss*.	147
9.1	Raghda in a moment of introspection, silently contemplating her youngest child. Still from *A Syrian Love Story* (2015).	158
9.2	The bound feet of a toddler killed in the Syrian war. Still from *For Sama* (2019).	164
9.3	A mother carries her dead child, Mohammad Ameen, from the hospital. Still from *For Sama*.	165
10.1	Marie Colvin on holiday in France in 2008. Image courtesy of Richard Flaye.	172
10.2	Marie Colvin on the Thames, on the old boat she shared with Richard Flaye. Image courtesy of Richard Flaye.	175
10.3	Marie Colvin and Richard Flaye at a family party in 2008. Image courtesy of Richard Flaye.	179
10.4	Marie Colvin on a river walk in Hammersmith near her home in 2010. Image courtesy of Richard Flaye.	188

Acknowledgements

Thank you to Gillian Leslie, Richard Strachan and the rest of the team at Edinburgh University Press for their excellent work preparing this book for publication and their patience as it was brought to fruition, and to Richard Flaye for giving permission to reproduce photographs from his private collection for the final chapter in the volume.

This book finds its origins in the lively discussions arising from a research workshop at the University of Reading in 2015, which was co-organised by the Department for Languages and Cultures and the Department of Film, Theatre and Television and hosted by the School of Law. The workshop was supported by the Rights and Representation Research Theme, in what was then the Faculty of Arts, Humanities and Social Sciences. We would like to thank the workshop's supporters and its participants, Thomas Ærvold Bjerre, Andreas Behnke, Susan Breau, Hilary Footitt, Alexander Hastie, Beatrice Heuser, Suheyla Tolunay İşlek, Karol Jóźwiak, Charles Leavitt, Sue Malvern, Jessica Sage, Heike Schmidt and Claudia Sternberg. More broadly, the book is the result of a dynamic interdisciplinary network of scholars working on war, conflict and representation at the University of Reading and elsewhere. We would like to thank the Heritage and Creativity Research Theme and in particular Roberta Gilchrist for encouraging this enriching interdisciplinary exchange in word and deed, and Jonathan Bignell, John Gibbs and Anna McMullan for their support throughout the writing process.

Lisa Purse thanks the students of her Representing Conflict on Stage and Screen module for willingly reflecting on often challenging films; Teresa Murjas, Sonya Chenery and Christina Hellmich for thought-provoking discussions on aspects of conflict representation, Iris Luppa for thinking breaks, Tamzin Morphy and Sandra and Rodney Purse for writing time, and Mia for being here. Ute Wölfel is grateful for the patience of her students on the War on Screen module who never tired of discussing lengthy theories on war, genre and treason. Her special thanks go to John Sandford who has accompanied all thinking and writing over the years with a scrutinising eye and inspiring challenges.

Notes on the Contributors

Thomas Ærvold Bjerre is Associate Professor in American Studies at the University of Southern Denmark. His research focuses on American popular culture with a particular interest in representations of 9/11 and the 'war on terror' in film, photography and literature. He has published on these topics in *Visualizing War* (2017), *Journal of War and Culture Studies* and *Orbis Litterarum*. He co-wrote the first Danish book about the American Western and has also published widely on southern literature and film in *Mississippi Quarterly*, *The Appalachian Journal*, *American Studies in Scandinavia* as well as in *Rough South, Rural South: Region and Class in Recent Southern Literature* and the forthcoming *The South in Fiction and Film: Essays in Adaptation*. Bjerre has also co-edited *Southern Exposure* (2017) and *The Scourges of the South* (2014).

Rebecca Clare Dolgoy was recently appointed Curator of Natural Resources and Industrial Technologies at Ingenium (Canada's Museums of Science and Innovation). She brings an interdisciplinary perspective to the portfolio. Her research on memory and museums explores relationships between material culture and public memory. She is committed to collaborative research and to developing creative processes of stakeholder engagement, partnership development and public scholarship. After completing her DPhil in Oxford, Rebecca has been Ottawa-based since 2015. In addition to her role at Ingenium, she is an Adjunct Research Professor in the School of Indigenous and Canadian Studies at Carleton University.

Emma Hanna is a Lecturer in the School of History, University of Kent. She has published widely in international journals and edited collections along themes of the First World War including contemporary memory and memorialisation, the media, wartime music and cinema. She is the author of *The Great War on the Small Screen: Representing the First World War in Contemporary Britain* (Edinburgh University Press, 2009) and *Sounds of*

War: Music in the British Armed Forces During the Great War (Cambridge University Press, 2020). Emma was a Co-Investigator on two major research and public engagement projects: *Gateways to the First World War* (AHRC, 2014–19) and *Reflections on the Centenary of the First World War: Learning and Legacies for the Future* (AHRC, 2017–20).

Patrick Major is Professor of Modern History at the University of Reading where he has taught since 2008, having previously lectured at Warwick University. He divides research between the history of Berlin (*Behind the Berlin Wall: East Germany and the Frontiers of Power*, OUP, 2010, currently investigating the wartime bombing of the city) and film representations of the 'good German', including most recently Erwin Rommel in 'Shooting Rommel: The Desert Fox (1951) and Hollywood's Public-Private Diplomacy', *Historical Journal of Film, Radio and Television*, 2019, 39 (2), pp. 209–32.

Agnieszka Piotrowska is an award-winning filmmaker and theorist. She is the Head of School, Film, Media and Performing Arts, and a Professor of Film and Cultural Studies at the University for the Creative Arts, UK. She is a Visiting Professor at Gdansk University, Poland. She is best known for her acclaimed documentary *Married to the Eiffel Tower* (2009) screened globally in sixty countries. She has worked extensively in Zimbabwe producing films in creative partnerships with artists there. Piotrowska has written extensively on psychoanalysis and cinema and is the author of the monographs *Psychoanalysis and Ethics in Documentary Film* (2014, Routledge), *Black and White: Cinema, Politics and the Arts in Zimbabwe* (2017) and *The Nasty Woman and Neo Femme Fatale in Contemporary Cinema* (2019). She has edited three books on psychoanalysis and cinema including *Femininity and Psychoanalysis* (2019) and *Creative Practice Research* (2020). She is a founding scholar at the British Psychoanalytic Council.

Lisa Purse is Professor of Film Studies at the University of Reading. She has published widely on genre cinema, digital film technologies, and the representation of war and conflict on screen. She is the author of *Contemporary Action Cinema* (EUP, 2011) and *Digital Imaging in Popular Cinema* (EUP, 2013), and the co-editor with Christina Hellmich of *Disappearing War: Interdisciplinary Perspectives on Cinema and Erasure in the Post- 9/11 World* (EUP, 2017). She is a member of the Ways of War Centre and an executive member of the Centre for Film Aesthetics and Cultures at the University of Reading.

Claudia Sternberg is Senior Lecturer in Cultural Studies at the University of Leeds. Her research and publications have focused on screenwriting, Black, Asian and Jewish British film and television, civilian internment and media representations of the First World War since 1919. She was a member of the Legacies of War hub at the University of Leeds, which facilitated research and public engagement connected to the First World War Centenary in 2014–18. Her books include *The First World War in Britain and the Media Discourses of Memory: Autobiography – Novel – Film, 1919–1999* (Könighausen & Neumann, 2005) and *European Cinema in Motion: Migrant and Diasporic Film in Contemporary Europe* (co-edited with D. Berghahn) (Palgrave Macmillan, 2010).

Guy Westwell is Reader in Film Studies at Queen Mary University of London and author of *War Cinema – Hollywood on the Front-line* (Wallflower, 2006), *Parallel Lines: Post-9/11 American Cinema* (Wallflower, 2012) and co-author of *The Oxford Dictionary of Film Studies* (Oxford University Press, 2020).

Ute Wölfel is Associate Professor in German Studies at the University of Reading. She has published widely in *Studies in European Cinema*, *Modern Languages Review*, *German Life and Letters* and *Oxford German Studies* among others on East German literature and film and on German war cinema. Among her edited and co-edited volumes are *Literarisches Feld DDR* (Königshausen & Neumann, 2005) and *Remembering the German Democratic Republic: Divided Memory in a United Germany* (Palgrave Macmillan 2011). She was PI of the project 'Children in German War (Con)-Texts 1945–1949' (British Academy 2014–16) and is currently working on East German antifascist film (Leverhulme, 2020–1).

CHAPTER 1

Introduction

Lisa Purse and Ute Wölfel

Conflict and war are constitutive. They shape and reshape international, intercultural and bodily territories, and shift how people feel about themselves and others. As Edward Said famously pointed out, twentieth-century human relations were structured by 'imaginative geograph[ies] and histor[ies]' of difference and distance (2003 [1978]: 55) rooted in a colonial fear of the other. Derek Gregory argues convincingly that public debate and thus public feeling about war's prospect, its spectacle and its consequences are still organised by such 'architectures of enmity', using as his case study the post-9/11 military campaigns of the US, Israel and Britain in Afghanistan, Palestine and Iraq, which 'turned on the cultural construction of their opponents as outsiders' (2004: 17, 28). In this way, as Christine Sylvester explains, war becomes a 'social institution', shaped by the relationship of fears, experiences and emotions to 'the prescribed war scripts' that dictate who are designated heroes and villains, victims and perpetrators in a particular geopolitical and historical moment (2013: 4, 6).

Cultural representation occupies an ambiguous position in relation to conflict and war. On the one hand, it can be weaponised. Audiovisual rhetoric can be deployed to persuade and reinforce state-sponsored or dominant cultural 'war scripts', to reinforce normative perceptions of who constitutes friend and foe, and how they should be treated. Judith Butler notes the extent to which this weaponisation often elides as much as it shows: 'states or other war perpetrators' seek 'to control the visual and narrative dimensions of war ... delimit[ing] public discourse by establishing and disposing the sensuous parameters of reality itself' (2010: xi). On the other hand, cultural representation can be a space for counternarratives to emerge, for thought and emotion to be provoked differently. And despite cinema's long history as a tool in the propaganda machinery of warfaring groups, Michael Shapiro (2009) argues that this is a cultural form which can also operate to bring spectators back from controlled narratives to the complexities and tensions of the real. Shapiro reaches back to Siegfried Kracauer's idea of cinema as an experiential encounter with 'things in their concreteness' rather than their abstraction (Kracauer 1960: 296), Walter Benjamin's description of cinema's capacity to invite the spectator into the 'position of a critic' (Benjamin 1968: 228), and Jacques Rancière's more recent assertion that cinema can disrupt 'the human tendency to place oneself at "the center of the universe of images"' (Shapiro 2009: 5, quoting Rancière 2006: 111), to argue for cinema as a privileged site at which conflict and its ramifications can be addressed: 'The worlds of pain, suffering, and grievance remain readily available for reflection and renegotiation' (2009: 155).

In this book, we look at those figures who sit in uncomfortable relation to architectures of enmity and prescribed war scripts; those figures who don't 'fit' dominant or state-sponsored narratives about war, either by accident or design; those figures who transgress the borders between 'us' and 'them', enemy and friend, perpetrator and victim. We call these 'figures of transgression', and we identify them as a crucial ingredient in cultural productions that seek to understand conflict and war and their aftermath, to reflect on dominant narratives about who wages war and why, and on its consequences for people, communities and nations. We examine their cultural function as a specific locus at which contested or competing ideas about war are aired and interrogated. Sharing Shapiro's view of the importance of cinema as a site for productive thought, we consider the occurrence of figures of transgression using the mass medium of cinema as our primary case study, but also signal how such an examination could be productively broadened out to other forms of cultural production by including case studies on television and the museum. The book looks at figures of transgression in relation to particular conflicts, to show how these figures often operate as a key site for reflection and renegotiation of dominant war scripts about collective injury, loss, violence, culpability and post-conflict national identity.

It is also important to acknowledge that this book emerges at a present moment mired in conflict's contemporary manifestations and its legacies from history, a moment at which political and social positions are expressed increasingly in terms of polarisation and opposition, public debate seems to find little common ground, and discussions of national identity are equally polarised and often protectionist. This is the era of US President Donald Trump and his isolationist approaches to immigration, war and international trade; of the resurgence of right-wing leaders and nationalist, populist movements in Europe and elsewhere; of domestic and extraterritorial attacks on journalists and democratic elections; and of a climate denialism whose vigour matches that of the climate protesters seeking to encourage leaders to address impending ecological disaster. This is the era of 'fake news' in which the rhetoric of injury, treachery and betrayal is frequently deployed by both right- and left-wing politicians and commentators. At such a moment, it is crucial to continue to argue for nuanced critical thinking, and to identify and celebrate those aspects of cultural production that encourage reflection, thought and an empathetic, inclusive attitude to others. It is in this spirit that we have brought together this collection of essays, and it is in this spirit that we have chosen to focus on the figure who declines easy or fixed positions within the public negotiation of war and conflict: the figure of transgression.

Transgression in a Polarised Present

As a frame for the articles that follow, some reflection is necessary on the ways in which the idea of transgression has gained currency in the contemporary moment. For Chris Jenks, transgression is 'to go beyond the bounds or limits set by a commandment, the law or the convention'; it is 'that conduct which breaks rules or exceeds boundaries' (2003: 2). Jenks describes transgression as a 'deeply reflexive act of denial and affirmation' (ibid.), an act that 'does not deny limits or boundaries, rather it exceeds them and thus complements them' (ibid.: 7). The radical potential of transgression can often be curtailed, precisely because transgressors, 'through their remarked differences . . . work to firm up the boundaries which give form and substance to the conceptual categories from which they are excluded' (ibid.: 185). Writing in 2003, Jenks situates the concept's importance in relation to the destabilisation of a shared social contract that he argues defines the late capitalist, postmodernist period, and the concomitant drive to exceed limits that characterises globalisation, technologisation and individualism in the twenty-first century (ibid.: 4–8). Yet the importance of the concept of transgression to geopolitics in particular, including war and conflict, cannot be understated. Transgression is often deployed as the designation for all who are not the category 'us', architectures of enmity dictating political rhetoric in particularly sharp ways around military action, its justification, initiation and aftermath.

Transgression can be dangerous, challenging accepted allegiances, disturbing dominant hierarchies, contesting received wisdom and asserted certainties, shining a light on and at the same time questioning the very core of authority that victory and even survival seems to depend on. As a result, in highly polarised contexts, the idea of transgression is invoked in public and political rhetoric in ways that sometimes very purposefully point away from transgression's actual radical potential. A much-discussed example is the aftermath of the terrorist attacks on the World Trade Center and the Pentagon in the US on 11 September 2001. The attacks precipitated a strident reiteration of the self/other binary: then-President George Bush Jnr's 2001 State of the Union address following the terrorist attacks made clear that, in his words, 'Either you are with us or with the terrorists' (Bush 2001: 69). This assertion categorised as transgressive any person who did not wholly embrace US domestic and foreign policy post-9/11, and in doing so purposefully obscured those who might seek to question the direction of government and military policy in the ensuing years.[1] More recently, social transgressions such as racist, homophobic, ableist and misogynist rhetoric and xenophobic nationalist discourse have been brandished by populist politicians to signal their authenticity and readiness to take action, and thus shore up their conservative world view, including Donald Trump in the US, Jair Bolsonaro in Brazil, Viktor Orbán in Hungary and Narendra Modi in India (see, for example, Winberg 2017). In this way, transgression can be radical or normative in its relationship with the 'norms' it transgresses, while the fixities it challenges are equally open to instability, contestation and renegotiation.

In the above brief examples, the deployment of and suppression of transgression is used to political ends. It is often tied to nationalist discourse, with the invocation of an idea of protecting the national interest, frequently steeped in a romanticisation of past conflicts and conquests and of the motherland or fatherland. This has, for example, characterised the public and political discourse around Britain's decision to leave the EU. From the 2016 referendum campaign and vote onwards, to Boris Johnson's election campaign in 2019 (the centrepiece of which was a commitment to 'get Brexit done'), pro-Leave commentators and politicians mobilised a set of slogans that emphasised sovereignty, territory and control of borders and laws, and characterised the UK as under threat from border transgressions by migrants and European bureaucrats. Moreover, the referendum result produced a polarisation of society predominantly along age and education lines in which both pro-Brexit and pro-EU contingents named each other as transgressors: pro-Brexit commentators and citizens were accused of the transgressions of racism and ignorance while pro-EU commentators and citizens were accused of the transgressions of fearmongering and unpatriotic sentiment (Norris and Inglehart 2019). The sudden strict divide thus activated transgression as a priority concept in the battle about political power.

Transgression exists as an act, a breaking of a demarcated norm, rule or law, but at the same time it is an interpretation of an act which might not be a conscious rule-breaking but is perceived and categorised as such. Extreme and polarised situations reinforce rules and laws per se, what is permitted and prohibited behaviour. In such situations both the breaking of a law or rule and the perceived breaking of one are commonly linked to 'treason', to the giving away of the country to the enemy. The term 'treason' here serves as a loose category summarising all severe forms of transgression, that is those judged (by the categoriser) as hostile or adverse in their effect on the national interest. In the current political climate of growing division, 'treason' has acquired the status of a war cry (Krischer 2019). Thus in the wake of the Brexit referendum, in which 48 per cent of voters sought to remain in the EU, and 52 per cent sought to leave, Brexit supporters charged Remainers (who were still campaigning to stay in the EU) with 'betraying the people' and 'giving away the country'; exemplary in this respect was the demand of the Tory MEP David Campbell Bannerman to try 'extreme EU loyalty' for treason (Chakelian 2018). In the US, those who defy President Trump are routinely accused of the same. House Intelligence chairman Adam Schiff and House Speaker Nancy Pelosi, both key to Trump's impeachment inquiry and subsequent impeachment, have been explicitly accused by Trump of 'treason' (Elfrink 2019: n.p.), while National Security Advisor to Trump, John Bolton, who has written a book which allegedly links Trump to the Ukraine scandal (in which Trump is accused of withholding aid to Ukraine to persuade them to find evidence of misconduct on the son of potential Democrat opponent Joe Biden) is called a 'traitor' (Dawsey et al. 2020: n.p.).

The relation of such accusations to the legislative frameworks of particular countries can be distant to say the least, but the socio-cultural frameworks of media reporting, political allegiance and lived experience in which they circulate is significant. Schiff, Pelosi and Bolton have not committed treason according to US law, but Trump supporters hear the language of treason and have their commitment to Trump emotionally reinforced as a result. In a similar way, Edward Snowden, who as a CIA subcontractor leaked highly classified National Security Agency information to reveal the extent of government surveillance in the US and elsewhere in 2013, was frequently accused of treason by politicians and commentators. Ex-CIA chief James Woolsey and Republican Mike Pompeo both suggested that the 'traitor' Snowden should receive a death sentence because the leaks hampered intelligence capability (McLaughlin 2015: n.p.; Kasperowicz 2016: n.p.). Yet these assertions are at odds with the criminal charges brought. As André Krischer points out:

> The question of whether Snowden really committed treason in the legal sense of the American constitution has been widely discussed and differently answered. The criminal prosecution authorities did not take up the charge – they have charged Snowden for espionage. However, that doesn't change the point that for many Americans Snowden is a 'traitor' at least in the moral sense. (Krischer 2019: 7)[2]

Notably these categorisations of Snowden as a traitor emerge during a period of increased threat perception, a product of an uptick in domestic US and European terrorist activity, and sustained threat rhetoric from politicians (Woolsey's comments were made in the wake of the Paris terrorist attacks).

Transgression, War and Cultural Representation

Krischer notes that '[c]oncepts of treason also imply scenarios of highest danger and collective threat' (ibid.), a moment most palpable in war. In military conflict and war as well as their beginnings and aftermaths, the figures of such 'existential' transgressions are usually the deserter, the conscientious objector, the actual traitor, the mutineer or others disobeying orders, such as the pacifist, the coward or the pillager. To label such figures as traitors simply because of their disengagement from what Sarah Cole has called the 'organizing oppositions of war' (2009: 27) marks them with highly negative connotations; for example, in Roman law treason was understood not to just damage but indeed destroy the community (Krischer 2019: 20), and the more recent reactions to Snowden's actions reveal the extent to which this meaning adheres. Audiovisual media that depict transgression in a military conflict or pre- or post-conflict setting catches these heightened moments and thus offers the opportunity to catalyse or intervene in the wider cultural debates focused on the act of transgression and the figure committing the act.

Film has a status as a significant mass media form in the twentieth century, a popular form which has often been deployed for propaganda purposes, as well as less strident forms of socio-cultural positioning; it continues to be important as a site for negotiations around national identity in the twenty-first century. Not only have cinema's technologies of vision developed alongside the war machine's technologies of vision, but so have concepts of national cinema which emerged with the media-war of the First World War. Cinema as a result has always been engaged in the documenting and cultural 'processing' of war and its legacies, with the war film being one of the most consistent genres. To illustrate, among the Academy Award nominations of the last five years were *1917* (Sam Mendes, 2019), *Jojo Rabbit* (Taika Waititi, 2019), *Darkest Hour* (Joe Wright, 2017) and *Dunkirk* (Christopher Nolan, 2017), *Hacksaw Ridge* (Mel Gibson, 2016), *13 Hours: The Secret Soldiers of Benghazi* (Michael Bay, 2016), *Land of Mine* (Martin Zandvliet, 2015), *A War* (Tobias Lindholm, 2015) and *American Sniper* (Clint Eastwood, 2014). This volume seeks to address that representational history, while acknowledging other visual and audiovisual contexts in which negotiations of transgressions generated by war and military conflict have taken place.

This book shines a light on figures of transgression because they are often marginalised in public discussion about war and conflict, yet play key roles in the re-thinking of cultural, national and community identity. Because their acts of transgression take place in extreme circumstances of stress for the whole community, they foreground the foundations of that community and offer them to scrutiny; in particular they raise questions of agency, moral responsibility and culpability. Even under severe circumstances such as war where an act of transgression may break a rule in the legal sense, transgression retains its characteristic as fundamentally and foremost an im/moral act (Parikh 2009; Jervis 1999; Åkerström 1991). These figures, and their cultural representations, may be marginalised, but their moral challenge serves as a site of intense public debate and negotiations. Transgression is, as Jenks reminds us, 'a touchstone of social relations' (ibid.: 33) and throws into the light the relation between centre and periphery, included and excluded, self and other.

Using an interdisciplinary lens that accommodates analysis of the narratives which frame these figures and their audiovisual depiction on the one hand, and analysis of the socio-cultural, political and historical context in which they emerge on the other, this book sets out to understand the complex function of transgressors in representations of war, and seeks to map a history of forms of identity negotiation linked to these figures. Within this process, we understand the figures of transgression to be 'rather a dynamic force of cultural reproduction' (Jenks 2003: 7); their analysis will help the reader to better comprehend how military conflict and cultural change intersect.

The book brings together scholars from a range of disciplines to understand the variety of mechanisms and connections that link military conflict, cultural change and cultural representation. With the focus on conflicts from the First World War to the 'war on terror', we look at the functions of figures of transgression as part of a wider cultural preoccupation with the connotations and consequences of acts of 'border crossing'. We argue that these figures operate as a crucial site for culturally vital processes of 'thinking through' architectures of enmity as complex processes of identity formation. We claim that the representation of transgression in war and military conflict is never just a question of showing illegal or im/moral acts but of exposing their wider social meaning linked to class, ethnicity, gender, sexuality, religion, political conviction and their role on the 'national stage' where the collective negotiates values.

The volume begins with representations of figures of transgression in the First World War from the interwar years to the present. The liminal space which conscientious objectors, pacifists, protesters, mutineers or alien nationals in occupied territories held with regard to the law as well as public perception has been used to negotiate the basis on which the national collective is founded in terms of territory, allies, class and voice, as well as gender. Applying different approaches to the minority position of the transgressors, the chapters describe strategies of othering and exclusion of the transgressor from national narratives of heroism, cohesion and homogeneity, but equally explore constellations that have opened up the traditional and often routinised stories of the nation to include the transgressors and their objection/antagonism. Claudia Sternberg's chapter on cultural representations of Edith Cavell offers an intriguing study of transgression as potential and as part of the rule. Taking the myth of Edith Cavell – the young and innocent nurse slaughtered by the 'relentless enemy' – as her starting point, Sternberg focuses on an early film adaptation, Wilcox's *Dawn* (UK, 1928), as an interpretation which actualised the figure's potential to transgress the very lines that have elsewhere confined her within narratives of British heroism and virtuousness vis-à-vis the German 'Hun'. Centrally, it was the rewriting of gender assumptions which permitted the film to question the national self-definition and politically polarised war narrative the figure of Cavell had – and has since – historically reinforced.

Sternberg's discussion of a momentary narrative shift to include the transgressive acts finds a complement in Rebecca Dolgoy's chapter on the Imperial War Museum's presentation of conscientious objectors, soldier-poets and their protest, and Irish Republicans. Dolgoy traces the curatorial strategies which stifle the perspective of the transgressive other in one exhibition while celebrating it in another, which allow, at least temporarily, the simultaneity of 'contesting narratives'. In both chapters, the situational specificity of transgression becomes palpable with regard to processes of historical re-evaluation of the act of transgression, linked to changing frames of interpretation but also of categorisation – that is, who is designated as a transgressor and for what transgressions at particular points in history. While it seems possible to include middle-class protest against the First World War's violence and futility to a point and celebrate conscientious objection in the context of the peace movement (though not in the context of the British war effort), Dolgoy highlights the difficulty in representing those acts defying the very territorial core of political self-understanding as Empire. Cultural and political shifts emerging around figures of transgression are often not permanent but resemble momentary visions of moral sympathy beyond self-entrenchment.

Impermanence is characteristic also of the continuous re-framing of deserters, mutineers and conscientious objectors in the British television productions analysed by Emma Hanna. The chapter follows small-screen productions from the 1960s to the 2010s and reveals the changing attitudes towards transgressors across that timeframe, ranging from their complete absence from representations of the First World War in early examples, to providing a perspective for rewriting the earlier war story, through to attempting to contain anew their transgressive potential. Hanna's overview reveals how closely the interpretation of the transgressor as either a destructive or productive force is linked to shifts in, for example, political questions of class justice but also concepts of historiography.

As a figure of negotiation within and beyond the collective, transgressors can play key roles in the aftermath of conflicts. The chapters on representations of transgressors following the Second World War explore the function that on-screen acts of transgression have to mediate the position of Germany as a morally defeated nation. Ute Wölfel's chapter looks at recent feature films about the re-émigré, jurist and attorney general Dr Fritz Bauer, whose efforts to confront the German majority with the atrocities committed, supported or condoned by Germans were perceived by many as a treacherous attack on the collective's self-definition as 'victim' of the war. While people like Bauer did successfully initiate a political and moral transformation, their representations still reveal resentment about the historical challenge which at the time questioned core notions of the self.

The transgressor as a much needed and yet distrusted mediator is central also to Patrick Major's contribution on the 1951 co-production *Decision before Dawn* (US, Anatol Litvak). The question of how defeated Germany could recover a sense of moral justice from within, and establish a tradition that would be acceptable to the compromised nation as well as the Allies and the wider world, gave the defector a special role to play. The chapter details the production process and the filmmaker's and producers' decisions, drawing out the difficulties the screen 'defector as mediator' posed to the task of attracting a German audience which could easily vent feelings of 'betrayal', and an American audience, on the other hand, which could fail to see what advantages defecting could bring.

Despite warnings Litvak received about presenting a German defector as a reliable and quite heroic ally of the Americans in 1951, the US have their own tradition of military counter-narratives, particularly organised around the figure of the deserter. Thomas Bjerre traces this tradition up to representations of the Iraq War. If the defector in the postwar film asked the question what a 'good' or 'moral' German looks like, the figure of the deserter in the recent *Stop-Loss* (Kimberley Peirce, 2008) helps to pose the question of what a 'good' man is in this fraught context. Bjerre's chapter outlines the tensions between the socially normative ideals of masculinity and their encapsulation and preservation in strictly guarded notions of 'soldierly masculinity' in the face of the traumas of war. The dictate of the military and masculine ideal exerts highly gendered constraints which shape their perception by society while clashing with the psychological responses of soldiers to war. The figure of transgression offers the opportunity to understand masculinity ideals outside of military confines and their gendered polarisation, though it remains temporary; the national quest of fighting a war in Iraq is reasserted at the film's close, preventing a fundamental undermining of the military or its campaigns.

The challenge war poses to the morally engaged military man is also explored through the figure of the pacifist, as Guy Westwell points out. A rare figure in popular American film due to its questioning of the very necessity and legitimacy of war, the pacifist, when he does appear on screen, is necessarily a religious pacifist. Here pacifism can be depicted because it is founded on a historically dominant US faith – Christianity. Westwell's comparison of two Hollywood films that focus on religious pacifism, *Sergeant York* (Howard Hawks, 1941) and *Hacksaw Ridge* (Mel Gibson, 2017), offers an insight into the reflexivity of transgression as manifested in this uncommon branch of the war film. The films explore the transgressive potential of pacifism, and while it might be easy to see these films as straightforwardly closing down pacifism's threat to the US military project, what emerges instead is a more nuanced picture in which the possibility of alternative ways of thinking about war and its effects are held open.

The final two chapters of the volume open up a different perspective on war and transgression in that they both discuss women whose political and humanitarian engagement with current violent conflicts, notably the Syrian civil war, demonstrate the complexity of transgression as a 'dynamic force in cultural reproduction' (Jenks 2003: 7). In Lisa Purse's chapter on activist mothers in Syria, the proliferation mechanisms of transgression are explored. The political activism of women against the Assad regime, a political transgression, generates the breaking of social norms for women, especially around gendered expectations of behaviour and agency. In the case of *For Sama* (Waad al-Kateab and Edward Watts, UK/Syria, 2019), a film by a woman 'citizen' filmmaker about life in the war zone, the norms of what western mainstream media is prepared to screen are also transgressed by the documentation of the death of children and the pain of their shocked parents. But even where the documentation of the violence does not include the dying and the dead, the transgressive activist mother defies western expectations in terms of private and political endings. For Raghda in *A Syrian Love Story* (Sean McAllister, UK, 2015) fulfilment is not the safety of France and family life, but the continued fight for Syria's freedom.

An acute concern over endings of activist women's lives also drives the chapter by Agnieszka Piotrowska. Like Purse, Piotrowska demonstrates the extent to which professional women's lives are still framed by patriarchal narratives that label them transgressive and unruly when they seek to work outside gendered norms around risk and self-determination. Fittingly for this final chapter of a book about the potential of transgression, Piotrowska chooses a transgressive form for her own reflections, drawing on feminist autobiographical forms alongside more traditional scholarly discussion to explore these pressing issues. Her memory of the war journalist and friend Marie Colvin, who was murdered in Syria in 2012, and the analysis of Colvin's representations, poses the same urgent question which was broached right at the outset of the anthology, in the first chapter on Edith Cavell: should we give in to the tendency to stifle the transgressor, whose commitment to human(ist) change and the consequent breaking of gender norms undermines social expectations, or can we actualise patterns of disruption in our cultural representations and in our wider social and national lives, to keep the transgressive potential alive and productive?

Notes

1. To read more about this moment of polarised rhetoric, excellent starting points include Roy (2001), Hunt (2002), McAllister (2002), Holloway (2008) and Westwell (2014).
2. Translation by Ute Wölfel.

Works Cited

Åkerström, Malin (1991) *Betrayal and Betrayers – The Sociology of Treachery*. New Brunswick, NJ: Routledge.

Benjamin, Walter (1968) [1935] 'The Work of Art in the Age of Mechanical Reproduction', trans. Harry Zohn, in Hannah Arendt (ed.), *Illuminations: Essays and Reflections*. New York: Schocken, pp. 217–51.

Bush Jnr, George W. (2001) 'Address to the Joint Session of the 107th Congress', United States Capitol, Washington, DC, 20 September, collected in *Selected Speeches of President George W. Bush, 2001–2008*. Washington, DC: White House Archives, pp. 65–73, available at <https://georgewbush-whitehouse.archives.gov/infocus/bushrecord/documents/Selected_Speeches_George_W_Bush.pdf> (last accessed 10 January 2020).

Butler, Judith (2010) *Frames of War: When Is Life Grievable?* London: Verso.

Chakelian, Anoosh (2018) 'From Jihadis to Remainers: Britain's Sinister Thirst for a New Law against Treason', *New Statesman*, 26 July <https://www.newstatesman.com/politics/uk/2018/07/jihadis-remainers-britain-s-sinister-thirst-new-law-against-treason> (last accessed 26 February 2020).

Cole, Sarah (2009) 'People in War', in Kate McLoughlin (ed.), *The Cambridge Companion to War Writing*. Cambridge: Cambridge University Press, pp. 25–37.

Cunningham, Karen (2002) *Imaginary Betrayals: Subjectivity and the Discourses of Treason in Early Modern England*. Philadelphia, PA: University of Philadelphia Press.

Dawsey, Josh, Hamburger, Tom and Leonnig, Carol D. (2020) 'Trump Wants to Block Bolton's Book, Claiming Most Conversations Are Classified', *Washington Post*, 22 February <https://www.washingtonpost.com/politics/trump-wants-to-block-boltons-book-claiming-all-conversations-are-classified/2020/02/21/6a4f4b34-54d1-11ea-9e47-59804be1dcfb_story.html> (last accessed 26 February 2020).

Elfrink, Tim (2019) 'Trump Suggests Pelosi, Schiff Committed "Treason," Should Be Impeached', *Washington Post*, 7 October <https://www.washingtonpost.com/nation/2019/10/07/trump-pelosi-schiff-impeach-treason-tweet/> (last accessed 26 February 2020).

Gregory, Derek (2004) *The Colonial Present*. Oxford: Blackwell.

Holloway, David (2008) *9/11 and the War on Terror*. Edinburgh: Edinburgh University Press.

Hunt, Michael H. (2002) 'In the Wake of September 11: The Clash of What?', *Journal of American History*, 89 (2), History and September 11: A Special Issue (September), pp. 416–25.

Norris, Pippa and Inglehart, Ronald (2019) *Cultural Backlash: Trump, Brexit, and Authoritarian Populism*. Cambridge: Cambridge University Press.

Jenks, Chris (2003) *Transgression*. London: Routledge.

Jervis, John (1999) *Transgressing the Modern: Explorations in the Western Experience of Otherness*. Oxford: Blackwell.

Kasperowicz, Pete (2016) 'Lawmaker: "Traitor" Snowden Deserves Death Penalty', *Washington Examiner*, 11 February <https://www.washingtonexaminer.com/lawmaker-traitor-snowden-deserves-death-penalty> (last accessed 26 February 2020).

Kracauer, Siegfried (1960) *Theory of Film: The Redemption of Physical Reality*. Princeton, NJ: Princeton University Press.

Krischer, André (2019) 'Von Judas bis zum Unwort des Jahres 2016: Verrat als Deutungsmuster und seine Deutungsrahmen im Wandel', in André Krischer (ed.), *Verräter: Geschichte eines Deutungsmusters*, Wien, Köln and Weimar: Böhlau Verlag, pp. 7–44.

McAlister, Melani (2002) 'A Cultural History of the War without End', *Journal of American History*, 89 (2), History and September 11: A Special Issue (September) pp. 439–55.

McLaughlin, Kelly (2015) '"It's Still a Capital Crime": Ex-CIA Head James Woolsey Said He'd Like to Watch Edward Snowden Be Hanged for Treason', *Daily Mail*, 20 November <httpws:// ww.dailymail.co.uk/news/article-3327298/Ex-CIA-head-James-Woolsey-said-d-like-watch-Edward-Snowden-hanged-treason.html> (last accessed 26 February 2020).

Parikh, Crystal (2009) *An Ethics of Betrayal: The Politics of Otherness in Emergent U.S. Literatures and Culture*. New York: Fordham University Press.

Rancière, Jacques (2006) *Film Fables*, trans. Emiliano Battista. New York: Berg.

Roy, Arundhati (2001) 'The Algebra of Infinite Justice', *The Guardian*, 29 September <https://www.theguardian.com/world/2001/sep/29/september11.afghanistan> (last accessed 26 February 2020).

Said, Edward (2003) [1978] *Orientalism*. London: Penguin.

Shapiro, Michael J. (2009) *Cinematic Geopolitics*. Abingdon and New York: Rouledge.

Sylvester, Christine (2013) *War as Experience: Contributions from International Relations and Feminist Analysis*. New York: Routledge.

Westwell, Guy (2014) *Parallel Lines: Post-9/11 American Cinema*. Bristol: Wallflower Press.

Winberg, Oscar (2017) 'Insult Politics: Donald Trump, Right-Wing Populism, and Incendiary Language', *European Journal of American Studies*, 12 (2) (August) <http://journals.openedition.org/ejas/12132> (last accessed 19 April 2019).

CHAPTER 2

Momentary Rupture? *Dawn* (1928) and the Transgressive Potential of the Edith Cavell Case

Claudia Sternberg

On 12 October 1915, the Englishwoman Edith Cavell was executed in Brussels by a German firing squad. Cavell had run a training school for professional nurses in the Belgian capital and was sentenced by a German military court because she had aided the escape of fugitive Allied soldiers to the neutral Netherlands. Her execution has been regarded – and represented – as a singular transgressive act. It served to confirm the German occupying forces as transgressors who had not only violated Belgian sovereignty but also shown contempt for caring femininity, embodied by the civilian nurse and educator. Cavell's death was widely reported internationally and posthumously bestowed on her the attributes of a First World War heroine and martyr; it was used in wartime propaganda and marked the beginning of an enduring process of commemoration. Over the years, Cavell became the subject matter of many publications and varied cultural productions. This far-reaching circulation suggests a transgressive potential that must be sought elsewhere than in her execution alone. This chapter proposes that a more complex picture of the Cavell case and the Cavell persona emerges if transgression is approached through a widened lens. This approach explores visual culture, which played a central role in constructing and remembering Cavell, and more specifically the British feature film *Dawn* (Herbert Wilcox, UK, 1928).[1]

Dawn tells the fictionalised story of Edith Cavell's incidental support for an escaped prisoner which leads to her building up an underground network that enables the flight from Belgium of a larger group of men. The production shows the efforts of the German occupiers to put an end to these activities, and their ultimate success after being tipped off by an informer. The film includes the trial proceedings in which Cavell confesses and is sentenced to death. Her time in prison and religious preparations are intercut with the unsuccessful interventions of various parties, including the American Delegation, to have the death penalty converted. *Dawn* concludes with Cavell's execution. By no means the first cinematic appropriation of the material,[2] *Dawn* was produced in England and Belgium by Herbert Wilcox and British and Dominions Film Corporation Ltd. Wilcox directed the picture based on story material and intertitles by Reginald Berkeley. Wilcox and Robert Cullen are credited for the scenario, and Cullen also served as assistant director. After the American Pauline Frederick withdrew from the role, the British stage actor Sybil Thorndike was cast as Edith Cavell.

From a position of film historical hindsight, Amy Sargeant attributes to *Dawn* an 'elephantine slowness' and critiques the abstraction with which the film 'mystifies war . . . by discounting political agency and disguising the ideological imperatives that obliged Britain to go to war'; she also assesses the production's anti-war mission as 'unremarkable for its date' (2011: 87). Some of the contemporary reviewers, however, presented a different view with regard to the latter. *Kinematograph Weekly* critic Lionel Collier observed: 'As an example of peace propaganda [*Dawn*] is almost unique' (1928: 40). His view was echoed by A. M. Sherwood, Jr, who wrote that the subject matter might have easily led to the film being a 'Hymn of Hate', but that 'war is war' and '*Dawn* becomes, not an anti-German film, but an anti-war film; one of the most effective pieces of anti-war propaganda we've ever seen' (1928: 847).

Dawn, as will be shown in more detail, indeed stands out in the history of Cavell representations because it deviates – by design as well as by contingency – from standard tropes and binary oppositions that have dominated this First World War narrative. As a consequence, Cavell herself is highlighted as a potentially transgressive rather than affirmative and unambiguous figure. As the editors of this volume assert, figures of transgression

> operate as a crucial site for culturally necessary processes of 'thinking through,' their liminal status permitting opportunity for visualizing and repositioning the enemy, the exploration of questions of legitimation and culpability, and the testing of moral and ethical grounds for future national and transnational or inter-cultural identity formation. (Purse and Wölfel 2014)

Instead of adding further detail to Cavell's case history or the attempts to ban the exhibition of *Dawn* (addressed later in this chapter), I want to direct attention at the film text itself. By looking closely at contextual, narrative and aesthetic choices in the divergent British and Belgian versions of *Dawn*, as well as in the novelisation of the same title by Reginald Berkeley (n.d.), I suggest that the way in which the Cavell affair was conceptualised for the screen in 1928 constitutes a contested departure from the mnemonic hegemony which persists to the present day. It does so by actualising certain aspects from the web of transgressions which have underlain the Cavell case from the beginning but have played a subordinate role in its legacy in visual culture.

The Cavell Case: Coexisting Acts of Transgression

War is a transgressive event, a 'grand transgression' (Jenks 2003: 2). It invalidates peacetime taboos by enforcing the militarisation of society and sanctioning the annexation and destruction of places and resources, which includes the maiming and killing of humans. For the First World War, Heather Jones has identified the killing of captive or incapacitated soldiers, the use of gas warfare and violence against civilians as central transgressions (2015: 125–30). Despite earlier large-scale deaths of civilians, including in colonial contexts, 'it was the scale of the violence against civilians that European populations at the time *believed* was unprecedented' (ibid.: 131, original emphasis). Shock reactions were particularly strong when women, like Cavell, were killed (ibid.: 134). Although what was considered transgressive changed over time, atrocities were ascribed to the opposing side and the 'idea of the enemy as transgressive . . . created new hatreds and lent the cultural impetus to keep populations fighting, because the concept dehumanised the enemy' (ibid.: 129).

Conditions of war undermine the given social orders and (national) boundaries; they create new binaries (such as friend/foe, invader/occupied) and activate alternative systems (for example martial law). If 'the story which always precedes the commission or acknowledgement of a transgressive act is the constitution of a centre, a centre that provides for a social structure, and a structure of meaning that is delimited or marked out by boundaries' (Jenks 2003: 15), then in wartime the shifting or emergence of coexisting 'centres' can bring forth new or double acts of transgression. The reordering of centres may be straightforward for combatants, but civilians like Cavell faced decisions of alignment or opposition in the contact zone of occupied Brussels. Location and situation furthermore fashioned transgressive figures like the *franc-tireur*, the spy,[3] the informant and, last but not least, the disarmed 'derelict soldier', who was a quasi-civilian figure while on the run but a combatant once he had been successfully trafficked.

As a civilian of 'enemy' nationality, displaced as a foreigner in a territory under an occupation that was based on the infringement of existing peacetime law, and embroiled in resistance activity which also poses questions of *jus in bello* legitimacy, Edith Cavell occupies a complex place, irrespective of the many affective factors that impacted on the way in which her trial and execution were perceived. Like Belgian civilians she was under occupational rule, and by transgressing the German military and penal codes she consciously risked exposure and punishment. Cavell also overstepped the boundaries of professional codes; her profession as a nurse placed her in the context of the neutral category of medical personnel according to the Geneva Conventions (Jones 2015: 132). By hiding soldiers on the premises of the Berkendael Institute, she furthermore implicated her staff, for example, her first assistant Sister Elisabeth Wilkins, who found herself, albeit temporarily, arrested (Pickles 2007: 16). As an accomplice of the Belgian resistance, Cavell was then also a witness whose statements in court were used by the occupying forces to their advantage and impacted on other organisations and individuals operating secretly (Speck 2001: 85).

The resulting 'civilian ambiguity' (Slim 2008: 181), which weakens notions of civilian innocence and immunity, featured in a number of official wartime and postwar assessments. In popular and propagandistic films, postcards and illustrations, however, the 'noncombatant strategies' (Barter 2012: 546) and actions that led to Cavell's arrest tend to be eclipsed. Instead she is shown in a nursing capacity, as the accused in a military court, as a condemned executee and finally as a transcending figure of veneration and memorialisation.[4] Her transgressions, if perceived as such at all, are regarded as virtuous, based on assumptions about a gendered morality and a natural propensity of women to preserve and care for lives. In representational terms, her intervention in affairs of war and engagement with able-bodied combatants are passed over while physical caregiving is foregrounded, as is her demise at the hands of male-identified violence.

Cavell's gender brought with it numerous opportunities of ascription, modification and embellishment. These helped to build and consolidate the Cavell myth while at the same transgressing representational limits. As Katie Pickles states: 'Although Cavell was a mature and independent new woman with a professional career, she was rendered a young, innocent, sacrificial and virginal woman. She was portrayed as requiring the protection of a patriarchy that, until the war, had not impinged upon her life' (2007: 32). Cavell's international professional orientation and work in the Belgian metropolis were replaced by images of prewar English pastoralism and bedside nursing scenes.[5]

In wartime visual culture, Cavell's death was turned into a motif of necrophiliac excess. Showing her killing and dead body played to a longstanding voyeuristic attraction of executions and the eroticism associated with a female corpse, both closely linked with theories and the art of transgression;[6] the image was also used in analogy to the motif of rape and violation, understood both literally and metaphorically as linked to the experience of Belgium and its population. The main purpose of using the woman's body as object was to express the barbarism of the enemy. Just one case in point is the much reproduced wartime postcard *Remember*, which shows a youthful Cavell on the ground and a German officer towering over her, phallic pistol in hand.[7] The caption on the reverse indulges in graphic violence and contains the following account of the execution:

> She faints: the German officer gives his soldiers the order to fire; they hesitate to shoot on the prostrate body of a woman. The fiend takes his revolver and leaning upon his victim, deliberately blows her brains out. REMEMBER!

Image and caption exemplify the scenic imagination of an undocumented event, but they also point to a deviation from an evasive historical truth. The story of the officer had its roots in rumours and reports about insubordination among the firing party, an unconscious Cavell and the urgency to conclude this hastily arranged execution by other means, but these occurrences were not confirmed by eyewitnesses.

Misinformation about the execution consistently accompanied the Cavell case and outlasted the war years. But not only additions were among the narrative transgressions. A further constant has been the erasure of the Belgian architect Philippe Baucq, who was executed alongside Cavell on 12 October 1915. He is notably absent not only from British, but also non-British and even Belgian visualisations.[8] Baucq's removal ensured that his gender and nationality would not diffuse the strong narrative of female martyrdom and English commitment to the war effort and the defence of a mainly passively enduring Belgium.[9] The full potential of eliminating Baucq was achieved not by erasure alone but by displacement. Rather than building a narrative of civilian solidarity among allies, the Cavell myth constructs the fictitious figure of Private Rammler, a German rank-and-file soldier, who replaces the real-life Baucq in the execution scene. Rammler personalises and enhances the insubordination story; his refusal to take aim at the nurse as a member of the firing squad leads to the disruption of due process: Rammler is shot on the scene and an officer concludes the execution of Cavell. To add credibility to this story, photographic postcards of disinterred remains, liberally attributed to 'Rammler, a German soldier, shot (without trial) . . . for refusing to fire on this nurse',[10] were brought into circulation and this episode, too, outlived the war.

In 1919, Cavell's body was exhumed in Brussels and she was repatriated with military honours. A memorial service was held at Westminster Abbey and she was reinterred in Norwich in May 1919. Her central London memorial, sculpted by George Frampton, was unveiled to the public in 1920. Soldiers with bugles and marching troops as well as speeches by uniformed men on the occasion denote the militarisation of Cavell's memory. It was not until 1924 that the National Council of Women successfully petitioned the Office of Works to have Cavell's own words added to the sculpture, approximating those recorded by the Anglican reverend H. Stirling Gahan on the eve of her execution: 'Patriotism is not enough / I must have no hatred or / bitterness for anyone'. It was the Frampton memorial which, according to Herbert Wilcox's own account, inspired him to make a film about Cavell (1967: 72–3). Almost ten years after the Armistice, in a different political climate and with old and new audiences attending the cinema, he decided to retell the charged events of 1914 and 1915. A set of claims for and against transgression would accompany the production and reception of *Dawn*, just as it had done during and after the represented events.

Dawn: Reconfiguring the Cavell Myth

Herbert Wilcox was among those who Christine Gledhill has called the '[p]ost-war entrants' (2008: 16) to the industry.

> [They] represented a new entrepreneurial generation who grasped both the workings of an internationally based film economics and the new ethos of mass culture – including, crucially, a modernising sexualisation of popular culture, with its concomitant class, gender and racial implications – to which large-scale filmmaking was now directed. (Ibid.)

Wilcox had an international orientation and specialised in biographical films about historical women central to national memory. For his Cavell film, he teamed up with Reginald Berkeley. A war veteran like Wilcox, Berkeley was a lawyer, politician and writer who wrote for the stage, radio and screen. His insights into legislation and legal proceedings were borne out in the detail that would inform the diversity of characters and details of the trial in the film and novelisation of *Dawn*. Together with documents, location shots and replica settings, the film approximated some of the documentary realism associated with the war-themed instructional films of the 1920s, of which *Q-Ships* (Geoffrey Barkas, Michael Barringer) was the last one, also released in 1928.

Berkeley had been engaged in the postwar reconciliation processes at the political level. He worked for the League of Nations in 1922 before standing as an independent Liberal for Central Nottingham.[11] In his maiden speech in the Commons on 24 November 1922, Berkeley critiqued 'basing our foreign policy on what I would call a group system, understandings between what we used to call the principal Allies during the War'; he urged the government of the day 'to consider whether the League of Nations is not a better basis for our foreign policy'.[12] He continued to lobby for the League and expressed an interest in returning to it in 1925.[13] Berkeley's affinity to the organisation may have reached further than British foreign policy. As Glenda Sluga has shown, the League with its international remit and multiplicity of future-oriented interventions, including those by transnational women's organisations, presented a forum for counter-discourses to patriarchal, imperial and nationalist approaches and logics, even if propositions were not realised (2013: 45–78). Had Cavell lived, she might have found a place in women's international activism which flourished in the 1920s inside and beyond the League.[14]

For Berkeley the commemorative project around the Cavell case provided an opportunity to recast the narrative as a reparative undoing of the 'group system'. *Dawn* can be seen, to some extent, as a continuation of his earlier work *The White Château* (1925), credited as the BBC's first full-length radio drama, which told an intertwined First World War story of civilians and soldiers, occupation and battle, death and survival, ruin and rebuilding using a Flemish estate as a symbolic site. Berkeley writes in the foreword of the published play script that *The White Château* is 'a play with a purpose', namely 'to reinforce the determination to abolish war' (1925: v). He continues: '[T]he story that I try to tell is such as might be true in any war between any civilized peoples; for the subject of the play is not the war between A and B, but War, the hideous Giant Despair of our times' (ibid.: vi). An abstraction of war is therefore programmatic for Berkeley, and the intertitles in *Dawn* are significant interventions of his own voice. The Cavell case is stripped of its wartime propaganda tone and becomes an object lesson in demilitarisation. Gender is employed critically here; Cavell is shown to resist being co-opted into the masculinist-militarist logic in anticipation of a 'feminist peace politics' (Ruddick 1993: 109).

Dawn remains, however, framed by the conventions of popular cinema. Neither Wilcox nor Berkeley set out to disassemble the Cavell mystique or alienate their audience through formal experimentation. Nevertheless, their reconfiguration of the myth requires new strategies to break the mould of previous representations. The first of these is to de-objectify Cavell as a sacrificial national heroine who is defined by the actions of the perpetrators and dominated by death and the paradox of a 'posthumous life' (Barney 2005: 218). In order to provide her with an *ante mortem* agency, screen time is dedicated to Cavell making decisions, arranging hiding places, instructing her personnel, building a team, installing hidden alarms and warding off search parties. Scenes between women are staged to highlight their independence and show how they employ their gendered roles and spaces for their clandestine activity. In the trial scene, the network is also shown as predominantly female. Included are the Irishwoman Ada Bodart (who played herself in the film as an additional marker of authenticity) and the rotund and resolute Madame Pitou. Crudely drawn for comic relief, Pitou's knitting in the courtroom nevertheless constitutes a form of female resistance to the (male) military order. A psychological rounding of Cavell is achieved by Thorndike's restrained acting style in moments of both contemplation and agitation. Wilcox and cinematographer Bernard Knowles, who would go on to work on Alfred Hitchcock's British films in the 1930s, furthermore use close frontal shots to create a sense of entangled space and destiny, even across enemy lines.

A further change to the Cavell narrative in *Dawn* is the rehumanisation of 'the enemy' which goes hand in hand with the agency of Cavell herself, whose decisions are deliberate within the confines of civilian options discussed above. Heather Jones suggests that 'reconciliation with the enemy was not about *realpolitik* only . . .; it was also about dismantling the dynamic of transgression – the series of wartime beliefs that the enemy had transgressed moral norms to the extent of dehumanising himself' (2015: 139). In the foreword to *The White Château*, Berkeley expressed a similar purpose of cultural production: 'the labour to remove the fears and mistrusts created by the War must be unremitting if it is to have success' (1925: v). By introducing a larger cast of real and imagined German characters, *Dawn* provides insights into the various pressures experienced by the military police who are expected to put an end to the escape of prisoners, underground papers and other forms of civil disobedience. Numerous scenes show differences between diplomatic and military needs and approaches, stipulations of martial law and how the informer's testimony and Cavell's confession contribute to the course of events.

The trial sequence shows the prosecution's hostility towards Cavell, but further scenes add nuance to undermine the notion of a national predisposition towards cruelty. In the novelisation, Colonel Schultz, Head of the Intelligence Police, and his staff pursue the fugitives

> not because they were any less humane than other people, or any less likely themselves to show pity for distress; but because it happened to be their duty . . . to enforce those very rules which the fugitives and their rescuers were breaking. (Berkeley n.d.: 16–17)

In addition to the rationalising element, fictional characters are introduced to diversify and humanise the occupying forces. They include a friendly young soldier in one of the search parties and an empathetic warder who looks after Cavell in prison. A further character is a German officer who surprises Cavell as she attends to the wounds of a British aviator in hiding. The officer takes in what is the only explicit nursing scene in the film and eventually leaves the locale in an unthreatening manner. Although he hesitates, he becomes complicit in the act of hiding and therefore, before he leaves the house, hides from his own comrades and waits until the street is clear.

Berkeley's 240-page novelisation offers even more opportunities for character development. The author frequently uses free indirect discourse to relate Cavell's thoughts and deliberations but also those of the German characters in an attempt to flesh out their mindsets, motivations and inner conflict. The literary technique also allows backstories to emerge. Cavell reminds a billeted soldier, for example, of his sister who trained to be a deaconess nurse at Kaiserswerth near Düsseldorf (Berkeley n.d.: 26). The location is carefully chosen to underline that women elsewhere, like Cavell, had come of age at a time when nursing became professionalised and was an attractive, often transnational, career option for unmarried women. Kaiserswerth, not too different from Berkendael, had instructed nurses from 1836, including the British nurse Florence Nightingale.

A third strategy to reconfigure the Cavell myth in *Dawn* is abstracting the 'war machine', which is mainly conveyed in Berkeley's extradiegetic intertitles. The first sets the tone of the film: 'This is a tale of heroic life and death and of a conflict of loyalties, told in reverence and without bitterness.' The story develops further along the juxtaposition of war as 'a dedication to brutal force' and nursing as 'a dedication to mercy and healing', each being 'the uncompromising foe of the other'. Cavell's anti-war position is established in a further title card: 'Out of her act of pity to one fugitive an organisation grew; and Nurse Cavell began her war on War.'

The concept of 'war on war' has a long-standing history in European thought and politics, from Immanuel Kant's *Zum ewigen Frieden/ Toward Perpetual Peace* (1795/6) to the international peace movement in Europe in the nineteenth and early twentieth centuries (Cooper 1991), the Women's Peace Congress in The Hague in April 1915 and the founding of the Women's International League for Peace and Freedom, Ernst Friedrich's multilingual publication of 1924, *Krieg dem Kriege! Guerre à la Guerre! War against War! Oorlog aan den Oorlog!*, and in proposals for international law, such as the failed *Geneva Protocol for the Pacific Settlement of International Disputes* (1924) and, importantly, the *General Treaty for Renunciation of War as an Instrument of National Policy* (Briand-Kellogg Pact) whose negotiations were under way when *Dawn* was in production.

Figure 2.1 'Woman and the War Machine': a proto-feminist peace politics? Still from *Dawn* (1928). (Source: Cinémathèque Royale de Belgique.)

Berkeley's intertitle sets up the 'Rulers of Europe' as the 'puppets of Carnage – some more willing than others; but all enslaved to the system of War.' The transformation from peace to war is inevitable: 'And then came the time when Europe played with fire once too often. The civilized world blazed into flames. The gods grew tired of Man and left him to be the plaything of War.' The metaphor of transgressive play is taken up in the first scenes of *Dawn*. At the Berkendael Institute, two hospitalised boys 'play war' in combination with hide-and-seek, using toy helmets and weapons. Cavell, in her first appearance, plays along, hiding the boys and humouring them: 'Great Big Soldier's after me!' Her phrase to one of the boys – 'You had better search' – is identical with what she will later say to the German patrols who repeatedly search her premises.

In her work on *Playing War*, Sabine Frühstück draws attention to the figure of the child which 'has emerged from a set of contradictory assumptions . . . : that children are innately attracted to war, and that they are exceptionally vulnerable to its violence' (2017: 1). With reference to the exploitation of the 'bifurcated notion of the child', Frühstück proposes that 'at its core, modern militarism – a juggernaut unto itself – is infantile' (ibid.). In the novelisation of *Dawn*, child's play is not scenic but a memory that flashes into Cavell's mind. When Colonel Schultz confronts her with the accusation that she is harbouring derelict soldiers and stands 'before her with suspicion in his eyes, and an odd mixture of arrogance and embarrassment on his face' (Berkeley n.d.: 71), Cavell's

> desire to laugh passed into something between a smile and a sigh. In the stern, efficient head of the German military police, she could only see the dressed-up child of two years before. What children men were. Destructive children, to lay waste the fertile earth and shatter their cities with explosives. Cruel children, to hunt each other down pitilessly . . . Bloodthirsty children, to organise slaughter on so gigantic a scale. But children, none the less, if only by virtue of their incurable solemnity about themselves, and their pathetic belief in the importance of their enthusiasms. (Ibid.: 72–3)

The first hunted down fugitive is an almost childlike young man who is already caught in the system for which boys are groomed and in which soldiers and older men of authority find themselves entangled. *Dawn* does not sanitise the fugitive's experience; the dialogue title establishes the young man as victim and perpetrator: 'Two of us escaped. We killed a sentry. They caught the other fellow and shot him . . . If they catch me . . .' In the novelisation, further details are provided about the miserable death of the Belgian soldier, the German sentry's funeral and the telegram to his wife (Berkeley n.d.: 18).

Figure 2.2 'We killed': Mars and the fugitive boy soldier. Still from *Dawn*. (Source: Cinémathèque Royale de Belgique.)

While it could be argued that the film's introduction of children, normally absent from Cavell stories, is a way of completing Cavell's childless femininity (cf. the construction of the maternal in the novelisation, 91–2), *Dawn* deviates in its dramaturgical use of children from earlier war-related films such as *Reveille* (George Pearson, UK, 1924) or *Blighty* (Adrian Brunel, UK, 1927) which used them as tokens of continuity of family and nation after the war's destruction. In combination with the hardly ennobling representation of caged fugitives in a basement who, as the novelisation makes clear, will either be reabsorbed by the war machine or hide in the Netherlands to avoid further active service (Berkeley n.d.: 183), Cavell's own painful process towards inevitable death makes *Dawn* not a story about heroic victory and the prospect of postwar reverence. Rather it endorses the ostracism of militarism in a production that pre-dated the male-centred front films which would emerge a few years later. While none of the above strategies were taken to any extreme, the mere prospect of having any visual representation based on Edith Cavell led to opposition from the outset. The reasons for regarding a Cavell biopic as transgressive, however, were manifold and directed both at the project and its execution.

Dawn as Transgression: Prohibitive and Productive Censorship

As Cynthia Enloe has observed, wars 'don't simply end', nor do they 'end simply' (2004: 193). *Dawn* made a film historical mark because its appearance in the entertainment industry was seen as disruptive in a period of incremental normalisation at the level of international relations. The Locarno Treaties of 1925 had been built on the collaboration of the foreign ministers Austen Chamberlain (United Kingdom), Aristide Briand (France) and Gustav Stresemann (Germany). Germany had joined the League of Nations in 1926 and the Briand-Kellogg Pact was under negotiation. From the German side, the Cavell story posed the threat of rekindling atrocity propaganda and historical misrepresentation. As Kai Nowak has shown in detail, other First World War films also came under scrutiny in the so-called *Hetzfilmdebatte* ('hate film' debate) and not only political but also market interests were at stake here (2015: 188–304). German diplomats hoped to effect a ban of Wilcox and Berkeley's production, but the British government had to involve the British Board of Film Censors and needed to tread carefully so as not to blur the boundaries between independent and political censorship (Robertson 1984).

The spectre of censorship, in turn, met with resistance not only from the producers, who had experienced difficulties before, but triggered responses in the press and trade press alike. Depending on political and other viewpoints, the notion of returning Cavell to the screen was seen as a transgressive endeavour of (misinformed and sensationalist) popular culture or a commercial exploitation of a human tragedy. Others saw a possible suppression of the film as unjustifiable, especially on grounds of foreign meddling in sovereign matters. Others again objected to political interference with cultural expression and self-regulation in the film industry. Just as in the Cavell case itself, the debate about the legitimacy of *Dawn* became an international news item and was debated in Germany (Nowak 2015: 239–64), the Netherlands (Knijff 2007, 2009) and of course Belgium (Biltereyst and Depauw 2006; Depauw 2007), but also further afield in the US and Australia. While the censor reached a decision to suppress the film's exhibition on grounds of inexpediency (Anonymous 1928a), Wilcox was able to circumvent a wholesale ban of *Dawn* in the UK by seeking screening permissions from local councils and the film was released in different countries.

As Annette Kuhn has shown, however, not all practices and processes that mark and possibly alter a film 'emanate from organisations with a specific remit to censor, nor are they all necessarily prohibitive in their effects' (1988: 126). Despite Wilcox's invitation to political stakeholders to assess the film itself, diplomats and politicians did not want to engage with film form and narrative. The latter, however, mattered for the version that was to be screened in Belgium, where any interference with *Dawn* had been renounced and rejected. A different set of sensibilities were at work here, closely linked to the visceral and localised memory of occupation. Media and publication censorship had been part of the measures that the German authorities imposed on the newly occupied country in 1914; the dissemination of the underground paper *La Libre Belgique* was a significant factor that led to the execution of Philippe Baucq. The break with film censorship in postwar Belgium must be seen as a response to the imposition during the war; it also explains the strong reactions to the narrative of political censorship in Britain.[15]

The Belgian embrace of Wilcox's production – and with it the acceptance of the erasure of Baucq – not only meant the screening of an uncensored 'original' version; it also entailed productive modifications that removed ambiguity from the film text and thus also for its viewers. The Belgian version of *Dawn* makes use of what Laura Isabel Serna calls a 'politics of title translation' (2014: 132). Presented in French and Flemish, the translated and modified intertitles achieve a different framing for Belgian cinemagoers which points explicitly to the domestic experience of warfare and occupation. They establish a clear binary between a distinctly German aggressor and non-German victims and relegate Berkeley's abstracted 'War' to a second order. *Dawn* is identified in the title card as a 'The Tragedy of

Miss Cavell'[16] and the story of 'The bloody dawn of the tragic day when "Miss Cavell" fell in the National Shooting Range under German bullets.'[17] Therefore, in a straightforward 'us/them' binary, it is Germany which 'wanted to play with fire to reduce to ashes the hard-won result of our civilisation'.[18] The verbal framing is complemented with an extended sequence of shots which sit outside the diegetic realm of *Dawn* and serve as visual memory cues. The compilation shows footage of exploding shells, mobilised soldiers, street fighting, displaced Belgian civilians, the destruction of towns and further impressions of the transgressive essence of the invasion.

Later changes to the intertitles follow a similar trajectory. The English title for the trial scene – 'The stage set for the trial between *the Woman and the War Machine*. The Senate House, Brussels. October 9th, 1915' – is translated into 'THE TRIAL The whole affair was a sham of justice, *a cover-up worthy of the Kaiser's henchmen who soiled the Senate chamber* with their presence' (my emphases).[19] The Kaiser, a central propaganda figure but otherwise absent from *Dawn*, and the transgressive appropriation of Belgian sovereign sites replace Berkeley's gendered anti-militarist juxtaposition.

The careful excision and re-editing of existing footage also impact on the aspiration of *Dawn* to differentiate and rehumanise the enemy. An example can be found in an early billeting scene. A German officer enters a private house to find accommodation for his men just at the moment in which Madame Rappard, whose fugitive son has just been hidden in her house, has collapsed and is assisted by Cavell. In the British version the officer takes in the situation and asks how many soldiers the household can accommodate. It is Cavell who answers and he acknowledges her and withdraws. In the Belgian version, the officer demands the billeting of four soldiers but Cavell's response has been cut. Albeit subtle, the sequential arrangements of individual shots make two very different points: one renders the unsuspecting German officer responsive and considerate when he sees the ailing woman, the other makes him appear callous and without empathy.

A further significant removal is that of the previously outlined encounter between Cavell and the German soldier who surprises her with the wounded aviator. In the Belgian version, the soldier is only seen outside the building, observing the arrival of the ambulance which creates the suspense of potential discovery for the viewer. The next shot of Cavell fades to black so that the scene is concluded. An inconsequential moment of cinematic tension is favoured over an equally ominous but narratively more laden scene that highlights the need for individual decision-making.

A major difference between the British and the Belgian version, however, exists in the execution scene for which both versions introduce Cavell's complementary figure of transgression, the German private Rammler who is called up as a member of the firing party. An analysis of the detail of this ending of the film demonstrates the way in which film form and narrative work to frame Cavell differently from other cultural representations.

Having already expressed anger at the task to his peers in the infantry guardroom, Rammler does not follow the order of his superiors at the scene of the execution. In the Belgian version the officer draws his pistol against the mutinous private and Wilcox cuts to Cavell who closes her eyes. The film returns to the squad, now with Rammler dead at their feet. Cavell becomes unstable, the German pastor reaches out in a futile gesture and the nurse faints. The squad is now ready to shoot, but their target is unconscious. The officer is ordered to sort it out, but he too displays discomfort at the task. He takes his pistol, with a look at the lifeless body of Cavell on the ground, implying he will make the shot. The moment of her death is elided, however, replaced by a cut to the priest closing the prayer book, followed by a shot of Cavell's fresh grave. The camera pans left to take in Private Rammler's adjacent grave, before coming back to rest on Cavell's simple wooden cross.

This ending, initially envisaged by Berkeley and directed by Wilcox, makes full use of the contested wartime narrative. Berkeley, in a letter to *The Times*, defended their choice on the grounds of conflicting reports *and* artistic licence (Berkeley 1928). But in the wake of the debates about *Dawn*, Wilcox made changes to the film based on his own judgement and in response to cuts suggested by representatives from local councils (Anon. 1928b). It is these changes that, inadvertently, offer a different, if equally imagined, account of events in the British version.[20]

As Cavell walks to her designated spot at the shooting range, eventually facing the firing party, the camera position reveals an open countryside behind the moribund character. The camera constructs an alignment that will reveal itself presently. The command to get ready is given, but the response is disorderly and hesitant. The men seek to reassure themselves by looking at each other. A connection between Cavell and Rammler is established through blocking and the gaze. He takes some resolve and stands at attention. An officer – the very same who did not give away Cavell's nursing of the aviator – challenges Rammler to get ready to shoot. The officer looks across, as if along the invisible connection. The next shots alternate between Cavell's face, the wider scene and Rammler. The exchange of glances is repeated, until Cavell – in a hardly noticeable gesture – shakes her head as if to discourage the man from disobeying orders. An intertitle reads: 'War makes no distinction between friends and foes. Those who break its rules are broken in its merciless fingers.' The British version ends on the German pastor's distraught face and his closing of the prayer book. The montage suggests that the deed is done. Two title cards follow: 'The tragedy of that dawn will be turned into rejoicing if the message of Edith Cavell can find a place in the hearts of men.' / '"Patriotism is not enough. I must have no hatred or bitterness towards anyone."' A short shot of Cavell's grave and cross concludes the picture.

The Rammler narrative, which dates back to wartime, served a number of purposes in the Cavell case. It heightened the transgressive nature of the execution by suggesting that ordinary enemy soldiers felt reluctant to realise the death penalty. It also added drama to the proceedings themselves, with a more drawn-out death struggle and even the glimpse of a last-minute rescue. On a more abstract level, the character of Rammler is the non-British other who stabilises the British identity on display and therefore also needs to die as a martyr. The 'self-censored' version of *Dawn*, however, maintains the violent supremacy of martial law and rule, even if both Cavell's and Rammler's resistance is indicated. For the Cavell character, the curtailed ending means that she is no longer consigned to the floor as passive victim and future martyr. Aided by Knowles's cinematography and Thorndike's performance, Cavell's final gesture is one of intimacy and civilian interposition. But the alignment and non-verbal exchange between Cavell and her executioner also underline that there cannot be heroism in war where killing or being killed are contingent on circumstance.

Figure 2.3 At eye level: Cavell's residual agency before death. Still from *Dawn* (1928). (Source: Cinémathèque Royale de Belgique.)

Conclusion: Moment(s) of Rupture and the Persistent Resistance to Transgression

In his *Work on Myth*, Hans Blumenberg states that '[m]yths are stories that are distinguished by a high degree of constancy in their narrative core and by an equally pronounced capacity for *marginal* variation' (1985: 34, my emphasis). It may be questioned therefore whether *Dawn*'s 'variation' of the Cavell myth is a transgressive deviation at all. Sufficient ambiguity in the British version of the film text itself and the way in which the censorship debate evolved without recourse to content or aesthetics, overrode a critical engagement with *Dawn* as a representational intervention. It is possible to make different selections from Berkeley's novelisation to construct the character of the nurse as foremost a patriot (for example Berkeley n.d.: 229). As a late silent production *Dawn* was part of the various turns towards futility narratives and wider anti-war discourses of its time, and had it not been for the debates about the proposed ban, it might have fallen into film historical obscurity.

At the level of film analysis, the two film versions compared here may not be identical with what audiences saw in various locations in the late 1920s. The observations draw on the 'British version' held at the British Film Institute and the 'Belgian version' from the archive of the Cinémathèque Royale de Belgique; the latter is a reconstruction of 2014 which combines an earlier Belgian restoration of 1985 and a Dutch version of which elements are conserved in the EYE Filmmuseum and Stiftung Deutsche Kinemathek. Further versions were in circulation; a promotional leaflet, for example, credits an *adapation française* to the French director Charles Burguet, with intertitles by screenwriter José Germain. Furthermore, *Dawn* has been analysed despite the absence of a score. As rare screenings of the British version at the British Silent Film Festival in Nottingham in 2004 and the Hyde Park Picture House in Leeds in 2015 demonstrated – with accompaniments by Neil Brand and Darius Battiwalla respectively – music adds a layer that can easily suggest different interpretations of the same production. With regard to my own understanding of *Dawn*, it may be more appropriate therefore to speak of a 'transgressive reading', which, according to Julian Wolfreys, 'is one that recognizes those traces in any text which are themselves disruptive of conventional and institutional codes' (2008: 12). I have argued in this chapter that Cavell in *Dawn* has been constructed as a figure of transgressive potential with agency and choices rather than objectified as martyr and national heroine. This effect has not been achieved by a stringent and purposeful strategy but rather by a number of contingent factors and decisions made not only by the writer and director of the film, but other agents who became implicated in the production at a crucial time in war memory, film history and international relations.

Transgression, states Georges Bataille, 'opens the door into what lies beyond the limits usually observed, but it maintains these limits just the same' (1986: 67). It is only at certain moments that Cavell is called upon in an actualisation of her *liminal status* as a figure of (potential) transgression in order to trigger a counter-memory or invite a counter-reading. In the First World War centenary years, the announcement of the Royal Mint that Lord Kitchener would be represented on the first uncirculated coin to mark the commemorations in 2014 led to a popular campaign, launched by Sheffield councillor Sioned-Mair Richards, to petition for a coin bearing a likeness of Edith Cavell – an action that resonates with the Council of Women's Frampton memorial intervention. Such a coin was struck in 2015, but the Mint's press release does not refer to the petition. The face of the coin 'depicts a scene with the ever-vigilant Edith tending to a wounded soldier with a portrait-style design of the selfless nurse in her uniform as the background' (Royal Mint 2015). The coin's edge carries the line 'SHE FACED THEM GENTLE AND BOLD', taken from Laurence Binyon's 1916 poem 'Edith Cavell' (in Clarke 2002), which also includes the insubordination narrative. A DVD of Herbert Wilcox's digitally remastered auto-remake *Nurse Edith Cavell* (USA 1939) was released in 2016. The sound film retained and even expanded the female agency of *Dawn*, adding screen time for Cavell's team of nurses and aristocratic network members, but it also made the title character younger and more attractive. Cavell's execution is suggested rather than shown, and no irregularities take place during the proceedings. The film closes instead with Cavell's memorial service at Westminster in 1919, the actor's superimposed face and her words: 'I realise that patriotism is not enough; I must have no hatred or bitterness towards anyone.'

Cavell's much quoted words also appeared as a closing credit for the last episode of *The Crimson Field* (2014), a six-part BBC1 television drama written by Sarah Phelps and set in a First World War field hospital in France. Cavell remains an off-screen and *post mortem* presence, but the production utilises her transgressive potential by association with one of the drama's central characters. Joan Livesey is a British nurse whose fiancé has been conscripted into the German army and both have become the 'playthings of war'. Livesey's relationship is found out and she faces a court martial and the death penalty for treacherous dealings with the enemy. On an explicit level, Phelps lets Livesey's interrogation coincide with Cavell's execution, an event which the male officers in the hospital refer to. But the screenwriter also draws more obliquely on elements from the repository of the Cavell case through characterisation (a professional nurse and new woman with transnational sympathies; a fugitive soldier) and discourse (martial law, the 'war machine' and 'examples to be made'; disruptions of the friend/foe dichotomy; the functionalisation of death).

The interweaving of two narratives in *The Crimson Field* received criticism from Kate Tompkins, then Chief Executive of the healthcare workers charity Cavell Nurses' Trust. Tompkins objected to the implied parallel between the fictional hospital sister and Edith Cavell, both facing execution: 'The two "offences" sit worlds apart. It is a pity that the courageous, caring exploits of Cavell were overlooked by the producers; she seems to have been included just to enable another character to remark that there is nothing like an executed nurse to get everyone behind the war effort' (2014). In *The Telegraph*, the image editor illustrates Tompkins's letter with a caricature by the French illustrator Paul Iribe. Entitled 'Death telling Kaiser Wilhelm that he is dishonoured by the killing of Edith Cavell', the image was originally published in 1916 in the French soldiers' magazine *La Baïonnette*. It shows the Kaiser with a smoking gun, cloaked by Death with a white sheet; to the right a young, quasi-naked Cavell with bare breasts and open hair has sunken down in a puddle of blood, still hanging from the ropes that tied her to a pole. As this example shows, then, Cavell continues to be a figure of transgression through whom, as in *Dawn*, ambivalences and contradictions of war and conflict can be crystallised. But even today, an actualisation of this potential remains contentious and in competition with the hegemonic legacy of wartime visual culture.

Notes

1. I would like to thank Regina De Martelaere (Cinémathèque Royale de Belgique, Brussels) and Jacques Oberson (United Nations Archives, Geneva) for their kind support. I also wish to thank Lisa Purse and Ute Wölfel for their unwavering trust and patience and Brenda Hollweg, as always, for her inspiration and sanity.
2. Earlier narrative films include *Nurse and Martyr* (Percy Moran, UK, 1915), *The Martyrdom of Nurse Cavell* (John Gavin and C. Post Mason, Australia, 1916), *Nurse Cavell* and *La Revanche* (both W. J. Lincoln, Australia, 1916) and *The Woman the Germans Shot* (released as *The Cavell Case*, John G. Adolfi, USA, 1918).
3. *Dawn* and other representations explicitly stress that Cavell was not a spy. Female spies in particular are an amply discussed figure of transgression. For a 'good/bad spy' juxtaposition of Cavell and Mata Hari see White (2008). The centenary radio programme *Secrets and Spies: The Untold Story of Edith Cavell*, presented by the former Director-General of MI5 Stella Rimington, suggests

women in intelligence are perceived as less transgressive in the twenty-first century (Rimington 2015).
4. Examples are the postcard series *Les plus odieux crimes des Boches: L'Assassinat de Miss Edith Cavell* and the set illustrated by Tito Corbella, as well as Cavell in image no. 11, *Panthéon de la Guerre*. Digitisations can be accessed at the Royal Library of Belgium and the Kay Seidenberg Nursing Postcard Collection. On the interwar years, see also Fell and Sternberg (2018).
5. See Souhami (2010: 107 and *passim*) on Cavell's mobility and professional internationalism.
6. Georges Bataille, who theorised transgression and created transgressive works, engaged with the visual representation of executions, sacrifice, death and the corpse (Richardson 1998). A fascination with execution scenes and calls for their restrictions also go back to the early years of filmmaking, as Hunnings relates for the late 1890s and the 1900s (1967: 41–2). On the conjunction of death, art and femininity in Western visual culture see also Elisabeth Bronfen's *Over Her Dead Body* (1992).
7. Kay Seidenberg Nursing Postcard Collection: <https://digital.library.vcu.edu/islandora/object/vcu%3A34151>
8. An example is the feature film *La guerre est une erreur / Oorlog is een dwaling* (Belgium 1928, dir. uncredited).
9. That there was some ambiguity when the news first travelled can be seen in the *Western Daily Press* which erroneously reported that 'one Belgian and one English lady' had been shot (Anon. 1915).
10. Kay Seidenberg Nursing Postcard Collection: <https://digital.library.vcu.edu/islandora/object/vcu%3A34319>
11. According to his personal file held at the League of Nations Archive, Berkeley was in the Information Section of the Secretariat from 1 January to 31 October 1922.
12. Hansard Commons, Deb Foreign Affairs, 24 November 1922, Vol. 159, cc185–224, here 186–7.
13. Hansard Commons, Deb Foreign Office Supervision, 18 February 1924, Vol. 169, c1291; an unsigned letter from Geneva to Berkeley, dated 15 August 1925, states that there is no capacity to 'introduce any new British element [to the League], as we are still somewhat above our numbers' (League of Nations Archive).
14. Recent scholarship has recovered the histories of organised and individual women and also shown how feminist approaches can provide new perspectives; see, for example, Bianchi and Ludbrook (2016) and Sharp and Stibbe (2017).
15. For a summary of wartime and postwar film culture in Belgium, see Engelen (2014).
16. 'La Tragedie de Miss Cavell / Het Treurspel van Miss Cavell'.
17. 'L'aube sanglante de la journée tragique où "Miss Cavell" tomba au Tir National sous les balles allemandes. / De bloedige morgenstond van den

tragischen dag toen "Miss Cavell" in de Nationale Schietbaan onder de Duitsche kogels viel.'

18. '[L]'Allemagne voulut jouer avec le feu pour réduire en cendres le pénible résultat de notre civilisation. / en toen wilde Duitschland met vuur spelen, om den zoo lastig verkregen uitslag onzer beschaving in rook le doen opgaan.'

19. 'LE PROCES Toute l'affaire fut un simulacre de justice, un escamotage digne des sbires du Kaiser qui souillaient de leur présence la salle de séances du Sénat. / HET PROCES Heel de zaak was een schijnrechtspleging, een goocheltoer Waardig van de gerechtsdienaars van den Keizer, die de zittingzaal van den Senaat met hunne tegenwoordigheid bezoedelden.'

20. Berkeley's novelisation presents yet another variation. Baucq is written back into history at the trial and execution, albeit as a minor character (Berkeley n.d.: 143, 162, 235, 237). The book's final pages relay the moments before the execution from inside Cavell's mind (237–40). Blindfolded, she hears that an insubordinate soldier is arrested and threatened with being shot, but she remains conscious and awaits the 'shock and stab of the volley . . .' (240).

Works Cited

Anon. (1915) 'German Ferocity: English and Belgian Ladies Shot', *Western Daily Press*, 16 October, p. 9.
Anon. (1928a) 'Censorship of Films', *The Times*, 1 March, p. 14.
Anon. (1928b) 'The Cavell Film', *The Times*, 30 March, p. 16.
Barney, Shane M. (2005) 'The Mythic Matters of Edith Cavell: Propaganda, Legend, Myth and Memory', *Historical Reflections/Réflexions Historiques*, 31 (2), pp. 217–33.
Barter, Shane Joshua (2012) 'Unarmed Forces: Civilian Strategy in Violent Conflicts', *Peace & Change*, 37 (4), pp. 544–71.
Bataille, Georges (1986 [1957]) *Eroticism: Death and Sensuality*, San Francisco: City Lights Books.
Berkeley, Reginald (1925) *The White Château*. London: Williams & Norgate.
Berkeley, Reginald (1928) 'Nurse Cavell Film' *The Times*, 6 March, p. 12.
Berkeley, Reginald (n.d. [1928]) *Dawn*. London: London Book Co.
Bianchi, Bruna, and Ludbrook, Geraldine (eds) (2016) *Living War, Thinking Peace (1914–1924): Women's Experiences, Feminist Thought, and International Relations*. Newcastle upon Tyne: Cambridge Scholars.
Biltereyst, Daniël, and Depauw, Liesbet (2006) 'Internationale diplomatie, film en de zaak *Dawn*: Over de historische receptie van en de diplomatieke problemen rond de film *Dawn* (1928) in België', *Revue belge d'Histoire contemporaine*, 36 (1–2), pp. 127–55.
Blumenberg, Hans (1985 [1979]) *Work on Myth*. Cambridge, MA: MIT Press.
Bronfen, Elisabeth (1992) *Over Her Dead Body: Death, Femininity and the Aesthetic*. Manchester: Manchester University Press.

Clarke, George Herbert (ed.) (2002) [1917], *A Treasury of War Poetry*, First Series. Boston: Houghton Mifflin; New York: Bartleby.com, <www.bartleby.com/266/> (last accessed 20 January 2019).
Collier, Lionel (1928) 'Reviews of the Weeks', *Kinematograph Weekly*, 12 April, p. 40.
Cooper, Sandi E. (1991) *Patriotic Pacifism: Waging War on War in Europe, 1815–1914*. Oxford: Oxford University Press.
Depauw, Liesbet (2007) 'Reframing the Past to Change the Future: Reflections on Herbert Wilcox's *Dawn* (1928) as a Historical Documentary and War Film', in Leen Engelen and Roel Vande Winkel (eds), *Perspectives on European Film and History*. Ghent: Academic Press, pp. 156–81.
Engelen, Leen (2014) 'Film/Cinema (Belgium)', in U. Daniel et al. (eds) *1914–1918-Online: International Encyclopedia of the First World War*. Berlin: Freie Universität Berlin. DOI: 10.15463/ie1418.10320 (last accessed 15 May 2019).
Enloe, Cynthia (2004) *The Curious Feminist: Searching for Women in a New Age of Empire*. Berkeley and Los Angeles, CA: University of California Press.
Fell, Alison, and Sternberg, Claudia (2018) 'Nurse-Martyr-Heroine: Representations of Edith Cavell in Interwar Britain, France and Belgium', *Journal of War & Culture Studies*, 11 (4), pp. 273–90.
Frühstück, Sabine (2017) *Playing War: Children and the Paradoxes of Modern Militarism in Japan*. Berkeley, CA: University of California Press.
Gledhill, Christine (2008) 'Play as Experiment in 1920s British Cinema', *Film History: An International Journal*, 20 (1), pp. 14–34.
Hunnings, Neville March (1967) *Film Censors and the Law*. London: George Allen & Unwin.
Jenks, Chris (2003) *Transgression*. London and New York: Routledge.
Jones, Heather (2015) 'Violent Transgression and the First World War', *Studies: An Irish Quarterly Review*, 104 (414), pp. 124–43.
Knijff, Christjan (2007) 'Edith Cavell: De problematische representatie van een oorlogsheldin', *Journal for Media History*, 10 (1), pp. 23–52.
Knijff, Christjan (2009) *Edith Cavell: Een bittere herinnering aan de Eerste Wereldoorlog. Problemen met de representatie van een oorlogsheldin tussen 1915 en 1928*. Soesterberg: Aspekt.
Kuhn, Annette (1988) *Cinema, Censorship and Sexuality, 1909–1925*. London: Routledge.
Nowak, Kai (2015) *Projektionen der Moral: Filmskandale in der Weimarer Republik*. Göttingen: Wallstein Verlag.
Pickles, Katie (2007) *Transnational Outrage: The Death and Commemoration of Edith Cavell*. Basingstoke and New York: Palgrave Macmillan.
Purse, Lisa, and Wölfel, Ute (2014) Call for Papers: Figures of Transgression in War Representation Workshop, University of Reading, 19 November, <https://www.jiscmail.ac.uk/cgi-bin/webadmin?A2=ind1411&L=GERMAN-STUDIES&P=R16935> (last accessed 27 February 2020).

Richardson, Michael (ed.) (1998) *Georges Bataille – Essential Writings*. London: Sage.

Rimington, Stella (2015) *Secrets and Spies: The Untold Story of Edith Cavell*. BBC Radio 4, 16 September <https://www.bbc.co.uk/programmes/b069wth6> (last accessed 30 June 2019).

Robertson, James C. (1984) '*Dawn* (1928): Edith Cavell and Anglo-German Relations', *Historical Journal of Film, Radio and Television*, 4 (1), pp. 15–28.

Royal Mint (2015) 'The Royal Mint Honours Edith Cavell', 27 May <https://www.royalmint.com/aboutus/news/royal-mint-honours-edith-cavell/> (last accessed 30 June 2019).

Ruddick, Sara (1993) 'Notes Toward a Feminist Peace Politics', in Miriam G. Cooke and Angela Woollacott (eds), *Gendering War Talk*. Princeton, NJ: Princeton University Press, pp. 109–27.

Sargeant, Amy (2011) '"A Victory and a Defeat as Glorious as a Victory": *The Battles of the Coronel and Falkland Islands* (Walter Summers, 1927)', in Michael Hammond and Michael Williams (eds), *British Silent Cinema and the Great War*. Basingstoke: Palgrave Macmillan, pp. 79–93.

Serna, Laura Isabel (2014) 'Translations and Transportation: Toward a Transnational History of the Intertitle', in Jennifer M. Bean, Laura Horak and Anupama Kapse (eds), *Silent Cinema and the Politics of Space*. Bloomington and Indianapolis, IN: Indiana University Press, pp. 121–46.

Sharp, Ingrid and Stibbe, Matthew (eds) (2017) *Women Activists between War and Peace: Europe, 1918–1923*. New York: Bloomsbury Academic.

Sherwood, A. M., Jr (1928) 'The Movies', *The Outlook*, 27 June, pp. 347–8.

Slim, Hugo (2008) *Killing Civilians: Method, Madness, and Morality in War*. New York: Columbia University Press.

Sluga, Glenda (2013) *Internationalism in the Age of Nationalism*. Philadelphia, PA: University of Pennsylvania Press.

Souhami, Diana (2010) *Edith Cavell*. London: Quercus.

Speck, Catherine (2001) 'Edith Cavell: Martyr or Patriot', *Australian and New Zealand Journal of Art*, 2 (1), pp. 83–98.

Tompkins, Kate (2014) 'BBC Drama Fails to Reflect Edith Cavell's Courage', Letter to the Editor, *The Telegraph* online, 15 May <https://www.telegraph.co.uk/comment/letters/10831551/BBC-drama-fails-to-reflect-Edith-Cavells-courage.html> (last accessed 30 June 2019).

White, Rosie (2008) 'Englishness and Espionage: Edith Cavell as the Good Spy', in Christopher Hart (ed.), *Heroines and Heroes: Symbolism, Embodiment, Narratives and Identities*. Kingswinford: Midrash, pp. 1–13.

Wilcox, Herbert (1967) *Twenty-Five Thousand Sunsets: The Autobiography of Herbert Wilcox*. London: Bodley Head.

Wolfreys, Julian (2008) *Transgression: Identity, Space, Time*. Basingstoke: Palgrave Macmillan.

CHAPTER 3

'An act of wilful defiance': Objection, Protest and Rebellion in the Imperial War Museum's First World War Galleries
Rebecca Clare Dolgoy

The Imperial War Museum (IWM)[1] is an unlikely place to look for figures of transgression. With its 'Extraordinary Heroes' (Ashcroft Gallery: George and Victoria Cross recipients) and its 'Everyday Heroes' (Family in Wartime Gallery: Allpress family), the IWM, like many national war museums, rarely deviates from familiar portrayals of heroes, perpetrators and victims (Thiemeyer 2010: 463) in order to convey 'sanitised', 'glorified' or 'pro-establishment' views to the public (Whitmarsh 2001: 45). Though each country has its own traditions (Arnold-de Simine 2013: 74–5), these types of portrayals reinforce rather than challenge dominant myths and narratives that underpin national cultural cohesion. A transgressor challenges these myths and narratives through acts of affirmative negation, which, according to Chris Jenks, are 'reflexive act(s) of denial and affirmation' (2003: 2) that assert the existence of limits and boundaries. Akin to a sudden 'awareness', described by Albert Camus in *The Rebel* (1991: 14), that attests to both one's own humanity and the humanity of others, the act of transgression, of asserting, of crossing boundaries or refusing to cross boundaries by objecting, protesting and rebelling is an act of transcendental solidarity: this act involves standing with those who came before, those who are among us and those who might come after by asserting that politics could be otherwise.

As one of the main stages of the British commemoration of World War I (WWI) Centenary, London's flagship IWM re-opened to the public after six months of extensive renovations in July 2014 sporting an atrium redesigned by Norman Foster and a new set of First World War Galleries (FWWG) conceived by Casson Mann. The centrality of WWI for British cultural memory is uncontested: WWI, as a phenomenon, is inextricable from both the founding of the museum one hundred years ago in the midst of ongoing conflict in order to serve archival, commemorative and pedagogical functions (Cooke and Jenkins 2001; Kavanaugh 1988; Malvern 2000) and its renewal today during the centenary commemorations. In spite of their purveyance of British stalwart tropes such as 'The Tommies and the Officers' and 'Your Country Needs You', the IWM's new FWWG do feature stories of those who resisted the First World War, and in so doing, transgressed contemporaneous norms. I have identified three different types of transgressors portrayed in the new Galleries: conscientious objectors, soldier-poets such as Siegfried Sassoon and Irish republicans.

I argue that both the curatorial apparatus surrounding them (e.g. texts, objects) and the IWM's current policy of historicising of the past, described by Senior Curator Paul Cornish as a 'policy of "contemporaneity"' (Cornish 2014), undercut the transgressor's 'capacity to challenge . . . or question the unquestionable' (Jenks 2003: 80). Each question raised in the Galleries is accompanied by an answer; every act of resistance is quelled. The new Galleries rely heavily on the word 'most' to suppress potential challenges to its dominant narratives. Similar to the shadowy part of the moon that is invisible during periods of waxing and waning, the voices of transgressors shadow the well represented albeit phantasmagoric majority. In other parts of the IWM some of these transgressors – conscientious objectors and soldier-poets – are brought out of the shadows and materialise before an audience. Irish republicans do not. How and why are certain transgressors palatable in Britain's national war museum and assimilable by prevailing conceptions of national identity while others are not?

This chapter is structured in three sections. In the first I analyse the IWM's curatorial approach in the new FWWG, the 'policy of "contemporaneity"', by outlining its effects and exploring the ensuing consequences. In the second, I offer close readings of these three figures of transgression as they are portrayed in the current galleries and in the wider IWM context. In the third, I contextualise these figures of transgression within the current FWWG's narratives of mythic togetherness and tacit imperialism as well as within wider conceptions of British identity.

Concept: A 'Policy of "Contemporaneity"'

The FWWG are divided into 14 'story areas'. Visitors walk along a prescribed and chronological path through the dark, loud and tight spaces. Upon entering the new Galleries via a gently inclining ramp, visitors look down at large-scale model ships seemingly docked on a sunken floor, and look up to see two screens joined at a right angle, where a film and photo presentation is projected. The theme – 'The people of Britain 1900–1914' – paints an ambivalent portrait of life at that time by addressing inequalities both between the classes and between men and women.

Turning the corner, the projection still in view, visitors come face to face with the first major gallery panel:

> These galleries are about the First World War . . . In Britain, everyone was affected by the Great War, whether they were fighting or on the home front. In these galleries, men, women and children who experienced the war will tell you their stories. They will help show you: Why the world went to war; Why it lasted so long; How the war was won; How it changed the world. They will do this in their own words and through the objects they gave to this museum.

This panel lays out both the 'how' and the 'what' of the new Galleries: the four questions account for their content and underpinning scholarship; the note that 'men, women and children . . . tell you their stories' signals their curatorial approach. On first glance, these questions appear objective: they neither promote nor critique. Furthermore, the emphasis on first-hand accounts appears apolitical and non-partisan, and fits within the IWM's main aim to 'help [their] visitors get close to the lives of those affected by war and to develop a deeper understanding of its effects on the world' (IWM 2018a) by letting people and objects appear to speak for themselves.

But despite this perceived objectivity and seeming withdrawal of an editorial voice, according to Donald Preziosi, museums are works of modern cultural fiction that often tell us more about the times in which they were constructed and curated than those they portray through their collections (2009: 489). Because museums are among the more trusted institutions in western cultures (Kendall 2013; Simon 2008), it becomes imperative to interrogate their contemporaneity by analysing how and why certain pasts are portrayed, and by extensionwhat these portrayals mean for contemporary culture. In Memory Studies, contemporaneity usually implies the presence of the past and a deep engagement with historicity, reception and interpretation. Core operations of Memory Studies emphasise tracing the changing uses and meanings of history, such as Jan and Aleida Assmann's *Funktions- und Speichergedächtnis* (functional and storage memory) (Assmann 1999), or various interpretations of the transnational flow of commemorative forms and museum practices (Bond and Rapson 2014; DeCesari and Rigney 2014; Sodaro 2018).

For the IWM's new FWWG, '"contemporaneity"' means something very different. Cornish defines the museum's 'policy of "contemporaneity"' as follows:

> We . . . portray the war as it was seen by people at the time, without the application of hindsight. This does not mean that there is not a 'museum voice' guiding visitors around the galleries; but just that our text attempts to avoid making judgements which were not made at the time. (Cornish 2014)

In opting to 'avoid making judgements' (Cornish 2014), the IWM's authorial voice ultimately abdicates its ethical obligations. Hindsight is one of the museum's greatest tools because it allows museums to acknowledge the origins of both the events they are portraying and of western museology more broadly, as well as acknowledge the attendant and ensuing ethical dilemmas. Hilde Hein writes that '[l]ong gone is the self-assured composure and elitism of the nineteenth-century institution. Today's museums are reflexive and wracked with the anguish of self-interrogation' (2011: 114). Museum Studies scholar Janet Marstine, whose research focuses on museum ethics, argues for the 'contingency' of contemporary museum ethics and cites curatorial mandates that demand 'social responsibility', 'radical transparency' and consideration for the 'ethics of guardianship' (2011: 8–20). Such curatorial practices take museums beyond representation of the past and into the domain of agency. According to Shelley Ruth Butler and Erica Lehrer the goal of curatorial work is no longer simply to represent but to make things happen (2016: 5). For Marstine, Hein and Butler and Lehrer, a museum's contemporaneity is its contingency: rather than attempt to do the impossible and stage the past of the present, a museum's social responsibility rests in its reflexivity and capacity to expose the presence of the past. A contingency-based approach to the IWM's collection would contextualise its objects within the present and would be open about what has changed between "how events appeared to people at that time" (Cambridge 2014: 7) and how they appear to people now. It would interrogate that distance.

While the historicised approach to the use of first-hand witness testimony is not confined to the new FWWG – historian Tony Kushner gives a nuanced analysis of the use of survivor testimony in the IWM's Holocaust Exhibition in which he notes how individual experiences become flattened and made uniform in subservience to the need to present a coherent exhibition concept (2001: 92) – the effect in the new Galleries is magnified. Carefully selected quotations are deployed on information panels and engraved in the Galleries' surfaces. These quotations are mostly attributed by name, rank and/or nationality, date. The source of the quotation is often omitted so the only context comes from its place in the exhibition. While these quotations offer the illusion of multiperspectivity, they also limit polysemic interpretation. An echo chamber is established, where the main through line of the narrative and the corroborating quotations bounce off one another in the dark and confined Gallery spaces.

For example, the FWWG uses Imperialism to frame its main narrative. The exhibition begins with a story area called 'Hope and Glory' that looks at shifting European alliances and celebrates the strength of the British

Empire, as is evidenced by its introductory panel: 'As the twentieth century dawned, Britain was one of the greatest powers on Earth. This small island nation ruled over a vast global empire.' The exhibition ends in a story area called 'War Without End', whose introductory panel states that 'Britain and its empire were triumphant but much was changed by four years of war . . . Old empires had fallen, new nations had been born'. The panels in 'Hope and Glory' also make use of the word 'most' in order to pre-emptively marginalise critical viewpoints, for example: 'Most Britons were proud of their empire, the greatest the world had ever seen', and 'Most Britons believed that Britain's empire was a force for good.' To further corroborate the portrayal of moral entitlement, the story area features a wall of embedded quotations, such as 'The Old Country must wake up if she intends to maintain her old position of pre-eminence in her colonial trade against foreign competition' (The Duke of York, the future King George V, 1901), and 'Your forefathers worked hard, fought hard, and died hard to make this Empire for you' (Robert Baden Powell, founder of the Scottish Movement, no date given). Interspersed with facts such as 'The British Empire spans 13 million square miles – a quarter of the planet's land mass', there is very little room for transgression. There is, however, one quotation that is critical of empire. Mahatma Gandhi is quoted, stating that 'It is not right that one people should rule another. British rule in India is an evil.' Gandhi's negation of British rule is an affirmation of Indian independence and decolonisation. While history has certainly demonstrated that this transgressive view was correct and drove significant political change, here this view is smothered and, without the benefits of hindsight, it is cut off from its affirmative potential.

Close Readings: Objection, Protest and Rebellion

Having outlined the IWM's 'policy of "contemporaneity"' I will now turn my attention to how this policy affects the museum's representation of transgressors by looking closely at conscientious objectors, soldier-poets (Siegfried Sassoon) and Irish republicans. Each reading will situate the transgressive figure in the new Galleries and in the wider context of the IWM.

Conscientious Objectors

In either a strange or a serendipitous manner, 'Feeding the Front' – the story area of the FWWG that engages with conscientious objectors – and the 'Your Country Needs You' story area, are presented on opposite sides of a dark wooden wall. But whereas 'Your Country Needs You' recounts the history of voluntary recruitment throughout the Empire, 'Feeding the Front' focuses on conscription, the establishment of the home front and the relationship between the two, thus laying the groundwork for the next story area, 'Total War'. Much of the texts and objects devoted to conscientious objectors attempt to contain them by describing them as abnormal 'social outcasts'. This is a multiphased process. First, according to panel text in 'Your Country Needs You', '[m]ost people in Britain put aside their differences to support the war effort . . . Most Britons needed little persuading to play their part in their country's cause.' This establishes conscientious objectors as a deviant minority. Second, the panel text in 'Feeding the Front' describing conscientious objectors states that 'their numbers were few. Of 2.5 million men conscripted less than one per cent raised moral or political objections' and 'A small number of men with ethical or religious objections appealed against conscription.' While 16,500 argued before tribunals, only '6,000 "absolutists" were imprisoned for their beliefs'. This further minimises the minority.

In addition to its use of the word 'most' and presentation of numbers, the Galleries portray conscientious objectors as 'social outcasts' by emphatically presenting the difficulties and brutalities faced by those who, by listening to the call of their conscience, refused the call of their King and their generals. While these brutalities included prison sentences and hard labour, conscientious objectors also faced 'a barrage of public hostility' that called their patriotism and masculinity into question. Among the objects included in the display, visitors can see a cartoon from the 'patriotic paper "John Bull"' that 'shows a conscientious objector lazily smoking at his fireside while his entire family is fighting or on war work'; a 'white feather symbolising cowardice . . . sent to pacifist Bernard Taylor'; a disc with the words 'At Home: A man from this house is now serving in his majesty's forces' that families could put in their window; an official albeit controversial recruiting poster featuring a pensive father looking outward as his son plays with toy soldiers at his feet and his daughter sits on his knee, with the words 'Daddy, what did YOU do in the Great War?' scrawled at the bottom; and the film *A Call to the Young* that, while not labelled as a propaganda film, according to the corresponding panel 'reflects the crushing pressure on the more reluctant British men to do their bit'. The display also features several personal effects including a letter that testifies on behalf of a conscientious objector, another that shows how difficult it was for conscientious objectors to find work, and a note labelled as from an 'anonymous "scoutmistress" to "Mr Brooks", a railway porter' inviting him to 'join the girls scouts as a washerup'. Surrounded by all of the other artefacts and texts, I could find only one object on display that gives visitors insight into why someone may have objected: a *Why We Object* pamphlet issued by the No Conscription Fellowship, a pacifist organisation.

Without giving visitors the opportunity to properly hear from conscientious objectors and without invoking some measure of hindsight, it is difficult for visitors to respond to a question posed on a small label in the middle of the display case: 'Why do you think some men wanted to stay at home?' This question is in itself misleading because it implies that the choice made by conscientious objectors was to 'stay at home' rather than to not fight. Similar questions are placed throughout the gallery and are aimed at younger visitors. In addition to the question, the label contains a subtle response to the question by way of a graphic of a white feather and the text 'Sometimes a man who didn't join the Army was given a white feather to bully him into joining – it meant he was being called a coward for not fighting.' Though the Museum is not directly saying that a man who objects is a coward, it simply lets the historicised 'most Britons' make the claim for them. During a time when every Briton was called to 'play their part', the conscientious objector does not appear to have a part to play. In the FWWG the conscientious objector is portrayed as eschewing solidarity with his contemporaries and with Britons of the past and the future.

But stepping out of the FWWG, conscientious objectors do have a part to play in British cultural memory and the construction of national identity, and these roles are thoughtfully and carefully represented elsewhere in the IWM. For example, the Museum's website boasts a publicly available web archive that documents conscientious objectors 'in their own words' through interviews, ephemera, photographs and texts (IWM 2018b). Writing about this initiative, Margaret Brooks states that: 'The number of COs may appear small compared with the six million who served, but the impact of these men on public opinion and on future governments was to be profound' (2018).

The depth and breadth of this impact was on full display in the summer of 2017 during the *People Power: Fighting for Peace* special exhibition (23 March – 28 August). The exhibition traced a lineage that began with conscientious objectors during the First World War, moved through the interwar years and the development of the Peace Movement, the Second World War, the Cold War and the anti-nuclear movement, and culminated in recent protest against the Iraq War, its aftermath and ongoing conflicts. The exhibition demonstrated how conscientious objection is assimilable for the national museum-going public. Here transgressors are portrayed as an important part of any war: George Dutch, an absolutist conscientious objector in the First World War era is quoted in the exhibition as saying:

'We started a movement which means that no war can be fought in the future without conscientious objection coming up.' Beneath the protest banners hanging from the ceiling, the text-heavy exhibition features a significant amount of audio, video and written testimony. The curators chose to allow different individuals – including many women – to share their own stories on their own terms resulting in nuanced portrayals of protest that avoid stereotypes. In a moving display, visitors could watch a short video in which Veterans for Peace stage a protest outside Downing Street in the summer of 2015. During the protest three veterans, wearing civilian suits and ties, discard their medals of service, army hats and Oath of Allegiance papers. Holding his hat, one veteran proclaims 'I reject militarism. I reject war and [the hat] means nothing to me.' By rejecting 'militarism' these veterans are, according to the Veterans for Peace website, 'affirm[ing their] greater responsibility to serve the cause of world peace' (Veterans for Peace 2018). These Veterans for Peace perform an act of transcendental solidarity that is reminiscent of Camus's rebel, or to be more precise, the slave who becomes the rebel once he refuses both to obey his master and to remain silent about what he considers to be 'unjust' commands (Camus 1991: 13–14).

Historian Lyn Smith, author of the book that accompanies *People Power*, writes that the exhibition offers a 'compelling counterpart to the myriad histories of war in the past hundred years' (Smith 2017: back cover). Smith cites First World War era conscientious objectors as an origin for her genealogy, but she also credits Gandhi 'whose philosophy of non-violence took a firm hold [in the interwar years] and has lasted to the present day . . .' (Smith, 2017: 10). Here we may note two simultaneous representations of one transgressor, Gandhi, in the same Museum: in the permanent gallery his critique of Empire is enveloped by other quotations and the weight of the historicised majority, and in the temporary exhibition, his non-violent resistance is cited as a source of power not only for protest in his own country, but as inspiration for protest beyond those boundaries. When liberated from the 'policy of "contemporaneity"', the transgressor's negation serves as an affirmation and reaches towards transcendental solidarities. The two simultaneous representations of Gandhi signal two different kinds of narrative in the IWM: the first are the dominant narratives in the FWWG and other permanent galleries where transgression is stifled, and the second are the interventions or critical narratives that are conveyed through the IWM's temporary exhibitions, where transgression is nourished. I will return to these narratives when examining the other two case studies.

Siegfried Sassoon: Soldier-Poets

Siegfried Sassoon's letter, *Finished With the War: A Soldier's Declaration* (1917), in which he accuses the political class of 'errors and insincerities for which the fighting men are being sacrificed' and critiques 'the callous complacency with which the majority of those at home regard the continuance of agonies which they do not share and which they have not enough imagination to realise', was read aloud at the time in the British House of Commons. It is a protest letter, an 'act of wilful defiance of military authority' (Sassoon 1917). In speaking 'on behalf of those who are suffering now' Sassoon's letter is also reminiscent of Camus's rebel who 'rebel[s] – therefore we exist' (Camus 1991: 22), or, perhaps paradoxically, emblematic of Jenks's understanding of the 'loneliness' of the contemporary transgressor, who without recourse to 'nihilism' or 'utopia' is temporally isolated (Jenks 2003: 6). Here the transgressor bridges the space between those who cannot see and those who can no longer speak by bearing witness and speaking truth to power. The transgressor also closes the temporal distance between past, present and future by leaving a marker for future generations to find. Unlike the portrayal of conscientious objectors, the portrayal of Sassoon gives visitors relatively direct access to the transgressor: the protest letter, photographs and additional documentary material – specifically a video that compiles biographic information and addresses Sassoon's postwar influence – are on display.

Sassoon's letter is one of the anchoring pieces in the 'Breaking Down' story area, the third to last in the exhibition. It is tucked away between 'Seizing Victory and 'War Without End' – both of which explore the lasting consequences of the First Word War – and right after 'Machines Against Men', one of the most brutal and visceral parts of the exhibition. Set approximately in 1917, 'Breaking Down' offers perhaps the only formal pause in the Galleries' unrelenting trajectory. Some panels display text that exposes the waning of the martial spirit: 'A growing number of civilians, politicians and soldiers were looking for a way out. Statesmen thought about negotiating an end to the war. On the battlefront soldiers went on strike and deserted. On home fronts there was hardship and often hunger. Public calls for peace became louder.' But even here, protest is quickly swallowed by surefooted recourse to the majority view: 'Most voices against the war were not outright pacifists but instead urged negotiation', and 'Why did more people not demand peace? The price already paid in blood by all the fighting nations meant that anything but victory would mean defeat.'

The gallery also contextualises Sassoon within a longer conversation about protest. In addition to depicting the breaking down in 1917, here visitors also catch a glimpse of an undercurrent of resistance that had been running since 1914. A panel claims that 'some political figures and intellectuals in Britain and Germany' were against the war and the display features a set of purple-hued photographic cards of public figures such as Karl Liebknecht, Sylvia Pankhurst, Rosa Luxemburg and Bertrand Russell. This set of cards is a rare instance in the FWWG where affinities between Germans and Britons are conveyed. While this points to larger transnational political projects and links between well-known citizens of enemy nations, this protest is cut off from the protest of ordinary conscientious objectors that was portrayed several story areas ago.

Sassoon's protest is depicted as something of which the British nation can be proud even if the 'policy of "contemporaneity"' ensures that it is also depicted as something that was deviant. The panel tells the story of how 'Sassoon risked heavy punishment for questioning the conduct of the war.' It also shows how this questioning was pathologised at that time: 'To dampen the controversy, the Army diagnosed him with "shell shock" and sent him home for treatment.' To further 'dampen the controversy' the panel concludes with the phrase 'He voluntarily returned to the Western Front in 1918.' While this panel does not challenge the portrayal of Sassoon as a sick man, it does somewhat reach outside the boundaries of 'contemporaneity' and signals a longer genealogy. A nearby panel situates Sassoon among the wider community of 'soldier-poets [who] expressed horror at the fighting and at the public ignorance of its realities'. Ever cautious, the panel continues 'at the time their poetry did not reach a wide audience'. Yet in a nearby video, Sassoon's protest is said to have 'influenced Britain's understanding of the war'.

In addition to the main difference, namely that a soldier-poet still took up arms, perhaps one reason for the discrepancy between the portrayal of conscientious objectors and these intellectuals and poets is the facility with which the 'great men and women' heroic narrative is co-opted by mainstream and neoliberal understandings of nation. Predominantly white middle- or upper-class soldier-poets are as much a familiar trope of British cultural memory traditions as the Tommies and the Officers. The importance of these soldier-poets is made evident by the ample sympathetic portrayals elsewhere in the Museum. For example, the *People Power* exhibit includes a large section on First World War poets and the Bloomsbury Group. There have also been several special exhibitions on war poets including *Poets of the First World War* (1974) and *Anthem for Doomed Youth: Twelve Soldier Poets of the First World War* (2002).

The IWM's use of the soldier-poets fits within a larger strategy of evoking critique through art. According to Sue Malvern, there are two different kinds of narrative presented in the IWM, one with artefacts and one with art (2000). Whereas the permanent galleries seem to move towards specific norm-confirming orders, the art exhibitions seem to leave space for interpretive plurality. Malvern gives the example of John Singer Sargent's painting *Gassed* (1919). It is possibly the most famous and discussed piece in the IWM's art collection partially because it has 'never yielded a fixed or consistent meaning' (Malvern 2000: 192–3). But there have also been provocative temporary art exhibitions, ranging from a display of David Smith's satirical *Medals for Dishonour* (1991) to a rotating series of contemporary artistic critical interventions that challenge the Museum's dominant narratives. Recent exhibitions include contemporary commissions such as Hew Locke's multimedia exhibition that offered a welcome critique of imperialism (2015) and sound installations by Imogen Stidworthy that explored the lingering effects of trauma and PTSD on returning soldiers and their families (2015). Through art, the IWM is able to portray transgressive ideas; however, these portrayals are always somewhat ambivalent. Furthermore, because these temporary exhibitions and artistic interventions may be seen as periphery, their important critical content does not unsettle the main narratives of the permanent galleries.

Irish Republicans

Because of their active rebellion that combines both a refusal and a reimagining of the status quo, Irish republicans perform the 'reflexive act of denial and affirmation' that Jenks designates as a hallmark of transgression (Jenks 2003: 2). The direct rebellion against British imperial rule during a time of mythic national togetherness might offer the clearest example of transgression portrayed in the FWWG. Yet this transgression is the most difficult for the museum to meaningfully represent. While the 'policy of "contemporaneity"' might be able to absorb some of the sting of this transgression through the museum panels – 'Most Irish people supported the war'; 'Many republicans opposed or were reluctant to engage in armed revolt. The Easter Rising was confined to Dublin, with around 1,000 rebels taking part' – there is no way for the IWM to recuperate or co-opt the narrative of the struggles for Irish independence into part of the greater British story. The area where visitors find material on the Easter Rising is called 'At All Costs' and the Irish story takes up very little space amid the accounts of German submarine warfare and America's eventual entrance into the conflict.

The Easter Rising is depicted as already doomed to fail. While lacking in foundational documents about the independent Irish Republic, the exhibit chooses to feature material on the rebels' submission and their treason. Towards the beginning of the story area, visitors are greeted by a proclamation that declares martial law and what is labelled as a 'sporting shotgun [that] was used by Irish republican rebels in 1916', because the 'modern rifles and machine guns which the Germans had shipped to arm them' were intercepted by the Royal Navy. Here we see a clear link between treasonous republicans and the enemies of the British nation. Similar to the portrayal of conscientious objectors, we encounter the transgression from the viewpoint of those in the majority, but specific to this instance we hear the voices of the victors. We do not have the chance to hear the reasons why the Irish republicans chose to revolt nor is the legitimacy of British rule ever questioned. When the visitors do hear from an Irish rebel leader, Patrick (Pádraig) Pearse, he is in the process of surrendering: Pearse offers 'safe passage to a wounded British prisoner needing treatment', and pleads with the other rebels to 'give up "to prevent the further slaughter of Dublin citizens, and in the hope of saving the lives of [their] followers now surrounded and hopelessly outnumbered"'. Pearse and the other leaders were court martialled and executed. Here transgression is featured only insofar as it is overcome and the normal order is restored.

Perhaps because of the Acts of Union 1800, British imperialism in Ireland is presented very differently to the depiction of imperialism in the rest of the Dominions. Ireland does not figure in the 'Hope and Glory' story area. Irish soldiers are well represented throughout the galleries (Peatfield 2018). The Easter Rising is the first indication of fissures in the union. While the British Army is not exonerated by the panels for their 'harsh' and 'brutal' response to the Easter Rising, and even though they are implicated in 'fann[ing] the flames of Irish nationalism' and stoking 'sympathy in Ireland for the republican cause', it is Irish nationalism itself that is cited as the precursor for post-WWI strife. This strife is taken up at the end of the exhibition in the 'War Without End' section that includes a discussion of the Irish War of Independence, the partition of Ireland, and actions taken by both the Irish Republican Army and British forces.

The topic of Irish republicanism appears to be very difficult for the IWM to address in general. While the permanent Galleries do explore the clashes in Northern Ireland in a section called 'War on the Doorstep', to my knowledge there has never been a special exhibition on any topic relating to Irish independence at IWM London. In fact, there does not appear to be any marker or trace of two IRA-planted incendiary devices that detonated in the IWM in September of 1992, though there is a plaque that commemorates the bombing sustained by the building in the Second World War. While conscientious objectors may signal a long running counter-narrative, and soldier-poets may occupy a heroic national pantheon, Irish republicans cannot be assimilated into British national/nationalist narratives. Not only does their act of transgression reject the war, but it also rejects the underpinning political structures of the British Empire.

Conclusion

Through looking at these three different examples of transgression, we can clearly note two things. The first is that while none of the acts of transgression break into the FWWG's main narrative thread, the IWM does feature stories of transgressors on the periphery of these narratives and as interventions. The second is that the transgression of Irish republicans remains both untethered and untethering in the IWM. This lack of representation in both the permanent galleries and temporary exhibitions demonstrates either a lack of capacity or a lack of willingness to deal with the relative recentness of 'The Troubles'. While both conscientious objectors and soldier-poets may be used to ground alternative constructions of national cultural cohesion myths, Irish republicans undermine the capacity to conceive of a British mythic togetherness.

This mythic togetherness is best expressed in how the IWM handles its own imperial past (and, I would argue, present). As I outlined earlier in this chapter, the new FWWG begins with an appraisal of the state of the British Empire in 1914, when 'most Britons were proud of their empire, the greatest the world had ever seen'. In a parallel move, the Galleries close with a reappraisal:

> Victory not only secured the British Empire: it expanded the territory under British control. But in the white Dominions, especially Australia and Canada, war had fostered a heightened sense of national identity. Their peoples expected the Empire to evolve into a more equal Commonwealth. In the non-white Empire, especially India, demands for self-rule became more vocal. Britain had to exert control and maintain its rule. The British Empire of Queen Victoria's days was gone forever.

While there is an indication and recognition that the First World War marked a turning point in attitudes towards independence in the various Dominions, the sentiment that appears to inform this text is one of nostalgia or regret coupled with the threat of violence. More corroboration of this point of view appears in the post-Second World War era part of the Museum, where visitors may read the following text on a panel entitled 'Your Britain 1945–1963': 'Britain was determined to remain a world power, with a global empire and international responsibilities.' Even during a period of significant decolonisation and decline, the Empire still served as an important part of Britain's self-identity.

The choice to emphasise Empire is unsurprising because, while 'Imperial' was initially included in the name and mission of the museum at the behest of those from the former 'Dominions' who wanted recognition for their contributions to the war effort (Kavanagh 1988), today it has become impossible to disentangle it from the Museum's brand. When asked by Stephen Moss of *The Guardian* whether it was time to re-think the Museum's name, Diane Lees, the museum's current director, claims that 'Imperial' in the museum is a 'historical fact as opposed to a political agenda' (Moss 2014). But, for me, such thoughts are symptomatic of a 'policy of "contemporaneity"' that makes it very difficult for visitors to read the actual contemporaneity of the museum's historicised narratives. It becomes easy to identify with the normative order presented in the Museum, to ignore the acts of affirmative transgression and to collapse the distance between then and now, that is to continue to assume that 'Britain's empire was a force for good' while ignoring the lingering effects of imperialism and colonialism even if temporary art exhibitions call this into question.

Paul Gilroy has identified this phenomenon as postcolonial melancholia – the systematic 'inability to mourn' the loss of empire (2005: 102) coupled with repression or the inability to acknowledge the evils perpetrated in the name of Britain's empire (ibid.: 94). It masks the lingering and often unexposed elements of empire in class relations and race relations that persist in British culture and inform nationalist, isolationist and exclusionary projects today. Gilroy suggests that 'martial images' (e.g. the Blitz, the war against the Nazis, Spitfires, Hurricanes) 'circulate' and continue to 'defin[e] the nation's finest hour . . . [and] provide the touchstone for the desirable forms of togetherness that are used continually to evaluate the chaotic, multicultural present and find it lacking' (ibid.: 87–8). For Gilroy this circulation results in a feedback loop that permits a transfer of moral authority from one historical instance to another, and that gives a kind of unquestioned legitimacy to current action (or inaction) on the world stage and at home: 'Brits can know who we are as well as who we were and then become certain that we are still good while our uncivilised enemies are irredeemably evil' (ibid.: 87–9). The mythical 'finest hour' in question is a contemporary creation. It offers the illusion of temporal solidarity with those who came before, who 'sacrificed' their lives for 'us', and with those yet to come, for whom we are maintaining the supposedly just character of society. While conscientious objectors and war poets may have a role to play in this 'us' because they signal a possible better or at least alternative version of this 'us', Irish republicans, whose transgression calls the very nature of the 'us' in question, have no role.

Bringing together this limited transcendental 'us' with the 'policy of "contemporaneity"' results in very real consequences. Several observers, such as Kehinde Andrews, have noted that 'colonial nostalgia is back in fashion' (2016). Evidence pointing to this includes examples such as Conservative MP Heather Wheeler's 'Empire goes for gold' tweet during the Rio Olympics in 2016, or trade secretary Liam Fox's effort to increase trade with Commonwealth nations that has been dubbed 'Empire 2.0'. Brexit itself has been linked with postcolonial melancholia (Andrews 2016; Ashe 2016) and nostalgia for a past that can only be conceived through a 'policy of "contemporaneity"'. Some of the Brexit campaigners, most notably both Boris Johnson, who, as part of his bid for the Prime Minister's job, published a biography of Winston Churchill, and Michael Gove, who, while Education Secretary, famously revamped the British school curriculum and critiqued 'the Left [for] belittling true British heroes' (Gove 2014), evoked military analogies that link the European Union with the Nazis, thus offering a perfect illustration of Gilroy's theories (Cowburn 2016; Merrick 2017). In a 2018 interview with Patrick Wintour of *The Guardian*, the outgoing German ambassador to the UK, Peter Ammon, noted that '[t]he image of Britain standing alone in the Second World War against German domination has fed Euroscepticism in the UK, but does little to solve the country's contemporary problems' (Wintour 2018). Different to the images of 'Britain standing alone' against a historical enemy, when a transgressor stands alone, she stands for and with a transcendental 'us', illuminating the presence of the past in order to see a 'country's contemporary problems'. Because the IWM is both a product and producer of these images, it is important to recognise the real contemporaneity of its curatorial choices.

Note

1. Five institutions make up the Imperial War Museums including: IWM London, IWM North (Manchester), IWM Duxford (Cambridgeshire), the Churchill War Rooms and HMS *Belfast*.

Works Cited

Andrews, Kehinde (2016) 'Colonial Nostalgia Is Back in Fashion Blinding Us to the Horrors of Empire', *The Guardian*, 24 August.

Arnold-de Simine, Silke (2013) *Mediating Memory in the Museum: Trauma, Empathy, Nostalgia*. London: Palgrave Macmillan.
Ashe, Stephen (2016) 'UKIP, Brexit and Postcolonial Melancholy', *Discover Society*, 1 June <https://discoversociety.org/2016/06/01/ukip-brexit-and-postcolonial-melancholy/> (last accessed 12 August 2018).
Assmann, Aleida (1999) *Erinnerungsräume Formen und Wandlungen des kulturellen Gedächtnisses*. Munich: C. H. Beck.
Bond, Lucy and Rapson, Jessica (eds) (2014) *The Transcultural Turn: Interrogating Memory Between and Beyond Borders*. Berlin: Walter de Gruyter.
Brooks, Margaret (2018) 'Conscientious Objectors: In Their Own Words', *Imperial War Museum*, 5 June <https://www.iwm.org.uk/history/conscientious-objectors-in-their-own-words> (last accessed 12 September 2018).
Butler, Shelley Ruth and Lehrer, Erica (eds) (2016) *Curatorial Dreams: Critics Imagine Exhibitions*. Montreal: McGill-Queen's University Press.
Cambridge, Duke of (2014) 'Foreword', in Paul Cornish, *The First World War Galleries*. London: IWM, p. 7.
Camus, Albert (1991) [1951] *The Rebel: An Essay on Man in Revolt*, trans. Anthony Bower. New York: Vintage International.
Cooke, Steven and Jenkins, Lloyd (2001) 'Discourses of Regeneration in Early Twentieth-Century Britain: From Bedlam to the Imperial War Museum', *Area*, 33 (4), pp. 382–90.
Cornish, Paul (2014) 'First World War Galleries Project', *First World War Studies*, 7 May <http://www.firstworldwarstudies.org/member-research.php?s=paul-cornish> (last accessed 12 August 2018).
Cowburn, Ashley (2016) 'Michael Gove Apologises for Comparing Economic Experts Warning Against Brexit to Nazis', *The Independent*, 22 June.
De Cesari, Chiara and Rigney, Ann (eds) (2014) *Transnational Memory*. Berlin: Walter de Gruyter.
Gilroy, Paul (2005) *Postcolonial Melancholia*. New York: Columbia University Press.
Gove, Michael (2014) 'Why Does the Left Insist on Belittling True British Heroes?', *Daily Mail*, 2 January.
Hein, Hilde (2011) 'The Responsibility of Representation", in Janet Marstine (ed.), *The Routledge Companion to Museum Ethics*. Abingdon: Routledge, pp. 112–26.
Imperial War Museum (2018a) 'About IWM', *Imperial War Museum* <https://www.iwm.org.uk/about> (last accessed 12 August 2018).
Imperial War Museum (2018b) 'Conscientious Objectors: In Their Own Words', *Imperial War Museum*, 5 June <https://www.iwm.org.uk/history/conscientious-objectors-in-their-own-words> (last accessed 12 September 2018).
Jenks, Chris (2003) *Transgression*. London: Routledge.
Kavanagh, Gaynor (1988) 'Museum as Memorial: The Origins of the Imperial War Museum', *Journal of Contemporary History*, 23 (1), pp. 77–97.

Kendall, Geraldine (2013) 'In Museums They Trust', *Museums Association – Museums Journal*, 113 (4), p. 17.
Kushner, Tony (2001) 'Oral History at the Extremes of Human Experience: Holocaust Testimony in a Museum Setting', *Oral History*, 29 (2), pp. 83–94.
Malvern, Sue (2000) 'War, Memory and Museums: Art and Artefact in the Imperial War Museum', *History Workshop Journal*, 49, pp. 177–203.
Marstine, Janet (2011) 'The Contingent Nature of New Museum Ethics', in Janet Marstine (ed.), *The Routledge Companion to Museum Ethics*. Abingdon: Routledge, pp. 3–25.
Merrick, Rob (2017) 'Boris Johnson Accuses EU of Contemplating Nazi-style "Punishment Beatings" in Revenge for Brexit', *The Independent*, 18 January.
Moss, Stephen (2014) 'The Imperial War Museum: As Much a Relic as its Spitfires and Doodlebugs?', *The Guardian*, 10 July.
Peatfield, Lisa (2018) 'Why Men of Ireland Volunteered to Fight in the First World War', *Imperial War Museum*, 21 June <https://www.iwm.org.uk/history/why-men-of-ireland-volunteered-to-fight-in-the-first-world-war> (last accessed 12 September 2018).
Preziosi, Donald (2009) 'Epilogue', in Donald Preziosi (ed.), *The Art of Art History*. Oxford: Oxford University Press, pp. 488–503.
Sassoon, Siegfried (1917) *An Act of Wilful Defiance*, statement of protest written 15 June. Read before the House of Commons, 30 July 1917, printed in *The Times*, 31 July.
Simon, Nina (2008) 'Trust Me, Know Me, Love Me: Trust in the Participatory Age', *Museum 2.0*, 28 March <http://museumtwo.blogspot.com/2008/03/trust-me-know-me-love-me-trust-in.html> (last accessed 12 August, 2018).
Smith, Lyn (2017) *People Power: Fighting for Peace from the First World War to the Present*. London: Thames & Hudson.
Sodaro, Amy (2018) *Exhibiting Atrocity: Memorial Museums and the Politics of Past Violence*. Newark, NJ: Rutgers University Press.
Thiemeyer, Thomas (2010) 'Zwischen Helden, Tätern und Opfern: Welchen Sinn deutsche, französische und englische Museen heute in den beiden Weltkriegen sehen', *Geschichte und Gesellschaft*, 36 (3), pp. 462–91.
Veterans for Peace (2018) 'Our Mission', *Veterans for Peace*, <https://www.veteransforpeace.org/who-we-are/our-mission> (last accessed 12 August 2018).
Whitmarsh, Andrew (2001) '"We Will Remember Them": Memory and Commemoration in War Museums', *Journal of Conservation and Museum Studies*, 7, pp. 11–15.
Wintour, Patrick (2018) 'German Ambassador: Second World War Image of Britain Has Fed Euroscepticism', *The Guardian*, 29 January.

CHAPTER 4

Figures of Transgression in Representations of the First World War on British Television

Emma Hanna

Since the 1960s British television programmes about 1914–18 have been produced, broadcast and received as memorials, small-screen alternatives to stone and bronze (Hanna 2007, 2009). The act of producing and viewing a programme about the conflict is an act of remembrance in its own right. This commemorative impulse – the visceral need to remember the war at significant points in time – means that British television has continued to be a powerful and influential platform for representations of 1914–18. Despite the fact that the Tommies of 1914–18 are now more than a century out of our reach, British television output shows that in Britain the memory of the First World War endures. However, the representations of 1914–18 curated in cultural responses to the First World War repeatedly emphasise particular imagery and ideas; the persistent tropes of mud, blood and poetry support the accepted national narrative that underscores the tragedy and futility of the war. The dominant narrative's emphasis on heroism, stoicism and sacrifice means that figures of transgression – those deemed to have broken a law or moral code, including spies, deserters, cowards, mutineers and conscientious objectors – have been largely absent from the national narrative. However, where they are included, those who had been seen to have betrayed their country, those whose courage was perceived to have been found wanting, and others who in various ways failed or refused to serve their King and Country, have provided a moral foil to underscore the right-ness of the conflict and those who made the ultimate sacrifice.

This chapter will explore British televisual representations of transgression in the First World War. It will focus on the ways in which mutiny, desertion and conscientious objection have been used to subvert normative narratives of the Great War and the notions of identity linked to them. It will also consider how the deployment of historical transgression has enabled critical reflections of contemporary political and social discourses. It will demonstrate how and why the intersection of the commemorative impulse in televisual representations of war encourages reflection on and negotiation of positions within and outside of the more reassuring cultural narratives about the conflict, within institutional and governmental contexts for production and reception. It will focus on texts that return to the figures of the mutineer, conscientious objector and deserter to show how these figures function in representations of the Great War, conflict, politics and nationhood, and how they have shifted over time. These examples indicate that such figures provide uncomfortable counter-narratives but that these are ultimately deployed to reinforce dominant ideas about the war. This chapter will therefore examine the ways in which the television medium has mediated public discourse about the historical and historiographical meanings of war and identity during and after the conflict of 1914–18.

The 1960s and 1970s: A Golden Age?

It has been said that British television experienced a 'golden age' of drama in the 1960s and 1970s, when television productions were relatively well funded and producers were allowed greater freedom and creativity compared to 'the more subservient roles played by their counterparts today' (Cooke 2003: 4). Britain's televisual representations of the First World War began in the 1960s with the production and broadcast of *The Great War* (BBC, 1964) to mark the fiftieth anniversary of the conflict. This 26-part series is acknowledged to be Britain's first modern history documentary which heralded a new age in television. *The Great War* broke new boundaries with its generous budget, the voluminous amount of archive footage it sourced from around the world and the number of people who were involved in its production. Sixty full-time staff interviewed more than 1,200 people from six different countries, assisted by seventy organisations from around the world (Staff Writer for *Kine Weekly* 1964: n.p.). *The Great War* was watched by approximately one-fifth of adults in Britain: a mean audience share of 16.5 per cent with an average of 8,167,500 viewers per episode (BBC 1988). The version of the First World War as presented by *The Great War* remained largely unquestioned because of the sheer weight of the series' size and authority: it was a televisual monument to the dead of 1914–18. Over 400 veterans were interviewed for the series.

However, the oral testimonies that were selected for inclusion in the series did not show the full range of wartime experiences. In *The Great War*, those whose deaths were ordered by courts martial as punishment for treachery, desertion, cowardice, mutiny, murder, striking or violence, disobedience, sleeping on post, quitting post and casting away arms were not discussed. Between August 1914 and March 1920, 3,080 British and

Commonwealth soldiers were sentenced to death by courts martial under the Army Act: 346 were confirmed and carried out. The death penalty was used by the British Army for all these offences bar treachery. Private Alan Bray, who served in the Wiltshire Regiment, was one of the 400 veterans interviewed on camera for the BBC series in the autumn of 1963. He spoke about his experiences of receiving an order to serve in a firing party to execute a man from another battalion who had been found guilty of desertion. Bray refused because

> I didn't think it was right in the first place that Englishmen should be shooting other Englishmen. I thought we were in France to fight the Germans. I thought that I knew why these men had deserted if they had deserted, because I understood their feelings which and what would make them desert . . . An old soldier in our battalion told me that . . . it is one thing in the army which you could refuse. So I straight away went back to the sergeant and said 'I am sorry I am not doing this' and I heard no more about it. (Bray 1963)

Bray's account, now held in the archives of the Imperial War Museum, is just one example where an individual believed that shooting a man on his own side was a morally transgressive act that he was not prepared to perform, but also because he himself understood the reasons why this man had lost his courage and deserted. However, Bray's account did not make the final cut of *The Great War* series. His testimony would have jarred with the overall tone of the series, which was written to provide a more heroic grand narrative account of Britain winning a costly and hard-won victory. A more palatable representation of the war was presented by the flagship dramatic series of this period, *Upstairs Downstairs* (LWT, 1971–5). The fourth series, which is set in the period of the First World War, features the lives of the Bellamy family and their servants at 165 Eaton Place, London. It was first broadcast in September 1974 during the sixtieth anniversary of the start of the conflict. *Upstairs Downstairs* closely followed the accepted narrative line of the British war experience. The eldest son goes off to join his battalion, the butler is horrified by the arrival of Belgian refugees, the elder daughter signs up to be a nurse in the Voluntary Aid Detachment (VAD) and the footman is handed a white feather before returning with shell shock, presented as a logical consequence of his wartime service.

With expanded production opportunities offered by developing camera technology and colour film, documentary makers in the 1970s looked to make programmes in a different style. However, the focus of these programmes would continue to be the concepts of heroism and sacrifice. Transgressive figures would not appear in Malcolm Brown's *Battle of the Somme* (BBC, 1976), the first British arts-style documentary to be made about the First World War. The programme utilised the cultural inheritance of the First World War by presenting history as tragic art in the form of Elegy: a poetic mode of mourning for the dead. Presented by the actor Leo McKern, the programme showed how television could utilise existing representations of the war's landscape found in well known cultural reworkings and recordings – such as the music of Ralph Vaughan Williams and the paintings of Paul Nash – to enhance the televisual narrative by resonating with the aural and visual impressions of loss, horror and futility that lie at the core of Britain's modern memory of the First World War. *Battle of the Somme* also showed how the voices of the men who fought could be prioritised over the work of historians and scriptwriters. The First World War on the small screen reflected the development of works about the war in print by mining relatively vast but disappearing seams of memory of the British Tommy at war. Television reflected the trend for more populist oral-based histories from the 1980s led by Lyn Macdonald, Max Hastings, Malcolm Brown, Max Arthur and Richard Van Emden. The increase in interest was reflected by 'memorial' programmes such as *Gone for a Soldier* (Scottish TV, 1985, written by Lyn Macdonald), *Very Exceptional Soldiers* (BBC, 1986), *A Time for Remembrance* (Channel 4, 1989) and *A Game of Ghosts* (BBC, 1991). These programmes focused on the established tropes of remembrance; scenes featuring be-medalled war veterans were recorded at local war memorials, Remembrance Day parades and commemorative ceremonies held in towns near the former battlefields in France and Belgium. In this period, therefore, figures of transgression were set aside in the service of the dominant narrative of heroic sacrifice.

Mutiny

The political unrest of the 1980s provided the backdrop for programmes which sought to attack the establishment. Anglo-Irish relations remained complicated, and the Falklands War (1982), Miners' Strike (1984–5) and a number of city-centre riots (for example Brixton and Handsworth 1981 and 1985) contributed to a period of social and political anxiety. The now ubiquitous 'butchers and bunglers' cliché – that the men of the British High Command, the majority members of the British upper class, thoughtlessly sacrificed millions of working-class men in successive failed offensives during the conflict – found an audience in this turbulent period. The battles waging between the Tory government and the National Union of Miners, of class conflict, mass unemployment and the rising tensions between minority racial groups and the police, for example, found analogical expression in televisual representations of the First World War. *Lions Led by Donkeys*

(Channel 4, 1985) was the first documentary programme to publicly attack the British High Command, particularly Field Marshal Sir Douglas Haig. One scene, for example, showed a still image from the audience watching the first *Live Aid* concert of July 1985 to demonstrate the number of British men who were killed in the first hours of the Somme offensive on 1 July 1916. Another example from the same documentary showed a young man approaching a Job Centre and seeing his reflection in the window dressed in the khaki uniform of a soldier from the First World War. The 1980s also saw the production and broadcast of cultural interpretations which buttressed ideas about the conflict's futility. Derek Jarman's cinematic interpretation of Benjamin Britten's *War Requiem* (1988) played heavily on the Christ-like sacrifice of young men, while the only comedy to be based in 1914–18, *Blackadder Goes Forth* (BBC, 1989), portrayed Haig planning his next infantry attack by sweeping up toy soldiers with a dustpan and brush. However, it was Alan Bleasdale's dramatisation of *The Monocled Mutineer* that caused a political and historiographical furore. The screenplay for the four-part series, written by Alan Bleasdale and broadcast in September 1986, attracted an average audience of 8.8 million viewers, a 40 per cent audience share (BARB 1986). Based on a book called *Toplis: The Monocled Mutineer: The Life and Death of the Incredible Percy Toplis – Mutineer, Racketeer, Master of Disguise, Rake and Rogue*, written by John Fairley and William Allinson in 1978, the series was a source of political and historiographical controversy. Percy Toplis (Paul McGann), a lower-class semi-criminal in the ranks of the Army, is said to have instigated mutiny at the infamously brutal military training camp in Étaples in Spring 1917. He evades the military police by fleeing to England where he adopts the identity of an officer who had been killed (see Figure 4.1). The portrayal of violent men in muddy khaki was perceived as offensive to the memory of the millions who went to fight. The swearing, drinking, robbing, raping and mutinous soldier characters portrayed in *The Monocled Mutineer* transgressed Britain's dominant memory of the First World War, which traditionally elides the less sanitary sides of life in the armed forces during wartime.

Bleasdale had already established a reputation for producing gritty real-life dramas such as *Boys from the Black Stuff* (BBC, 1982), a five-part series about the effect of unemployment on a gang of road workers from Liverpool. Bleasdale drew further comparisons with the socio-political condition of Britain in other interviews. In another reference to First World War soldiers as 'cannon fodder' he underlined that 'like today, with unemployment and the Falklands, hopes and dreams were dying in the gutter' (Bleasdale 1986). It is not without irony that the trench scenes in *The Monocled Mutineer*, which were filmed at a peat works on the Somerset Levels, featured approximately one hundred extras who were 'enlisted' from local job centres.

FIGURES OF TRANSGRESSION ON BRITISH TV 59

Figure 4.1 Percy Toplis (Paul McGann) impersonating a dead officer. Still from *The Monocled Mutineer* (BBC, 1986).

Claims by right-wing political commentators and the British press that *The Monocled Mutineer* is an overtly left-wing piece are somewhat wide of the mark but are symptomatic of the backdrop of industrial unrest, for example the Miners' Strike (1984–5), against which the programme was written, filmed and broadcast. Toplis (Paul McGann) is not presented as a socialist, nor is he portrayed as a particularly political character. That role is fulfilled by the character Charles Strange (Matthew Marsh). In the second episode, Toplis and many of the soldiers in the camp are angered when they witness the harsh military punishments administered to some of their fellow soldiers. Violence against the camp commanders ensues and the deserting soldiers establish their own camp. A key exchange in a scene between the mutineers expounds Toplis's and Strange's different political attitudes:

Strange: But there's many reasons for deserting. And you never know, education could be one of them.
Toplis: A reluctance to get killed must come high on the list.
Strange: Aye it does, as well as a reluctance to kill your own kind.
Toplis: Germans?
Strange: Young men. Cannon fodder, just like you and me.
Toplis: Listen. If you're talking politics, talk to someone else with your grammar school ideas. It's politics got us into this sodding mess.
Strange: And it's politics that'll get us out. The politics of socialism. I'm a socialist.
Toplis: But of course, I mean, aren't we all . . .
Strange: And, after being conscripted into this madness, I'm a pacifist as well.

Nor is the disturbance in the camp presented as an organised mutiny. Indeed, the mutiny scenes are directed as a confused and brutal burst of the soldiers' frustrations at their treatment rather than an organised mini-revolution. The odd red flag can be seen in the background but the traditional socialist symbol is outnumbered on screen by flags displaying the skull and crossbones motif. Bleasdale himself said that:

> I tried to make it clear that the mutiny, like the Brixton and Toxteth riots, wasn't politically motivated although it also happened because of politics, because of the condition of the people, which is brought about by political factors. The mutineers were like the rioters – they were just fed up, had had enough and hit back. Toplis is in no way a socialist, although Strange is, but he isn't the central character, not in any sense a mouthpiece or exemplary. I suppose he is as near as I'd go to putting my own personal beliefs in a piece, which is probably why I killed him off! I don't want to stand up on a soapbox and preach to people, any more than I want to be preached to . . . What my films are saying is not think this or that . . . here's a different view of history, think about it. (Bleasdale, quoted in Petley 1987: 131)

It remains a difficult series for British viewers to watch. The representation of a large body of British soldiers transgressing military discipline goes against the ways in which the majority of these men are remembered. The idea that a group of soldiers who fought for King and Country turned against the British Army and were involved in the willing destruction of a French village and its inhabitants does not fit with key concepts in Britain's memory such as honour and duty.

Figure 4.2 A scene from the deserters' camp. Still from *The Monocled Mutineer*.

The 'Memory Boom' and Victimhood

In parallel with the 'memory boom' of the 1990s (referring to the prominence of memory and memory studies both inside and outside of academia), there was a cultural shift in British televisual representations of the First World War which reinforced old narratives of the war but elsewhere also opened opportunities to explore alternative perspectives. Around the time of the eightieth anniversary commemorations, documentaries appeared to split into two broad camps: there was a revival of the military-diplomatic series, such as Richard Holmes's *Western Front* (BBC, 1999), but there was also a noticeable emphasis on cultural aspects of the war such as poetry, music and individual narratives from the home front, for example the series *1914–18* (BBC, 1996) and the development of reality reconstruction programmes such as *The Trench* (BBC, 2002). The commemorations also stimulated a heightened interest in the production and broadcast of more investigative programmes, particularly those which featured the direct testimonies of elderly veterans. A number of First World War documentaries broadcast during the late 1990s placed the remaining veterans of 1914–18 at the centre of onscreen remembrance. The ninetieth anniversary of the armistice added to programme-makers' anxiety that the last representatives of the First World War generation must not be allowed to slip away without first recording their wartime memories for the nation. By the time *Veterans: The Last Survivors of the Great War* (BBC, 1998) was broadcast, veterans' roles in remembrance rituals had reached a prevalent status which has remained largely unquestioned since. Veterans on camera have given the war a human dimension, and viewers can respond to one man's experiences of war more easily than large and faceless statistics. On the other hand, the use of veterans has contributed to the creation of myths about the First World War by buttressing the traditional narratives of the conflict. It has been suggested that television has encouraged a 'tyranny of the witness', the pretext that only the men who have lived through the war have the moral, generational and historical right to discuss it (Audoin-Rouzeau and Becker 2000: 37–9). Significantly, none of the men featuring in these documentaries were those who had transgressed accepted notions of duty and service. Harry Patch, the eponymous 'Last Tommy', was a pacifist who was conscripted into the Army, but he did not apply to be a conscientious objector, so along with the majority of veterans featured on British television, he did not transgress the soldier role which was expected of him.

In the same period, Field Marshal Sir Douglas Haig became a figure whose actions were revisited in the context of more challenging aspects of the war. After his death in 1928, influential memoirs such as those published by the wartime Prime Minister David Lloyd-George in the 1930s portrayed Haig as an uncaring and careless military commander who had thoughtlessly sacrificed the lives of his men. The anti-war sentiments of the 1960s proved fertile ground for further representations of Haig as a figure of ridicule. The veteran historian Basil Liddell Hart was highly critical of the British High Command, led by Haig, and popular histories such as Alan Clark's *The Donkeys* (1961) were particularly scathing. The popular stage play *Oh, What a Lovely War* (1963) and subsequent film *Oh! What a Lovely War* (1969) used allegory and satire to criticise the ways in which the war was fought. In the film, Field Marshal Haig (John Mills) is seen counting British casualties from the Battle of the Somme on a cricket scoreboard. *Haig: The Unknown Soldier* (BBC, 1996) attempted to show that Haig's reputation as a 'butcher' and 'bungler' was inaccurate and undeserved. At a time when the Shot at Dawn campaign[1] was gaining momentum to get the executed men exonerated of their 'crimes', Haig's authorisation to execute those soldiers designated figures of transgression by the court martial process, including deserters and those accused of cowardice, was seen as particularly problematic. In some ways Haig was being reframed as himself a figure of transgression. However, the negative public reaction to the programme showed that not everyone appreciated this. Two years after the programme was broadcast, *The Express* launched a campaign to pull down Haig's statue in Whitehall.

Haig's reputation was again under fire in *Shot at Dawn* (Carlton, 1998), and in this programme a significant shift to consider the perspective of those soldiers falling foul of military rules on cowardice and desertion is evident. As the following analysis illustrates, the programme's commitment to its marginalised soldier subjects is strong enough to sometimes elide aspects of the historical record. *Shot at Dawn* showed just how intense the debate over pardons for the 306 British soldiers executed during the war had become. Out of 324 soldiers executed from Britain and the Dominions, ninety-one men (28 per cent) were subject to suspended sentences for previous offences and forty had been sentenced to death before. One soldier had been handed the death sentence on two previous occasions. These figures do not give the impression of an unrelentingly harsh military system, but instead 'suggest a system of military justice that could be tough but was usually prepared to give a man another chance' (Peaty 1999: 199). Yet *Shot at Dawn*'s presentation suggests otherwise. During the programme's discussion of individual cases, interspersed with interviews with living relatives of the deceased, the camera pans to rostrum shots of documents, among them a death warrant, focusing on the words 'confirmed: Haig'. Often there are a few poppies placed on the paper for added pathos. The granddaughter of executed soldier Harry Farr seems disgusted with Haig as she proclaims: 'I don't think he ever refused [to sign] one.' She is unaware of the fact that Haig authorised only 11 per cent of the total sentenced to death, and that more than 80 per cent of death sentences were commuted to lesser punishments (Corrigan 2003: 229) The principal charge laid against Haig in *Shot at Dawn* is the authorised murder of men based on distinction of class, which is expressed in the language of left-wing class struggle. What the programme fails to illustrate is that men were tried by officers from neighbouring units and executed by men from their own units: they were judged and punished by those who were facing the same dangers and hardships as the accused. *Shot at Dawn* does not inform the viewer of the actual legal process that was followed by the British Army as it leaves the audience to infer that Haig was the ultimate judge and jury. As John Peaty has shown, the courts martial system was full of checks and balances. The surviving proceedings provide no evidence that the chain of command was circumvented, or that those in the chain of command discharged their responsibilities frivolously or incompetently (Peaty 1999: 219).

The programme's purpose is to posit the *Catch-22* style irony that not only did British commanders purposely execute their own men on grounds of class, but that their battle tactics were also responsible for the mass slaughter of the men who carried out their orders. *Shot at Dawn* underlines this sense of irony at the beginning of the programme. Over the most well-known 'over the top' scene from the official film *Battle of the Somme* (1916), an actor's voice reads Private Albert Troughton's last letter to his family: 'Think how we were being slaughtered at the beginning of the war. You would think that they would have a bit of pity and mercy for those who are living and fighting for their country.' This reading is followed by aerial shots of military cemeteries to underline that behind the official commemoration of British sacrifice, there are 306 'unremembered' souls who were killed by their own side. The camera then pans to other graves surrounded by masses of flowers to signify that along with those who died in action, the executed were also cut down while their lives were in full bloom. The broadcast and positive reception of *Shot at Dawn* is evidence of the shift in the public's perception of this divisive element in First World War history. Military executions had never before featured in a mainstream documentary, certainly not in the grand narrative of the Great War. It can be seen that, during the 1980s and 1990s, greater acceptance of terms such as post-traumatic stress disorder – officially recognised as a legitimate medical condition in 1980 – previously termed shell shock or combat fatigue, validated entitlements to public sympathy (Winter 2000).

Shot at Dawn is a good example of how the past is subject to judgements from the present imposed retrospectively on past events. The programme is influenced more by today's civilian standards rather than the historical context of the military regimen of 1914. One scene shows the niece of an executed soldier, Private Billy Nelson of the Durham Light Infantry, visiting her uncle's grave in Flanders for the first time. At the graveside she recalls that her mother, the sister of the executed man, had told her that he had been murdered. Kneeling in front of the uniform headstone she sobs:

> I'm here, I'm here. I'd thought I'd lost you. I'm here for Mum. I've got your Bible, and I've got all the things of Mum's like the poppy she bought the second year after you were gone. She was only fifteen and she's kept it eighty years and she loved you. You loved your sister and your brother – who you never saw grow up; to know a mother's love, a wife's love, or a family. You never had that chance – they took it away from you and God forgive them because I never will and never will Mum. Goodbye sweet uncle.

The relatives who featured on *Shot at Dawn* asserted on the programme that the executed men 'were just as much victims of that war' and that 'it's a shame we have this stain on our history'. Executed men's graves were indistinguishable from those of their comrades who died in action, but *Shot at Dawn* does not pay heed to this important point: 'in some corner of a foreign field that is forever England the dust of those who died bravely and those whose deaths were shaming are irretrievably mixed' (Peaty 1999: 221). By the 2000s, support for the 'Shot at Dawn' campaign had shifted towards being part of established remembrance rituals. In November 2000, the families of fifteen British soldiers executed during the war took part in the official march past the Cenotaph for the first time, an event organised by the British Legion, who were said to have sympathy with the families' cause (Ward 2000: 5). In 2005, the family of Private Harry Farr took the government to the High Court in an attempt to win a posthumous pardon for his execution for cowardice, and on 6 November 2006 MPs agreed that all of the men executed in the First World War should be given a posthumous conditional pardon. In a similar vein, the 2000s saw a flourishing of sympathetic televisual depictions of another figure of transgression: the conscientious objector.

Approximately 16,000 men claimed conscientious objection once the Military Service Act was passed to allow conscription in January 1916. There were two categories of conscientious objection: 'alternativists' refused to bear arms but would be involved in non-combatant work while 'absolutists' refused to have anything to do with the war. The BBC's commemorative programming for the ninetieth anniversary of the armistice in 2008 was the first to discuss conscientious objection among less well-known histories from the First World War. Programmes such as *Not Forgotten: The Men Who Wouldn't Fight* (Channel 4, 2008) and *Timewatch: The Last Day of World War One* (BBC, 2008), featured conscientious objectors and the severely disfigured survivors of 1914–18. *Not Forgotten: The Men Who Wouldn't Fight*, presented by Ian Hislop, looked at the history of conscientious objectors during the conflict and asked: 'Ninety years on were they cowards or shirkers, or were they in their own way courageous for refusing to fight?' Standing at the less well-known memorial to conscientious objectors in Tavistock Square, London, Hislop asserts that 'it's important that these individuals are not forgotten'. The programme underlines that several thousand individuals did not lack courage: they served on or near the front line on the Western Front unarmed and unpaid. The documentary also exposes some rather shameful behaviour on the side of the British Army, who at one point pretended that a large group of 'absolutists' were to be executed for refusing to be involved in the war effort before 'commuting' their sentence to imprisonment and hard labour.

Contemporary Traces of the Great War

Television dramas about the First World War can be divided into five types: dramatic series made about the war, such as *The Monocled Mutineer* (BBC, 1986), *The Unknown Soldier* (BBC, 1996), *The Red Baron* (BBC2, 2012), *The Crimson Field* (BBC2, 2014), *Our World War* (BBC3, 2015), *The Passing Bells* (BBC1, 2014), *37 Days* (BBC2, 2014) and *Anzac Girls* (Channel 4, 2014); dramatic series which include episodes/wartime narratives such as *Upstairs Downstairs – series 4* (ITV, 1974), *Downton Abbey – series 2* (ITV, 2011), *The Village – series 1* (ITV, 2012) and *Life in Squares* (BBC, 2015); literary adaptations such as *My Boy Jack* (ITV1, 2007), *Birdsong* (BBC, 2011) and *Parade's End* (BBC, 2012); comedies – *Blackadder Goes Forth* (BBC, 1989), *Chickens* (Sky, 2013) and *The Wipers Times* (BBC, 2013); and finally dramatic series set in the immediate postwar period, for example *Peaky Blinders – series 1 and 2* (BBC, 2013–14). The majority of these dramatic narratives engage with the themes of loss and futility that are well established in Britain's modern memory of the First World War. This final section of the essay explores how the Great War's normative narratives and progressive portrayals of figures of transgression interweave through popular historical television drama – to provide dramatic pathos or historical context. The themes that emerge in these contemporary dramas reveal much about how the objector and traumatised soldier are now understood.

Although new programmes have been produced, televisual output about the First World War still refers back to images and ideas which resonate with the accepted stories of the conflict: the established tropes of mud, blood and poetry, that the majority of women served as nurses, that most servicemen were liable to become mutinously left-wing, and of trauma, punishment and executions on the orders of an unfeeling High Command. This accepted view of the war was perpetuated by *Downton Abbey* (ITV, 2011–15), the natural heir to *Upstairs, Downstairs*. As the popularity of the series testifies, even in the 2010s it remains that 'the British usually look back [to] the trenches as a lost Edwardian Eden' (Reynolds 2013: 430). The first series of *Downton Abbey* had already established itself as a national Sunday evening favourite with approximately twelve million viewers (BARB 2011). The second series of *Downton Abbey* is set against the backdrop of the second half of the war, from the Battle of the Somme in 1916 to the 1918 flu pandemic. The storyline details how many of the town's men go off to fight in the war, as Downton Abbey is converted into an officers' hospital. Matthew Crawley (Dan Stevens), the heir to the estate, enlists as an officer in the British Army along with Downton's footman William Mason (Thomas Howes) as his batman. While William dies from his war wounds after a deathbed marriage, the only transgressive episodes occur when the cook discovers her nephew has been shot for cowardice, and the footman allows himself to be shot in the hand in order to be sent back to safety in England.

A more social realist portrayal of wartime life was provided by *The Village* (ITV, 2013). Set in a Derbyshire village, the first six-episode series covered the years 1914–20. The story is narrated by the character of Bert, a twelve-year-old boy in a working-class farming family who are experiencing hard times. His brother Joe Middleton is encouraged to go to war by his mother Grace as an opportunity to leave the village, but he returns with shell shock after fighting on the Somme and being subjected to the harsh military punishment of being tied to a stake and exposed to enemy fire overnight. When he fails to return to his regiment he is caught in the village by the military police and executed for desertion. A man from the village is imprisoned as a conscientious objector. Striking cinematic shots of the vast panoramas of the English countryside provided a counterpoint to the microcosm of village life, albeit during a period of intense suffering and trauma. The nature of the series was 'unremittingly grim, and offered few moments of escapism' (Lawrence 2013). The programme's audience decreased throughout the series, the final episode being watched by 5.48 million viewers (BARB 2013). This implies that the events of the wartime narrative were not enough to keep viewers' interest or that they may have found the series too harrowing. One reviewer suggested that the scheduling of the programme was an issue. Viewers tended 'not to want challenging fare on Sunday nights. The costume dramas that have succeeded on Sundays – *Lark Rise to Candleford* (BBC, 2008–11), *Downton Abbey*, *Mr Selfridge* (ITV, 2013–16) – have seduced audiences by rejecting any sort of reality and aiming for a cosy candlelit view of the past, or big, bold storylines with a soap-like quality' (Lawrence 2013).

After a number of literary adaptations in the 1990s and early 2000s, the heir to Percy Toplis arrived on British television screens in 2013. After returning from his wartime service in a tunnelling company on the Western Front, Tommy Shelby (Cillian Murphy), the lead character in *Peaky Blinders* (BBC2, 2013–), is running a gang in the lawless streets of 1920s Birmingham. The series was compared to the American *Boardwalk Empire* (HBO, 2010–14) and was voted number one in *The Guardian*'s 'Best TV Shows of 2014: Readers' Picks' (Bausells 2014). The first series of *Peaky Blinders* was watched by an average of 3.3 million viewers, while the fourth and final season was seen by 6.2 million viewers (Bond 2019). This is significantly more viewers than any documentary broadcast in the centenary period, so its depiction of war veterans is worth examining. Exceeding the levels of violence seen in *The Monocled Mutineer*, the behaviour of the rival gang members is in part explained and contextualised by the men's wartime experiences, and the assumption that most British veterans 'were not hypersensitively reflective about their own manhood, sexuality or even suffering' (Reynolds 2013: 231). Opening scenes include a line of men blinded in the war begging for pennies singing 'Molly Malone' and, in the gang leader Thomas Shelby's family home, a close-up showing a photograph of the three brothers (Arthur, Tommy and John) smiling in the khaki uniform of the Warwickshire Yeomanry with a freshly dug trench behind them. During the war Thomas Shelby was awarded the King's Medal for gallantry, but he is now suspected of robbing a factory of firearms to supply to Irish dissidents. The men who served their country in France and Flanders have returned home, disregarded their medals and resumed their criminal careers on the streets of Birmingham.

The war is present in the interplay between the characters. Freddie Thorne (Iddo Goldberg), a Factory Union organiser and former wartime comrade of Thomas Shelby, admits that 'there are days when I hear about the cuttings and beatings that I wish I'd let you take that bullet in France.' Thomas is privately amused and retorts almost instantly, 'There are nights I wish you had.' Shell-shocked veteran Danny 'Whizz Bang' (Samuel Edward-Cook) has episodes where he believes he is a bomb and destroys the local pub. The script directs that:

> *Thomas and Freddie swap a half-amused glance before silently resolving to act. [. . .] in restraining a madman we see that they are used to working together in violent situations. [. . .] Thomas hisses in Danny's ear:*
>
> Danny, you're home. You're home. We're all home in England.'
>
> *Danny*: 'Had to go bang, had to go bang, had to go bang'
>
> *Thomas*: 'You're not an artillery shell, Danny, you're a man'
>
> *Danny roars and struggles some more*
>
> *Thomas*: 'You're not a whizz bang, you're a human being. Now get yourself together for Christ's sake.'
>
> *After a moment Danny takes a huge breath and then takes this on board*
>
> *Danny*: 'Ah, hell. Did I do it again?'
>
> *Thomas*: 'Yeah you did it again Danny. Got to stop doing this, man. [. . .] Go home to your wife, Danny. Try to get all that smoke and mud out of your head.'
>
> (*Peaky Blinders* 2014: 17)

When Danny 'Whizz Bang' murders a man shouting 'fix bayonets!', he tells Tommy: 'I died over there [. . .] I left my fucking brains in the mud.' Tommy Shelby, likewise, has a number of flashbacks to hand-to-hand fighting in underground tunnels during the war. He habitually uses opium and imagines that he can hear tapping on his wall and that people are digging through it. When Tommy's gang require reinforcements against a London gang, he calls on fellow veteran and rival gang leader Billy Kitchen (Paul Bullion) and his Black Country Boys:

> *Billy Kitchen*: [to Tommy] Ready for active service.
>
> *Tommy*: That's alright Billy, you don't have to stand in line for us, you're just the man we're looking for, but you'll have to pass the medical first. [. . .]
>
> *Tommy*: It's been a long time, eh, Billy? What did you do with your medals?
>
> *Billy*: I threw them in the cut, same as you.
>
> *Tommy*: It was never an hardship having you Black Country boys on our left flank.
>
> *Billy*: You Brummies did alright on our right.
>
> *John*: Damn right.
>
> *Tommy*: I want you to be the head of a brigade, Bill. You'll be Brigadier Kitchen from now on, you'll have a hundred men under your command. [. . .] Go home Bill.

> Round up any good men you can trust and put the word out. Black Country boys and Brummie boys are on the same side again.

This sense of wartime camaraderie among the criminals is seen in how they relate to Tommy's brother Arthur (Paul Anderson), another man suffering acute psychological damage as a result of the war. Addicted to drink and drugs, and prone to murderously violent outbursts, one reviewer underlined that Arthur's depiction might '[provoke] viewers to consider how many other men like him went on after the Somme to kill and kill again in pub fight, gang battle and prison brawl . . . it became difficult to know if he believed the war was truly over' (Dent 2015). Wartime vocabulary and phrasing is constantly referenced. Arthur asks Tommy to look out for his two sons, asking him to help them get apprenticeships:

> See they get apprenticeships. [. . .] Just ordinary men. And they won't get told to do that shit, that *shit*, that shit we got told to do. [. . .] Those fucking guns blew God right out of my head. [. . .] Don't bury me where there's mud, ok? Promise me. Bury me on a hill.

Thomas tells him 'You were a good man and a good soldier' Danny replies, 'Yes sergeant major.' When two policemen indicate that Thomas's reign of terror is over, Thomas replies 'See you in No-Man's land, boys', but in another scene Tommy's lack of respect for the head of police, Campbell (Sam Neill), illustrates that Campbell is seen as a figure of transgression because he 'didn't serve' as Tommy and his colleagues had done. Most significantly, transgression of accepted moral codes of behaviour, particularly the experience of violence, even against fellow soldiers in the trenches, acts to explain the psychopathic tendencies of some of the main characters. In the second episode of series 2, Tommy Shelby meets with Jewish gang leader, Alfie Solomons (Tom Hardy). Solomons is using a bakery as a front to an illegal rum distillery and is at war with a gang of Italians relating to racing and drink. In a tense scene full of menace, Solomons faces up to Shelby: 'You were in the war. I once carried out my own personal form of stigmata on an Italian. [. . .] It was fucking biblical mate.' Dramas such as *The Village* and *Peaky Blinders* show that wartime trauma can be depicted for today's audiences via a range of transgressive characters who can convey disturbing elements of the conflict in the context of their dramatic settings without disturbing the accepted national narrative of mud, blood and futility.

Figure 4.3 Tommy Shelby (Cillian Murphy, right) comforts Danny 'Whiz Bang' (Samuel Edward-Cook). Still from series 1 of *Peaky Blinders* (BBC, 2014).

Coda: Return to Commemoration

British television drama since the 1970s has increasingly utilised figures of transgression to enable the exploration of the darker sides of 1914–18. The dramatic explorations of figures of the mutineer, conscientious objector and deserter discussed in this article have shown how these characters have functioned in representations of the conflict, and how they have shifted it over time to provide uncomfortable counter-narratives which are then ultimately deployed to reinforce dominant ideas about the war. This further underlines the importance and cultural functionalisation of transgression. Representations of mutineers, conscientious objectors and deserters have at certain times been brought to the foreground of televisual narratives about the First World War, particularly in complex circumstances that can encourage shifts in audience perception including socio-political developments such as social unrest and economic downturn such as that experienced in the 1980s. The heightened focus and sensitivity to memory in the following decade, described as the 'memory boom', sought to retrieve and in some cases rehabilitate figures previously regarded as transgressive, particularly in the cases of the men who were executed as deserters and cowards. The television medium was able to increase the emotional engagement with a difficult and disturbing part of First World War history, which then formed part of a trend to normalise – and ultimately exonerate – the transgressive figure.

Alongside these contemporary references in television drama – and no doubt driving their occurrence – is the centenary itself, which provided a site for the reinforcement once again of traditional narratives of heroism and sacrifice. In October 2013, the BBC announced an unprecedented broadcasting project in its commemoration of the First World War: 2,500 hours of programming across all platforms, to be transmitted throughout 2014–18. Certainly 'it is pertinent to consider how commemoration of events key to national identity are [filtered] through broadcaster's preconceptions of audience preferences and their own institutional identities' (Bell and Gray 2013: 20). Historian Rowan Aust has asserted:

> This self-billed '4 year-season' is far more than the BBC's fulfilment of its Public Service Broadcasting charter in the Reithian sense of informing, educating and entertaining. Coming as it does after a tumultuous period of crisis where trust in the BBC has been quantified as declining, and when the corporation remains under extended assault from the competing media that have proliferated in the digital era, the commemorative season is the BBC's attempt to bolster and secure its own place as a repository for public history and public memory. (Aust 2014)

The flagship series of the BBC's commemorative programme was *Britain's Great War*, a four-part series presented by Jeremy Paxman, broadcast in a primetime slot in January 2014. A BBC press release in October 2013 underlined that the aim of the series was to explore 'how Britain and the lives of British people were transformed by the Great War'. It was designed to attract attention in its content and telling: the emphasis on Britain, *our* story, a story for all our ancestors. Most notably this series shows how television continues to be consumed as a form of public history (de Groot 2009). The use of Paxman in presenter mode delivers a 'knowledge brand' – where persona and authority converge to create a particular style of delivery and sense of authorship (Corner 2010: 13–27). The occasional pronouncement from the cantankerous former *Newsnight* anchor, such as his assertion that conscientious objectors were 'cranks', gained for the series additional and predictable attention in the press, and one reviewer said that Paxman 'goes over the top more than the infantry' and described the series as 'a theatrical documentary' (Simon 2014). The series received largely positive reviews. However, the BBC repeated the 1964 series *The Great War*, and it is unsurprising that the organisation reprised the established national televisual memorial. As a precursor to this the BBC has released extended versions of the veterans' interviews filmed for the original series, titled *The Great War Interviews*. This asserts the veterans' testimonies as *the* oral history of the conflict, especially given that the last surviving veteran of the war, Harry Patch, died in 2009. The BBC assumed the role of custodian of this valuable first-hand material: television has preserved the veterans for posterity, and the authority of the voices of what one historian called 'the nation's grandparents' is still a powerful force weighted with the authority of men who witnessed the war first-hand (Haggith 2004).

By the end of the centenary period, the repeats of programmes already made meant that British television programmes, both drama and documentary, rarely transgressed the accepted narrative of the First World War: mud, blood and futility were firmly held in place as the nation marked the passing of one hundred years since the conflict began. On the one hundredth anniversary of the signing of the Armistice, Peter Jackson's *They Shall Not Grow Old* (2018) was broadcast on BBC2. Original footage from the war was taken from the 'sacred archive' of official war films and transformed with modern production techniques including sound effects and colourisation (Napper 2018). Commissioned by *14–18 Now*, the centenary arts organisation, veterans' recorded testimonies were used as narration. Here was the nation's new on-screen memorial, unchallengeable in its retelling of the accepted narrative of Britain's wartime experience. The memory of those who had transgressed accepted notions of duty and sacrifice were once again faded out of the televisual representations of 1914–18.

Note

1. A campaign by relatives of the executed men for a pardon (see Taylor-Whiffen 2011).

Works Cited

Audoin-Rouzeau, Stéphane and Becker, Annette (2000) *1914–1918*. London: Profile.
Aust, Rowan (2014) *The Presentation of the First World War: History, Crisis and Recovery at the BBC*, CATH conference, De Montfort University, Leicester, June (conference presentation).
BARB (1986) Viewing figures from 1986 were obtained from the British Audience Research Board at the request of the author.
Bausells, Marta (2014) 'The Best TV Shows of 2014: Readers Picks', *The Guardian*, 30 December <http://www.theguardian.com/tv-and-radio/tvandradioblog/2014/dec/30/the-best-tv-shows-of-2014-readers-picks-peaky-blinders> (last accessed 23 September 2015).
BBC WAC (1986) *Broadcast*, 29 August.
BBC WAC (1988) 'Audience Figures', 15 June.
Bell, Erin and Gray, Ann (2013) *History on Television*. London: Routledge.
Bond, Kimberley (2019) 'Peaky Blinders Gets Its Highest Audience Figures Ever', *Radio Times*, 3 September <https://www.radiotimes.com/news/tv/2019-09-03/peaky-blinders-gets-its-highest-audience-figures-ever/> (last accessed 12 December 2019).

Bray, Alan (1963) IWM 4035: Private Alan Bray, Oral History recording, BBC.
Broadcasters' Audience Research Board (BARB) (2011) 'Top 10 Programmes 2011' <http://www.barb.co.uk/resources/tv-facts/tv-since-1981/2011/top10?_s=5> (last accessed 23 September 2015).
Broadcasters' Audience Research Board (BARB) (2013) 'Top 30 Programmes / BBC1 / Mar 25 – Mar 31' <https://www.barb.co.uk/viewing-data/weekly-top-30/?station%5B0%5D=1&period_year%5B0%5D=2013&period_month=3&period_week=31&period%5B0%5D=201303060131> (last accessed 20 April 2013).
Cooke, Lez (2003) *British Television Drama: A History*. London: BFI Publishing.
Corner, John (2010) '"Once Upon a Time . . .": Visual Design and Documentary Openings', in Erin Bell and Ann Gray (eds), *Televising History: Mediating the Past in Postwar Europe*. London: Palgrave, pp. 13–27.
Corrigan, Gordon (2003) *Mud, Blood and Poppycock: Britain and the Great War*. London: Cassell.
de Groot, Jerome (2009) *Consuming History: Heritage and Historians in Contemporary Popular Culture*. London: Routledge.
Dent, Grace (2015) 'Grace Dent on TV: *Peaky Blinders* Needs a Third Series', *The Independent*, 7 November <http://www.independent.co.uk/arts-entertainment/tv/reviews/grace-dent-on-tv-this-gangland-tale-needs-a-third-series-9845780.html> (last accessed 23 September 2015).
Haggith, Toby (2004) *It's History But Is It True?* IAMHIST Conference presentation, Imperial War Museum, October.
Hanna, Emma (2007) 'A Small Screen Alternative to Stone and Bronze: "The Great War" (BBC, 1964)', *European Journal of Cultural Studies*, 10 (1), pp. 89–111.
Hanna, Emma (2009) *The Great War on the Small Screen: Representing the First World War in Contemporary Britain*. Edinburgh: Edinburgh University Press.
Kine Weekly (1964) '*The Great War* Series', 28 May, n.p., Staff Writer, Liddell Hart Centre for Military Archives, LH 13/62.
Knight, Steven (2013) *Peaky Blinders* Script, Episode 1: 17, available at <downloads.bbc.co.uk/writersroom/scripts/Peaky-Blinders-S1-Ep1.pdf> (last accessed 23 September 2015).
Lawrence, Ben (2013) '*The Village* episode six, BBC One review', *The Telegraph*, 5 May <http://www.telegraph.co.uk/culture/tvandradio/10036702/The-Village-episode-six-BBC-One-review.html> (last accessed 25 September 2015).
Napper, Lawrence (2018) 'They Shall Not Grow Old (2): The Abject Archive . . . The Sacred Archive', October 12 <https://atthepictures.photo.blog/2018/10/12/they-shall-not-grow-old-2-the-abject-archive-the-sacred-archive/> (last accessed 12 December 2019).
Peaty, John (1999) 'Haig and Military Discipline', in Brian Bond and Nigel Cave (eds), *Haig: A Reappraisal 70 Years On*. London: Leo Cooper.
Petley, Julian (1987) 'Over the Top', *Sight and Sound*, 56 (2), pp. 126–31.
Reynolds, David (2013) *The Long Shadow: The Great War and the Twentieth Century*. London: Simon & Schuster.

Simon, Jane (2014) 'Jeremy Paxman Goes Over the Top More Than the Infantry in *Britain's Great War*', *The Mirror*, 27 January <http://www.mirror.co.uk/tv/tv-previews/jeremy-paxman-goes-over-top-3064145> (last accessed 25 September 2015).

Taylor-Whiffen, Peter (2011) 'Shot at Dawn: Cowards, Traitors or Victims?' *BBC History*, 3 March <http://www.bbc.co.uk/history/british/britain_wwone/shot_at_dawn_01.shtml#four> (last accessed 15 February 2020).

Ward, David (2000) 'Battle for Recognition: Shamed Soldiers Acknowledged', *The Guardian*, 10 November, p. 5.

Winter, Jay (2000) 'The Generation of Memory: Reflections on the "Memory Boom" in Contemporary Historical Studies', *Bulletin of the German Historical Institute*, 27, pp. 69–92.

CHAPTER 5

The End of Transgression: Fritz Bauer as Traitor on the German Screen
Ute Wölfel

Introduction

This chapter looks at two recent German feature films about the eminent figure of Dr Fritz Bauer (1903–68) whose work as attorney general and intellectual in the West Germany of the 1950s and 1960s was key to the regeneration of the West German postwar jurisdiction and, more generally, to the revival of a democratic mentality and culture. As historian Norbert Frei put it, even someone who estimates the influence of an individual on social developments as small, has to acknowledge that it was first and foremost due to Fritz Bauer's singular commitment that judicial prosecution did not die completely in the so-called 'quiet' of the 1950s (in Wojak 2016: 23–4).[1]

Bauer worked to restore a sense of justice to the defeated and compromised society and, as a central part, demanded the critical confrontation of the West Germans with their recent Nazi past. The most prominent effort in this respect was the Frankfurt Auschwitz Trials (1963–5), which he initiated. Yet with his death in 1968, Bauer disappeared from public discourse and West German memory almost entirely (Wojak 2016: 12). Only recently have researchers, journalists, museum curators and filmmakers turned to Bauer again in order to salvage his achievements from oblivion. As part of the new interest in Bauer, the feature film *Der Staat gegen Fritz Bauer/The People vs. Fritz Bauer* (Lars Kraume, 2015) and the TV production *Die Akte General/The General* (SWR, Stephan Wagner, 2016), which both have the figure of Bauer at their centre, seem a late tribute and an attempt to re-introduce him to the wider public.[2]

This chapter discusses in what role Fritz Bauer is re-admitted to German cultural memory and analyses the key aspects that have shaped his latest screen depictions. My hypothesis is that at the (hidden) core of Bauer's representation is, still, seventy years after the end of the Second World War, his historical perception as 'traitor' by a majority of the West

German public, including many of the political class and most of Bauer's colleagues in the West German jurisdiction. This chapter will offer close readings of the films which expose the 'markings' of the traitor in the depiction of Bauer and will scrutinise the function the historical 'traitor' is allocated decades after his 'treason'.

Bauer's efforts to confront the West German majority with the crimes of the Nazi regime and the support it had from them, and his attempts to encourage the West Germans to acknowledge the Nazi regime's character as fundamentally unlawful and inhuman, met with denial and rejection in the West Germany of the economic postwar boom, the so-called 'economic miracle'. The re-emergence of West Germany 'as a responsible and necessary partner in a number of transnational activities, both economic and political, in the Western world', allowed the past to 'be ignored, except in so far as the privations of recent years of war and occupation were contrasted with the modest but increasing prosperity of the present' (Fulbrook 2015: 156).

Historians have described in detail the public attitudes and official measures which resulted in the termination of denazification and of debates on German crimes and guilt. Instead, the 1950s saw the amnesty of those sentenced by the Allies and their re-integration (Frei 2002, 2009; Moeller 2003). Given this desire to 'draw a line' under the past, Bauer's efforts were perceived by many as 'treason', that is as going against the heavily guarded lines which defined West German postwar identity. Describing Bauer as a 'traitor' acknowledges the 'situation-specific' character of transgression, the meaning of which 'resides within the context of the act's reception . . . within the social situation' (Jenks 2003: 8). 'Whether the act and actors will be defined as treacherous depends on who is defining and on more general values that may change over time' (Åkerström 1991: 17). In the 1950s and beyond, the defining was done by a majority that saw itself not as perpetrators but as victims, 'an imagined community defined by the experience of loss and displacement during the Second World War' (Moeller 2003: 6). Bauer's challenge of this resolutely defended victim identity was registered as a treason.

Today, Bauer's historical challenge is (still) the officially agreed stance in German politics and the public sphere. It forms a central part of the (still) widely shared understanding of the Nazi regime on the one hand and notions of democracy and citizenship on the other. The conviction of the few re-emigrants and resistance fighters in the postwar period has become the conviction of the many, and it seems impossible that anyone would be tolerated today calling Bauer a 'traitor'. And yet the films display a lingering unease with the figure of Bauer, a reservation which remains indissoluble and marks the 'traitor' across time and change, reverberating with the seriousness of his historical transgression. While the two films differ, they share aspects that facilitate the ambivalence of the traitor figure who is presented as hero and at the same time marked by the 'retribution' (Jenks 2003: 34) of the challenged community. This strategy of ambivalence, showing Bauer as role model while undermining him at the same time, is typical for the representation of the 'traitor', who is morally right to broach the question of agency 'and change through constitutive . . . relations of responsibility' (Parikh 2009: 2) but is also seen to endanger the 'tribe' (Norris and Inglehart 2019).

To be clear from the start, the films do not deserve analysis for their filmic merits: both productions are highly conventional and offer standard conflict solutions while not asking new questions; their aesthetics are unattractive, even outright boring; within the national film production context they mark the decline of the historical genre into *Staatsbürgerliches Erziehungskino*/civic education cinema (Pilarczyk 2019), which employs 'big stories' to produce socio-political standardised meaning (Gass and Suchsland 2019). Nevertheless, the films should be taken seriously not least because they are watched by considerably more people than artistically innovative films which unsettle prejudices and sensibilities.[3] Their popularity suggests the attractiveness of an approach to national history which appropriates the outsiders, particularly the transgressors, in order to reinvest their moral capital in a narrative that supports the 'bitter' community which got 'injured' (Parikh 2009: 2) by the transgression.

Bauer as 'Traitor'

Historically, Fritz Bauer was perceived as a traitor in at least two ways – as emigrant and as dedicated antifascist. Large parts of postwar West German society saw those who had fled Nazi Germany or actively fought against it as betraying the nation. The fact that Fritz Bauer – who came from a Jewish family, was an active Social Democrat, member of the *Reichsbanner Schwarz-Rot-Gold*[4] and outspoken opponent of the Nazis – was among the first to be excluded from the Nazis's 'people's collective', to be persecuted and under threat of being murdered, did not interfere with common allegations of 'treason' after the war. It is indicative that in 1966, twenty-one years after the defeat of the Nazi regime, a TV documentary (SWR) still addressed the issue as urgent. In *Der Emigrant – Patriot oder Verräter?/ The Emigrant – Patriot or Traitor?*, Wolf Littmann followed the often exhausting, materially deprived and lonely lives of German emigrants. Interviews with those who had re-emigrated after the war, among them Bauer, stated unanimously the reason to return to Germany was the aspiration to build a better country. Yet, as Littmann found, this met with deep-seated rejection from the majority which, since the end of the immediate postwar period, had increased rather than decreased. Discussing the reasons why, psychoanalyst Alexander Mitscherlich explains that:

> None of us wants to be reminded of the Hitler past and that the emigrant is a figure which appears from this suppressed past, a memorial, a trace of memory which cannot easily be removed. (*Der Emigrant* 1966)

Bauer, in particular, reminded the public of this past tirelessly and with high media impact – he gave speeches, published in journals, appeared on TV and invited the public to attend Nazi-criminal trials. As attorney general in the courts of Brunswick (1949–56) and Hesse (1956–68), he was responsible for some of the ground-breaking trials in West German postwar history, particularly the Remer Trial (1952) and the First Frankfurt Auschwitz Trials (1963–5). While the first resulted in the official rehabilitation of the conservative resistance against Hitler (20 July 1944 plot), the second, for the first time, brought 'normal Germans'[5] to a German court and wider public attention for their atrocities committed at Auschwitz concentration camp. That Bauer, at the peak of the Cold War, cooperated with countries behind the Iron Curtain to gather evidence against the accused, particularly Poland and East Germany, which for different reasons were both symbols of national defeat,[6] must have added to the rejection, even hate, he met with.

It is of particular interest in the context of this chapter, that Bauer's historical work as prosecutor and jurist was not only perceived as 'treason' by large parts of the West German public but was indeed consistently linked to the legal definition of the very offence. The prominent Remer Trial sued former army major-general Otto Ernst Remer for libel as he continued after the war to publicly brand the participants of the 20 July 1944 plot around Claus von Stauffenberg as 'traitors', thus reiterating the actual Nazi verdict which, at the time, sought to justify their executions. The wider legal crux of the matter was that in the West Germany of the 1950s and 1960s, resistance against the Nazi state was still deemed 'treason' and that, at the same time, the law still allowed political nonconformity to fall under this offence, potentially including Bauer's own activities.

Irmtrud Wojak describes the Remer Trial as the first turning point in the ongoing public and juridical attempts in West Germany to discredit the antifascist resistance as unjustified by law per se (2016: 252–3). Bauer's successful prosecution of one such attempt had therefore the status of a 'piece of public pedagogy, indeed . . . a normative act' (Frei 2002: 267). In order to have antifascist opposition publicly and officially acknowledged as ethically right and legal, Bauer had to expose the Nazi dictatorship's character as *Unrechtsstaat*/a fundamentally unlawful state. He did this in his final speech with the argument that 'ein Unrechtsstaat wie das Dritte Reich ist überhaupt nicht hochverratsfähig' (Bauer 1952, in Foljanti and Johst 2018: 334) / 'an unjust state like the Third Reich is not subject to treason in any manner' (translation from Frei 2002: 268). Supported by the Allies, the West German government rehabilitated the conservative military resistance though the rearmament of the new German NATO partner was a decisive reason (Pfeifer 2001). Bauer's efforts did not yet initiate a general reappraisal of antifascist resistance activities. Hermann Weinkauff, then Head of the Federal Court of Justice (1950–60), took the Stauffenberg example to confirm and at the same time restrict the legal right to oppose the Nazi state to a small elite. According to Wojak, Weinkauff established that only those capable of forming a clear and infallible judgement of the state's infringement of the law could 'afford' to resist (Wojak 2016: 262–3). Furthermore, there would have to be the well-founded hope that the resistance would be successful. This stance, as Wojak explains, restricted the group of people 'entitled' to acts of resistance dramatically. At the same time, Weinkauff determined that desertion and insubordination by members of the military would not be acknowledged as lawful resistance, not even with the justification that the Second World War had been an unjust war.

This tight restriction of the legality of resistance absolved Nazi criminals, supporters and followers from any notion of human responsibility and moral guilt while at the same time confirming Nazi jurisdiction over many of those who had had the courage to breach Nazi laws at the risk of their lives. It also reactivated a highly authoritarian model of citizenship for the new West German democracy. Bauer's attempts to legalise the 'right to oppose the state'[7] thus formed a juncture where demands to engage with the society's Nazi past and to build a better one coincided. As it was, West Germany had not only retained the old Empire's treason laws in the Nazis' revised version but had added more detail of the offence (Bauer 1962). That these laws still served the political purpose of suppressing critical engagement with state policy became obvious in the so-called '*Spiegel* Affair'. On 26 October 1962, the rooms of the political weekly magazine *Der Spiegel* in Bonn and Hamburg were searched and a number of staff arrested on suspicion of treason. The magazine had published an article about the military defence strategy of NATO and the West German government, criticising atomic armament as a means of deterrence in the Cold War as facilitated by the West German government and particularly the Minister of Defence, the ultraconservative Franz Josef Strauss. Bauer, who had been campaigning for a 'right to oppose', seized this opportunity to expose the West German treason laws' highly problematic heritage and status and to defend the freedom of a critical press with an article in *Der Spiegel* itself. Under the title 'Was ist Landesverrat?'/What is treason?, Bauer traces the historical abuse of the treason laws to silence political opponents back to the 1920s, where he finds them applied to the advantage of conservative and nationalist circles. He points out that references to the treason laws increased proportionally with the growing *inner* political conflicts after the First World War, while nominally they were meant to safeguard the country against its *external* enemies. During National Socialism, resistance was generally punished as 'treason'. The Allied Control Council then suspended the treason laws in 1946, though West Germany reintroduced and extended them in 1951. One of Bauer's major objections is the complete lack of a feasible definition of what constitutes a 'state secret' and in which cases the state is really under threat. Bauer goes on to criticise:

> Even today in our democracy, leading circles are of the opinion . . . that [governmental] politics has to be feigned as serving the welfare of the state per se, that citizens only have the limited understanding of subjects and therefore the opposition can only be permitted to wait for the next federal election and new government. (Bauer 1962)

Yet can there be a democratic opposition, Bauer asks, if it is thus silenced?

The '*Spiegel* Affair' highlighted the topicality and urgency of Bauer's commitment to a self-critical engagement with the crimes of the Nazi past and their authoritarian roots. The imminent question of what should be regarded as treason in past and present, of what, in other words, should be deemed a betrayal of the people or the state that leaves them vulnerable and weak in the face of an enemy, was a focal point of public debates about the Nazi dictatorship as much as about the character of West German democracy. Last but not least, this highlights the role and character of the 'traitor', who is not just a 'rebel' challenging 'the very thoughts' his collective is based on (Åkerström 1991: 17). As someone questioning the relation between self and other in terms of ethical responsibility – for transgression is situated 'within the realm of the moral' (Jervis, in Jenks 2003: 8) – the 'traitor' has an imminently political role 'such that the ethical always ruptures "the political", rendering it continually unfinished and open' (Parikh 2009: 8). In the words of Parikh, which describe Bauer's kind of 'ethical treason' well, to point to the crimes of the past and its victims, to that which 'remains unintelligible and unintegrated to laws, norms and representations, is to seek out the ethical possibility of justice to come and democracy to come' (ibid.). In this sense Bauer's 'treason' was a 'political transgression by which the subject negotiated the heterogeneities of social formation' (ibid.: 11) and 'open[ed] a future that [was] unimaginable and unintelligible from within the bonds of fidelity and identification' (ibid.: 12). The two films about Fritz Bauer feed on the vision of a democratic future made possible by transgressions such as Bauer's. At the same time, they undermine his very effort and courage, and deflect attention away from his challenge of the 'German self' that tried (and tries) to preserve itself in narratives of victimhood.

Fritz Bauer on Screen

While it is generally more productive to look at what a film *does* rather than what it *does not* do, the latter offers a useful way of understanding what prior choices the filmmakers took. The first obvious decision of the filmmakers was to ignore all of Bauer's major contributions, that is not just the mentioned trials and debates surrounding them, but also his efforts to bring euthanasia to court and to fundamentally reform the law. Instead, the films focus on an aspect of Bauer's work that was not known at the time, namely his secret contributions to the capture of SS Obersturmbannführer Adolf Eichmann, the main organiser of the Holocaust, in Argentina in 1960 by the Israeli secret service. Following Ronen Steinke's Bauer biography (2013), they further emphasise an aspect of Bauer's private life which was neither part of the highly public figure of Bauer, nor has it been ultimately proven: his suspected homosexuality.[8] The filmic rediscovery of Bauer for a wider audience is thus motivated by new discoveries which have the spectacular element of 'revelation'.[9] These choices feed into dominant big- and small-screen practices, 'a consumerist quest for the new', 'to present the "never-seen-before"' (Halle 2008: 114) side of history as the most relevant, inviting highly emotional stories and sensationalising effects. This generally happens to the detriment of the historical context as 'history gives way to story' (ibid.: 96). Such stimulation of the public's appetite for history has prepared the main course on the menu of German cinema and TV since the 1990s,[10] offering chunks of national history in easily digestible, attractively dressed servings. In the case of *Der Staat* and *Die Akte*, the question is what effect these choices have on the cultural framing of Bauer, the figure of the 'traitor'.

The sensationalisation of Bauer is supported by the films' reliance on the topic's currency and on genre traditions of international cinema. Both films tie in with recent productions on Eichmann.[11] In the run-up to the 50th anniversary of Eichmann's capture, the UK released *Adolf Eichmann*

(Robert Young, 2007) followed by the German public broadcasting production *Eichmanns Ende: Liebe, Verrat, Tod/Eichmann's Ending: Love, Treason, Death* (NDR, Raymond Ley, 2010). These films rediscover the 'Eichmann case' through previously marginalised figures, including Fritz Bauer in the German production, though the prominent historical figures are the Holocaust survivor and Argentine-emigrant Lothar Hermann, who had discovered Eichmann; Willem Sassen, the Dutch fascist journalist who interviewed Eichmann in Buenos Aires (*Eichmann's Ende*); and Avner Less, the Israeli police officer interrogating Eichmann in preparation for the trial in Jerusalem (*Adolf Eichmann*). These previously minor characters provide a new perspective also because they are private people with families, hobbies and health problems. Similarly, two other productions, *The Eichmann Show* (BBC2, Paul Andrew Williams, 2015) and the internationally successful German big-screen film *Hannah Arendt* (Margarete von Trotta, 2013), treat the 'Eichmann case' from novel points of view, namely that of the camera team filming the trial in 1961 and that of Hannah Arendt, the German philosopher and exile, who reported about the trial for the *New York Times* and turned these reports into the widely and controversially debated *Eichmann in Jerusalem: A Report on the Banality of Evil* (1963). Again, the individual with his or her fears, love affairs and unpaid bills is the point that makes 'big history' come alive, according to the filmmakers. Both *Der Staat* and *Die Akte* add to the string of productions offering a private perspective on the known 'case'.

At the same time, the two films fit into an older tradition on small and big screen linked to Eichmann, such as the US TV-films *The House on Garibaldi Street* (Peter Collinson, 1979) and *The Man Who Captured Eichmann* (William A. Graham, 1996). More generally these films belong to the 'Nazi hunter' film, a thematic interpretation of the thriller. Nazi hunter thrillers have been part of particularly American cinema since the Second World War, with famous postwar examples from Orson Welles's film noir *The Stranger* (1946) and Alfred Hitchcock's *Notorious* (1946) to Ronald Neame's *The Odessa File* (1974), John Schlesinger's *Marathon Man* (1976) and Franklin J. Schaffner's *The Boys from Brazil* (1978). A recent example like *Operation Finale* (Chris Weitz, 2018) continues this tradition while films like *Shutter Island* (Martin Scorsese, 2010) or *Remember* (Atom Egoyan, 2015) have brought about a shift, retaining the thriller plot and merging it with trauma and amnesia narratives; they have turned the 'hunt' into a psychological battle over memory and selfhood. I will come back to these versions of the Nazi hunter thriller in my conclusion. For now, they are neglectable, as the two popular German films remain indebted to the older patterns.

The Nazi hunter film draws its narrative energy from the Nazi criminal, his notoriety linked to atrocities past and present. The crime, however horrific, lends the story appeal and promises the pleasure of fear and horror as well as action: the bigger the criminal, the more danger the hunter (frequently an underdog figure) is in, and the more cunning, action and revelation on the hunter's part can be expected. The Nazi in these thrillers is a historical incarnation of the mesmerising screen villain (from Fritz Lang's eponymous Mabuse (1922) to Sam Mendes's Blofeld/Oberhauser in *Spectre* (2015)) who is supported and protected by his criminal organisation, in the Nazi case a network of old comrades. Personal betrayals as well as treason form staple elements of these films as their narratives are driven by a search for someone unknown posing a national or even international threat; the hunter can never be sure who is who in the hunt and who can be trusted; often it is those closest to the hunter who betray him in a situation of utmost danger. And the other way around, it may be the Nazi criminal and the hunter respectively who hide their identity, thus betraying the one (beloved) who trusts the mask. The need to keep identity secret turns the old Nazi hunter thriller into a round of masquerades.

Der Staat and *Die Akte* rely on the formula of the old Nazi hunter thrillers in two ways. Firstly, they restrict their perspective on Bauer to his secret search for Eichmann, which activates the typical constellation of the (underdog) hunter and his (unsafe) ally vs. the hunted perpetrator and his network of old comrades. Secondly, they indulge in staple thriller elements like meetings in the middle of the night with shady informants; encounters with secret service agents wearing dark glasses; the stealing of and dealing with information; enormous camera lenses for monitoring suspects; blackmailing outsiders into cooperation; warnings and threats conveyed by the network of old comrades; the concealing of knowledge, intentions, identities; suspected treason and personal betrayal; state corruption and Cold War fears. Both films recycle elements of the thriller *mise-en-scène*, from the grey and blue tints, long shadows and fast-cut cinematography to suspense-building sound effects such as a clock ticking.

The films reflect that tradition. In *Der Staat*, the hunting-plot is explicitly acknowledged when prosecutor Kreidler (Sebastian Blomberg), one of the old comrades, mockingly invites Bauer (Burghart Klaußner) to join a 'hunt' at his estate:

> *Kreidler*: You look pale. A bit of fresh air would do you good.
>
> *Bauer*: Yes, you are quite right.
>
> *Kreidler*: Wouldn't you like to join me at my country estate? Are you interested in hunting?
>
> *Bauer*: Sure, but not animals.

In the two films, Eichmann functions as the notorious super-criminal (whose name everybody in the audience recognises) even though the films restrict him as a character. Eichmann makes the hunt a just and unquestionable undertaking and at the same time a spectacular (screen) event starting with the secrecy of the investigation and ending with the abduction of Eichmann from Argentina by the Mossad in a cloak-and-dagger operation which both films include. The historical 'treason' committed by Bauer is thus interpreted through a film genre which has formalised betrayal and treason in terms of action plot and suspense, sidelining the socially, culturally, politically transformational work of transgression. This, I would argue, undermines Bauer's 'treason' retrospectively.

In keeping with the genre, *Der Staat* and *Die Akte* develop the hunt as a process of hiding and revealing in which personal betrayal and state treason figure first of all as plot triggers. Bauer needs to identify reliable helpers among the state authorities (police, court, federal police, government) which, however, make up the network of old comrades. The network for its part not only tries to foil Bauer's search but to find a fault which would allow them to remove him from office all together. Bauer works to unmask Eichmann, who is hiding behind a false name, and to get him arrested. This involves treason in the legal sense as Bauer secretly cooperates with the Mossad in a case that could – as both films explicitly stress – compromise West German state officials and thus weaken the West German front-line NATO partner in the Cold War. Both films offer two occasions on which treason is discussed, the first between Fritz Bauer and Georg-August Zinn, the Social Democrat Minister-President of Hesse (1950–69), who made Bauer general prosecutor in Frankfurt am Main, and the second between Bauer and a young attorney working with him, Dr Karl Angermann (Ronald Zehrfeld) in *Der Staat* and Dr Joachim Hell (David Kross) in *Die Akte*. The latter discussions are of particular importance as Angermann and Hell represent the new generation of Germans to be won over for the cause of democracy. The test for the young is their willingness to commit treason in order to bring Nazi criminals to justice.

> *Angermann*: I think we are committing treason. The Federal Intelligence Service is our executive power.
>
> *Bauer*: Do you really think the Federal Intelligence Service wouldn't know where these people hide? Probably the CIA knows it, too. They would at the most warn Eichmann. [. . .] Nobody from Bonn to Washington wants Eichmann in court.
>
> *Angermann*: But treason can't be the solution.
>
> *Bauer*: Damn it, Angermann! Do you want justice or just a new kitchen? If we want to do something for our country, we have to betray it in this case.

Similarly, *Die Akte* includes explicit considerations of the treason Bauer (Ulrich Noethen) is committing to capture perpetrators. After the successful arrest of Eichmann, which his young assistant Hell accepted in silence though not without doubts about its legality, Bauer hopes to prosecute Hans Globke, the Secretary of State and Chief of Staff of the Chancellery (1953–63) under Konrad Adenauer and former civil servant in the Nazis's Ministry of Interior, where he contributed to the Nuremberg Laws and thus the Holocaust.

> *Bauer*: We'll institute preliminary proceedings against Globke.
>
> *Hell*: Against the Chief of Staff of the Chancellery? Haven't we got enough to do? [. . .]
>
> *Hell*: Do you really want to support the Zone [East Germany] in its attack on the Adenauer government? That is a highly political case. [. . .]
>
> *Bauer*: Doktor Hell, I have noted your doubts [. . .] I'm also not a friend of the show trials in the East. But injustice remains injustice. [. . .] We can't let these people get away. It is our duty to be uncomfortable. Otherwise, we're no better than a man like Globke.

Both discussions reveal that the aspect of Bauer's 'treason' which is presented as most disconcerting and relevant to the next generation (of the 1950s or 2010s), is the political reverberation of Eichmann's or Globke's prosecution in the context of the Cold War confrontation, *not* the realisation that German postwar 'normality' was based on the suppression of an abyss of crime, guilt and trauma. Applying the formula of the Nazi hunter thriller to Bauer's postwar work results in an equation of punishment of the worst perpetrators with mental and moral regeneration, and Bauer's 'treason' as legal offence. The films pursue a 'policy of containment' which leaves unexamined the majority's types of involvement with the National Socialist regime, its mentality that found inhumanity and blaring injustice acceptable, and its conviction that the 'German people' were the first victims of the Nazi regime. In other words, the films cut short the engagement with society, which was key for Bauer. Even the 'baddies', the old comrades, never get a backstory and remain (in the fashion of the genre) flat. The *mise-en-scène* allows the occasional glimpse of the old comrades' self-disciplining and their effort to deny responsibility. Thus prosecutor Kreidler (*Der Staat*) communicates with stiff and smirking facial expressions and gestures; surrounded by dark brown and heavy furniture, his movements seem repressed and strained. Generally, the darkness and stuffiness of rooms has to stand in for the old comrades' denial of the truth. *Die Akte* on the other hand does even less to explore the perpetrators: short moments of tension are all the figure of Globke gets. Some reviewers criticised this highly schematic approach (Dell 2015); 'it feels like Bauer is fighting cardboard cut-outs rather than actual people, which makes him and his struggle less interesting' (van Hoeij 2015).

The genre-based deflection of 'treason' onto a schematic legal Cold War frame weakens the screen representation of Bauer as 'ethical traitor'. This, it will be argued, permits other aspects of Bauer to become meaningful and enriched with the moral capital that the historical Fritz Bauer accumulated with his transgression.

Exploiting the Figure of the Traitor

German cinema screens, particularly in West Germany, developed the figure of the traitor during the 1950s, historically coinciding with Bauer's first phase of postwar work. The moral and legal debates of the period were reflected on screen in the distinction between *Landesverrat*/treason against the people or country and *Hochverrat*/high treason. In many of the 1950s war films, both kinds of traitors had the important function to raise the question of German moral failure without giving it too much relevance and weight (Wölfel 2015). The sheer threat posed by the question to notions of German identity was neutralised on 1950s screens by the traitor's highly ambivalent character, generally marked by his social, physical or sexual deviation (ibid.). I want to argue that it is deviation, the traitor's 'marking' accessory, which the films under discussion here re-evaluate and to which they transfer moral capital.

To begin with, the filmmakers fit Bauer with the chain-smoking habit of the real man, as well as with substantial consumption of sedatives and alcohol, with coughing, choking and shaking fits, that is with the typical physical deviation of the traitor figure. No doubt these physical deviations, which no other single character in either film shares, are re-evaluated as signs of loneliness, exertion and the paranoia of the 'hunted hunter'. However, the physical deviation of the screen Bauer is not particularly significant. The deviation which does carry meaning is Bauer's assumed sexual orientation. Like the physical deviation, homosexuality is being re-evaluated. Already the fact that the network of old comrades reflects it as 'deviant' and tries to sue the dangerous 'Nazi hunter' for homosexual practices, still a legal offence in West Germany in the 1950s and 1960s, ennobles the sexual orientation. However, on the level of film ideology, homosexuality loses the negative connotation of deviation also because it is the feature which does not isolate Bauer but links him to others. Furthermore, homosexuality acquires meaning within the context of social and mental change. While Bauer's physical otherness, his coughing, smoking, drinking, is linked to the Nazi past and the fight against the old comrades' power, his sexual orientation is, in both films, closely tied to the new generation which is to build a democratic West Germany. The two films implement this narrative in different ways, but both are keen on salvaging homosexuality as a central aspect of moral credibility.

In *Der Staat*, the young prosecutor Angermann is gay himself. His suggestion of a lenient sentence for a young man sued for homosexual practices sparks outrage within the court.[12] This in turn inspires Bauer to make Angermann his assistant in the search for Nazi criminals. The status of homosexual men in West Germany, particularly the retention of the Nazis's version of §175 after the war, introduces gay men not only as outsiders but as the group of Nazi victims still legally persecuted after the war. In the logic of the film, this precarious and marginalised position predestines them to be more democratic and just than other, that is heterosexual, Germans. The argument is supported by the film's editing, which relates homosexuality directly to dealing with the Nazi past.

Der Staat introduces Fritz Bauer as a 'dead man walking' not just because the very first scene shows him passing out and almost drowning in his own bathtub (a glass of red wine and a jar of pills on the rim), but because the first fifteen minutes of the film offer a succession of scenes presenting Bauer as isolated, threatened, angry and paralysed, while in a parallel strand of action with which these scenes are cross-cut, we see Eichmann moving freely in sunny Argentina spreading his anti-Semitic poison. A first trail to Eichmann ends in defeat when the Mossad excludes further investigation. This scene is cross-cut with Angermann's defeat in court pleading for the mild sentence in the homosexuality trial. Both cases of failed justice are here linked. Angermann has become a (homosexual) *persona non grata*, which directly results in Bauer trusting him. Their effective cooperation starts when Angermann begins to resist his wife and her family. Confronted with his wife's wish to have a child, his father-in-law's authoritarian attitude and the family's consumerism and political indifference, Angermann leaves the family gathering to engage a shady informant in support of Bauer's attempt to find Eichmann. The hunt is thus passed on to the young German homosexual the minute he rejects traditional heterosexual family life. At the same time as Angermann begins to be involved in illegal doings, he gradually lives out his sexuality, visiting the gay club 'kokett' and having a short affair with the club's singer (Lillith Stangenberg), a young transvestite. It is not by chance that her song *Inkognito* describes both the political and the sexual events.

Figure 5.1 Karl Angermann as an outsider in his wife's conservative family. Still from *Der Staat gegen Fritz Bauer* (2015).

The tight knitting of sexual orientation and change is highlighted again at the end of the film. After Eichmann's capture, the two 'traitors' Bauer and Angermann celebrate their success, which Bauer takes as the opportunity to confess his own moral failure and guilt. Remembering his nine months' imprisonment in the concentration camp Heuberg in 1933, Bauer admits to having signed a statement submitting himself to Nazi rule. His political comrade and friend Kurt Schumacher, Member of Parliament for the Social Democrats until 1933 and Chairman of the SPD after the war until his death in 1952, refused to sign and therefore spent twelve years in camps. The film Bauer recapitulates: 'I never forgave myself. Schumacher didn't submit. One must never bow to tyranny, Karl. Never.'[13]

Within the logic of the film, Bauer's signing of a 'loyalty declaration' is a moral failure; indeed, the film's director understands it as the secret motor of all of Bauer's postwar efforts:

> Oliver [Guez] and I have always understood the declaration of compliance extorted by the Nazis as the inner motor of Fritz Bauer's work: Someone who has allowed himself to be defeated and chased into exile,[14] fights unwaveringly against all failings after his return home. (Presseheft 2015: 10)[15]

The pseudo-psychological explanation misses Bauer's commitment to justice and democracy pre-1933, but it is also a sign of the film's inversion of the victim status. The victim of the Holocaust is here presented as 'giving in' to the Nazis rather than being persecuted by them on all grounds. What makes it worse is that, after redefining 'escaping total persecution' as 'having submitted' and, secondly, making 'refusal to submit' the law of morality, Angermann gets an opportunity to prove his steadfastness. By now the West German Federal Police have worked on a case against Bauer. Having documented Angermann's homosexual affair, they offer him impunity and silence in return for information on Bauer's treason. Angermann refuses, turning himself in for homosexual practices before the Federal Police can blackmail him. The building of a new West Germany needs a sacrifice which only the young German homosexual seems able to make to the full extent.

The rewriting of the West German founding narrative in terms of sexuality is also present in *Die Akte*. Here, too, the figure of the young prosecutor remains central to the interconnectedness of change and sexual orientation, although this representative of the new generation serves as a contrast to Bauer. Hell's democratic awakening is a vital part of the film narrative and takes up most of it. Implicitly, it takes so long because Hell is not gay. In *Die Akte* Bauer surrounds himself with young gay men, which he calls his 'salon'. This group represent 1950s modernism: they are fashionable, politically and aesthetically educated, listen to jazz, and further the cause of democracy and critical engagement with the past. The figure of Thomas Harlan, one of these young modernists, is the incarnation of a changed Germany (the son who learnt from his father's 'mistakes'[16]). Like Angermann in *Der Staat*, Harlan proves his moral standing by supporting Bauer's efforts even where they are illegal. Harlan, however, is a minor character; the film's focus is on Hell.

Bauer decides to have Hell in his team because the young man does not bow to the old authorities. However, Hell's courage and insubordination falter where treason in the legal sense is concerned. While Hell does what Bauer asks of him, he also reports on Bauer to the Federal Intelligence Service. Hell does not give Bauer away by reporting his homosexuality, but by the time Hell overcomes his doubts, it is too late to pursue the case of Hans Globke. According to the film, a central part of Bauer's efforts has thus failed.

Neither *Der Staat* nor *Die Akte* motivate their characters through individual stories about the Hitler and the postwar years in terms of political conviction, involvement and war experience, or class, gender, ethnic origin, religion or occupation. Not surprisingly, *Die Akte* fails to motivate Hell's reluctance with any sort of explanation; the new generation in both films appears completely without biography (and it is indicative that both young Germans are fictional characters, not the prosecutors Bauer actually worked with). Given their 'flatness', the only aspect of differentiation

Figure 5.2 Bauer and Hell with the 'salon' in the background: 'A reckoning with the past is necessary not because the old Germany deserves it, but because the new Germany needs it.' Still from *Die Akte General* (2016).

is again sexual orientation. Hell's heterosexuality is what clearly sets him apart from Bauer and the 'salon'. Compared to them (or Angermann), Hell is a conventionalist with a young pregnant wife and a big house in a wealthy area who is comfortable in his heterosexual set-up and does not mind the trivialities of his housewife or the Intelligence Service's money to support his young family. The film cuts between new information Bauer receives on Eichmann and Hell's argument with an old judge which leads to Hell's employment for Bauer and the start of the 'hunt'. Every step that brings the 'hunters' closer to Eichmann is accompanied by a glimpse of Bauer's 'secret life' and often a 'lesson' for Hell, too. Hell's first 'lesson' is about the failed denazification in West Germany and it takes place in Bauer's flat amid the hustle and bustle of the 'salon'.

The next revelation takes place in Israel, where Bauer and his supposedly lesbian Danish wife discuss social and legal problems of homosexuality before Bauer meets representatives of the Mossad to push the Eichmann case further. Once Eichmann is captured, Bauer exchanges desiring gazes with a young man while Hell witnesses postwar anti-Semitism. Last but not least, when evidence against Globke is found, we see Bauer in his flat with a naked young man. This parallelism of the hunt and homosexuality explains why, in an extremely wooden final scene, Bauer passes his credo on to Harlan and the 'salon', not to Hell. In a balcony box at the opera just before the beginning of the overture, Bauer whispers the lasts words of the film:

> To resist Nazi crimes, barbarity, is an eternally valid human right. To draw on it, is the least the German judiciary can do in the face of its complete failure, or else the earth will swallow it up. Laws are nor written on parchment but on sensitive human skin.

Conclusion

Bauer's assumed homosexuality becomes a main signifier of morality and justice in both films; it is meaningful also because the next generation lends it the connotation of 'future'. At first glance, this may seem like a successful 'negotiation of the heterogeneities of social formation' (Parikh 2009: 11) issued by the intervention of ethical betrayal. However, the fact that the full dimension of Bauer's 'treason', its 'traumatic rupture' (ibid.: 3), is bypassed, also affects the sexuality tale. What van Hoeij said about the depiction of homosexuality in *Der Staat* is as true for *Die Akte*: it is 'more of a plot convenience than an innate part of their character' (2015). There is not a single scene in either film in which homosexuality is depicted in any depth as lived (historical) experience. It could be seen as indicative of the accessory-status of sexuality in the films that the attractive transvestite in *Der Staat* was played by a woman (with digitally added male genitals) because, as the director explains, the boys cast and made up 'could not walk elegantly in high heels' (Presseheft 2015: 12).

Why focus on homosexuality if there is no perceptibly genuine interest in it? I suggest that the answer brings us back to the postwar national self, historically injured by Bauer's 'treason'. The only graspable gain from the perpetuated deflection mechanism of the films is the diversification of the national, ethnically widely homogenised German post-Hitler 'tribe', whose claim to victimhood is retrospectively fulfilled by the films – doubtlessly, homosexuals were victims of the Nazis, though they were not persecuted on racial grounds. Unlike other non-racial victims such as communists, homosexuals are politically uncontested in contemporary Germany and offer routinised opportunities for lifestyle statements with regard to fashion and art, elements that both films employ to appeal to their audiences.

Figure 5.3 Angermann and Bauer in Bauer's modernist flat with a Feininger painting. Still from *Der Staat gegen Fritz Bauer* (2015).

Pilarczyk calls films like *Der Staat* and *Die Akte* the 'bubble of meaningless significance'; they have nothing to say about the past or the present (2019). This is true, though with the hidden national story, both films perpetuate the victim collective which Bauer had challenged. 'What is remarkable', writes Helmut Schmitz, 'is that the shift from memory centred on the victims of Nazism to a "perpetrator-centred" memory occurs, almost antithetically, subsequently to the institutionalisation of the memory of the Holocaust at the heart of contemporary German historical identity' (2007: 4). Internationally, the shift to a perpetrator-centred memory has generated compelling stories of guilt and trauma, suppression and identity loss. The psychological turn of the Nazi hunter thriller in Scorsese's *Shutter Island* or Egoyan's *Remember* explores the chasm of the self, its mechanisms of denial and the haunting uncanniness of encounters with the self's horrible deeds. The truly extraordinary aspect is, however, that the perpetrator-centred memory in German films still appropriates the other's – not just the victim's but the transgressor's – discourse to deflect its own history.

Notes

1. All quotations in English from German sources were translated by the author.
2. Other recent German films which deal with Bauer are *Fritz Bauer – Tod auf Raten* (Ilona Ziok, 2010) and *Im Labyrinth des Schweigens* (Giulio Ricciarelli, 2015). However, they are not discussed in the present chapter. *Tod auf Raten* is a documentary and *Im Labyrinth*, on the other hand, makes Bauer a minor character. Thus the films lack the developed fictionalisation of Bauer which *Der Staat* and *Die Akte* deploy at their centre.
3. Since 2015, *Der Staat gegen Fritz Bauer* has been watched by 274,814 in Germany (514,460 viewers in Europe) while Christian Petzold's cinematic gem *Phoenix* (2014), which he dedicated to Fritz Bauer and which, though not telling Bauer's 'story', understood his work much more thoroughly than any of the other films, has since 2014 been seen by only 99,365 viewers in Germany (529,821 in Europe) (http://lumiere.obs.coe.int/web/search/). This public preference is also reflected in the number and kinds of German film awards given to the productions: *Der Staat* was awarded Best German Film in 2016 and also won in the categories Best Script, Best Director, Best Supporting Actor, Best Costume Design, Best Set; in 2015 it was awarded the Prize of German Film Critics, the Bavarian Film Prize, the Günter-Rohrbach Film Prize and the Hessian Film Prize. *Phoenix*, on the other hand, received only one German award, namely the German Film Prize 2015 in the category Best Supporting Actress (www.filmportal.de). Surprisingly, *Die Akte General* also had a considerable success with a market share of 11.3 per cent (3.63 million viewers) when first broadcast on 24 February 2016 (Prime-check, http://www.quotenmeter.de/n/84001/).

4. This was a paramilitary unit linked to the Social Democrat Party protecting the democracy of the interwar years, the Weimar Republic.
5. In the context of Nazi crimes, the 'normal German' of the 1950s was the 'Peiniger, [. . .] der längst in der Familie, im Berufsleben und in seiner Gemeinde wieder die Rolle eines ehrenwerten Biedermanns [. . .] zu spielen begonnen hatte'/ 'the torturer, who had again started to play the role of the honest man in his family, work place and community' (Bauer 1958, in Foljanti and Johst 2018: 529).
6. The division of Germany after the Second World War and the loss of German territory in the East to Poland (formalised in the Oder-Neisse border in 1945) were central moments of the (West) German victimhood narrative and its Cold War frame.
7. In articles and speeches such as 'Die Stärke der Demokratie' (1954), 'Wer verteidigt die Freiheit?' (1955), 'Im Kampf um des Menschen Recht' (1955), 'Widerstand heißt Verantwortung' (1956) and 'Wir aber wollen Male richten euch zum Gedächtnis' (1961), Bauer detailed the right of the individual to resist unjust and inhuman authority, and defined it as a basic requirement for a democracy (see Foljanti and Johst 2018). In 1968, the year of Bauer's death, 'the right to oppose' was included in the Basic Law.
8. That the films pay so much attention to Bauer's assumed homosexuality (following Steinke's biography of Bauer (2013)) caused one of the fierce debates about them. What links Bauer to homosexuality is a report by the Danish police from 1936, according to which Bauer was seen with homosexual men and admitted homosexual proclivities. While some critics stress that this is the only indication of a homosexual orientation, that there is no evidence of any other sexual activities before or after, and that none of Bauer's friends could ever confirm the assumption (Wojak 2015; Rautenberg 2014; Nelhiebel 2014a), others maintain that there is evidence enough and that those who fulminate at Bauer's homosexuality are homophobic (Boll 2017; Renz 2017; Kramer 2014).
9. This is what critics had already reproached Steinke's biography with (Nelhiebel 2014b).
10. For the commercialisation of historical drama after unification see also Hake (2012).
11. The Eichmann films provide only one context. German big and small screen has disseminated heaps of historical dramas roughly covering the period 1871–1960, and the Nazi regime, particularly the Holocaust, have figured prominently among those (Hake 2012; Halle 2008; Schmitz 2007; Rentschler 2000).
12. It is remarkable that both films introduce their young prosecutors through a court scene in which the old judges fail their legal and moral duty. However, these scenes do not show Nazi trials, which immediately shifts the focus and depicts the West German judiciary vaguely as generally 'failing'.
13. The 'confession scene' sparked a second debate. Interestingly, the bone of contention was not that everybody released from a German concentration

camp had to sign a letter of submission; the 'loyalty letter' was seen as a slightly different matter. For Rautenberg (2014) and Wojak (2015) the problem is that the film (again adopting Steinke's biography (2013)) accepts the Nazi press's publication and claim without having seen the original. This, they argue, reiterates Nazi practice in that it accepts Nazi publications as true and reliable and ignores the highly likely possibility that the Nazis forged and published the letter to undermine solidarity among the persecuted. Renz (2017) on the other hand sees the existence of the letter as proven and justifies it as a way to allow the persecuted to continue fighting.
14. Kraume's phrasing ('klein kriegen und ins Exil jagen ließ') interprets the total persecution as a lack of power to resist or stamina on the victim's side.
15. The word *Heimat* further underlines the relentless ignorance or naiveté of the film's conception, as postwar Germany was certainly not simply a 'home' for those coming back after twelve years of persecution.
16. Thomas Harlan, indeed a friend of Bauer's, was the son of Veit Harlan, beside Leni Riefenstahl the most prominent director of Nazi propaganda films, most notably the anti-Semitic *Jud Süß* (1941).

Works Cited

Åkerström, Malin (1991) *Betrayal and Betrayers – The Sociology of Treachery*. New Brunswick, NJ: Routledge.

Bauer, Fritz (1962) 'Was ist Landesverrat?', *Der Spiegel*, 7 November <https://www.spiegel.de/spiegel/print/d-45124528.html> (last accessed 24 February 2020).

Bauer, Fritz (2018a) [1952], 'Der Generalstaatsanwalt hat das Wort. Das Plädoyer des Anklägers Dr. Bauer im Prozeß gegen Remer', in Lena Foljanty and David Johst (eds), *Fritz Bauer: Kleine Schriften (1921–1961)*. Frankfurt am Main and New York: Campus Verlag, pp. 323–36.

Bauer, Fritz (2018b) [1958], 'Mörder unter uns!', in Lena Foljanty and David Johst (eds), *Fritz Bauer: Kleine Schriften (1921–1961)*. Frankfurt am Main and New York: Campus Verlag, pp. 529–31.

Boll, Monika (2017) 'Rede zur Eröffnung der Ausstellung: Fritz Bauer. Der Staatsanwalt. NS-Verbrechen vor Gericht', exhibition catalogue, Militärhistorisches Museum der Bundeswehr, Dresden, 9 March <https://www.fritz-bauer-institut.de/fileadmin/editorial/download/aktuelles/2017-03-09_Monika-Boll_FB-Eroeffnung-Dresden.pdf> (last accessed 25 January 2020).

Dell, Matthias (2015) 'Von den Socken', *Der Freitag*, 39 <https://www.freitag.de/autoren/mdell/von-den-socken> (last accessed 24 February 2020).

Filmportal.de, Alles zum deutschen Film <https://www.filmportal.de/> (last accessed 24 February 2020).

Foljanty, Lena and Johst, David (eds) (2018) *Fritz Bauer: Kleine Schriften (1921–1961)*, vol. 1, Wissenschaftliche Reihe des Fritz Bauer Instituts, Frankfurt am Main and New York: Campus Verlag.

Frank, Arno (2015) 'Großes Nazijäger-Kino', *Der Spiegel* Online, 2 October <https://www.spiegel.de/kultur/kino/der-staat-gegen-fritz-bauer-grosses-nazijaeger-kino-a-1055561.html> (last accessed 19 November 2019).

Frank, Arno (2016) 'Die Akte General', *Der Spiegel* Online, 24 February <https://www.spiegel.de/kultur/tv/die-akte-general-ard-film-ueber-fritz-bauer-a-1078813.html> (last accessed 19 November 2019).

Frei Norbert (2002) *Adenauer's Germany and the Nazi Past*. New York: Columbia University Press.

Frei, Norbert (2009) *1945 und Wir: Das Dritte Reich im Bewußtsein der Deutschen*. München: dtv.

Fulbrook, Mary (2015) *A History of Germany, 1919–2014: The Divided Nation*. Chichester: Wiley-Blackwell.

Gass, Lars Henrik and Suchsland, Rüdiger (2019) 'Gegen die Kultur-Abwicklung: Ein Gastbeitrag', *Der Spiegel* Online, 18 October <https://www.spiegel.de/kultur/kino/filmfoerderung-gegen-die-kultur-abwicklung-gastbeitrag-a-1291850.html> (last accessed 22 October 2019).

Hake, Sabine (2012) *Screen Nazis: Cinema, History, and Democracy*. Madison, WI: University of Wisconsin Press.

Halle, Randall (2008) *German Film after Germany: Toward a Transnational Aesthetic*. Urbana and Chicago, IL: University of Illinois Press.

Jenks, Chris (2003) *Transgression*. London: Routledge.

Kaever, Oliver (2015) 'Der Held will keine Rache', *Die Zeit*, 30 September <https://www.zeit.de/kultur/film/2015-09/staat-gegen-fritz-bauer-lars-kraume> (last accessed 11 May 2018).

Kramer, Helmut (2014) 'Ein großes Vorbild, ein Mensch. Zum Streit um Fritz Bauer, den Generalstaatsanwalt der Auschwitz-Prozesse: eine Erwiderung auf Kurt Nelhiebels Tagesspiegel-Beitrag', *Der Tagesspiegel*, 22 December, <https://www.tagesspiegel.de/kultur/debatte-um-fritz-bauer-ein-grosses-vorbild-ein-mensch/11150190.html> (last accessed 8 November 2018).

Lumiere: Database on Admissions of Films Released in Europe <http://lumiere.obs.coe.int/web/search/> (last accessed 22 October 2019).

Moeller, Robert (2003) *War Stories: The Search for a Usable Past in the Federal Republic of Germany*. Berkeley, CA and London: University of California Press.

Nelhiebel, Kurt (2014a) 'Die Nestbeschützer', *Der Tagesspiegel*, 8 November, <https://www.tagesspiegel.de/kultur/deutungskampf-um-das-werk-von-fritz-bauer-die-nestbeschuetzer/11087028.html> (last accessed 14 February 2020).

Nelhiebel, Kurt (2014b) 'Fritz Bauer als Zerrbild – Eine Biografie mit Lücken und Tücken', State Association of Bremen: Association of Anti-Fascists (WN-BdA), 21 August <https://bremen.vvn-bda.de/2014/08/21/fritz-bauer-als-zerrbild-eine-biografie-mit-lucken-und-tucken/> (last accessed 25 February 2020).

Norris, Pippa and Inglehart, Ronald (2019) *Cultural Backlash: Trump, Brexit, and Authoritarian Populism*. Cambridge: Cambridge University Press.

Parikh, Crystal (2009) *An Ethics of Betrayal: The Politics of Otherness in Emergent U.S. Literatures and Culture*. New York: Fordham University Press.

Pfeifer, Douglas (2001) 'Commemoration of Mutiny, Rebellion, and Resistance in Postwar Germany: Public Memory, History, and the Formation of "Memory Beacons"', *Journal of Military History*, 65 (4), pp. 1013–52.

Pilarczyk, Hannah (2019) 'Bedeutungslose Bedeutsamkeit: Ein Kommentar', *Spiegel* Online, 2 October <https://www.spiegel.de/kultur/kino/deutschstunde-zwischen-uns-die-mauer-kritik-am-deutschen-kino-a-1289352.html> (last accessed 22 October 2019).

Presseheft *Der Staat gegen Fritz Bauer* (2015) https://www.zeroone.de/wp-content/uploads/DER-STAAT-GEGEN-FRITZ-BAUER_Presseheft.pdf (last accessed 22 May 2020).

Quotenmeter.de <http://www.quotenmeter.de/cms/> (last accessed 10 February 2020).

Rautenberg, Erardo C. (2014) 'Die Demontage des Generalstaatsanwalts Dr. Fritz Bauer: Nicht nur eine Kritik der Biographie von Ronen Steinke', *Neue Justiz*, 9, pp. 369–76.

Rentschler, Eric (2000) 'From New German Cinema to the Post-Wall Cinema of Consensus', in Mette Hjort and Scott MacKenzie (eds), *Cinema and Nation*. London and New York: Routledge, pp. 260–77.

Renz, Werner (2017) 'Einführung: Fritz Bauer. Der Staatsanwalt. NS-Verbrechen vor Gericht', Dorsten, Jüdisches Museum Westfalen, 15 October <https://www.jmw-dorsten.de/wp-content/uploads/2018/06/Einf%C3%BChrung-Renz-FritzBauerDorsten_2017_10_15.pdf> (last accessed 4 February 2020).

Schmitz, Helmut (2007) 'Introduction: The Return of Wartime Suffering in Contemporary German Memory Culture, Literature, and Film', in Helmut Schmitz (ed.), *A Nation of Victims? Representations of German Wartime Suffering from 1945 to the Present*. Amsterdam and New York: Rodopi, pp. 1–20.

Steinke, Ronen (2013) *Fritz Bauer oder: Auschwitz vor Gericht*. München: Piper.

van Hoeij, Boyd (2014) '"The People vs. Fritz Bauer": "Der Staat gegen Fritz Bauer": Locarno Review', *Hollywood Reporter*, 8 July <https://www.hollywoodreporter.com/review/people-fritz-bauer-der-staat-813278> (last accessed 19 November 2019).

Wojak, Irmtrud (2015) '"Der Staat gegen Fritz Bauer" oder "Der Jude ist schwul"', *Forschungsjournal Soziale Bewegungen*, Heft 4 <http://forschungsjournal.de/sites/default/files/downloads/fjsb_2015-4_wojak.pdf> (last accessed 10 December 2019).

Wojak, Irmtrud (2016) *Fritz Bauer (1903–1968): Eine Biographie*. München: Buxus Edition.

Wölfel, Ute (2015) 'At the Front: Common Traitors in West German War Films of the 1950s', *Modern Language Review*, 110 (3), pp. 739–58.

CHAPTER 6

'Just another Kraut'? The Wehrmacht Traitor as 'Good German' in Hollywood's *Decision before Dawn* (1951)

Patrick Major

Decision before Dawn (Anatole Litvak, 1951) is a story of line-crossing and moral realignment, reflecting shifting loyalties between World War and Cold War.[1] In a film designed for a global but also a post-fascist German audience, universal notions of what constituted a 'good German', based on humanistic morality, vied with legalistic and nationalistic attitudes in a postwar West Germany emerging from occupation. It was a film, therefore, which trod carefully in the no-man's-land of postwar national identity, but still managed to trigger some of the hidden hazards buried there. The Twentieth Century-Fox film tells of Karl Maurer (Oskar Werner), a German Luftwaffe medic captured by American forces during the battle for Alsace in December 1944. As a prisoner of war he is recruited by US intelligence and parachuted on a so-called 'tourist mission' back into Nazi Germany. As Maurer – code name 'Happy' – roams wartorn southern Germany, non-German audiences become vicarious tourists, catching an imaginary glimpse of the other side, of conflicted 'good Germans' beyond previous SS/Gestapo stereotypes. In its export print, as *Entscheidung vor Morgengrauen*, it also allowed German audiences an empathetic, if not sympathetic, view of the 'other Germany', until so recently vilified by Nazi propaganda (Hake 2012: 69).

As a film designed for multiple audiences, its transgression does not operate in a single dimension, but speaks to different notions of loyalty, finding resonances with anglophone viewers habituated to antifascist messages, but also Germans seeking moral certainties in an age of denazification but also partial rehabilitation of anti-communist *Feindbilder*. Studio publicity called it 'a picture of the people who fought and suffered on both sides separated by the almost indefinable hairline boundary that made one a hero and the next a traitor'.[2] US audiences, too, were experiencing an inquisitorial age of McCarthyism, joining a crusade against communism which many Germans felt they had been waging for a decade already. Hollywood publicity departments therefore had to remain ambivalent when inviting home audiences to consider whether a line-crosser was a 'patriot or traitor'.³ In order to square the circle of these contradictions, the filmmakers used a number of subtle post-production techniques to produce two slightly different versions of the same film. The inherent risk, nonetheless, was that one film could never satisfy two sets of audiences.

An act of treachery might not seem propitious for audience sympathy. West German attitudes to the acceptable limits of treason were still in flux in the early 1950s (Kleine 2016). Leading resisters such as Stauffenberg had not yet become official martyrs. When former army major-general Otto-Ernst Remer, who had helped quell the ill-fated July 1944 putsch, accused the would-be assassins of being 'Landesverräter' or traitors to the country, a high-profile libel trial ensued in 1952 in the run-up to the movie's German release. Conservative critics would not accept that the price of defeating the greater evil of National Socialism might be the deaths of German soldiers, 'stabbed in the back'. Exculpation risked opening the floodgates to legalised pacifism at a time of Cold War rearmament. As late as 1967, during civil disobedience against the so-called Emergency Laws, right-wing publicist Karl Balzer still categorised the 1944 conspirators as 'traitors', not 'rebels' with a just cause (Balzer 1967: 8).

As Ute Wölfel has already noted of West German cinema, many Germans distinguished between *Hochverrat*, or high treason against the Nazi state, and *Landesverrat* or 'treason against the country' (Wölfel 2015). *Landesverrat*, which usually involves direct collusion with the enemy, betrays the nation. Yet both state and nation were shifting concepts under the Third Reich. National Socialism had turned the inclusive concept of nation into the exclusionary dogma of the *Volk*. Defending the 'people's community' involved combatting not only foreigners but compatriots now ostracised as second-class 'community aliens', notably the Jews. By 1945 the NS leadership ultimately betrayed even 'people's comrades', sacrificing them as human shields and cannon fodder (Keller 2013: 365–417). Capitulationists were *Volksverräter* as the party-cum-state became a law unto itself. It was only at the Remer trial in March 1952 that Braunschweig's attorney general, Fritz Bauer, forced the court to redefine the NS regime as an *Unrechtsstaat*, or unlawful state, thus breaking the jurisprudential logjam (Steinbach 2000: 105).

Decision before Dawn deals not with prominent resisters but forgotten resistance by an anonymous corporal. Following the Wehrmacht Exhibition controversy of the 1990s, which accused rank-and-file soldiers of complicity in Hitler's race war, interest grew in the 'other soldiers' who did not simply obey orders: pacifists, defeatists and deserters. Desertion incurred charges of aiding and 'abetting the enemy' (*Feindbegünstigung*), 'war treason' (*Kriegsverrat*) or even 'preparation for high treason' (*Vorbereitung zum Hochverrat*).

The penalty was often death and even persecution of family members. Only the end of the Cold War signalled greater public willingness to exonerate Wehrmacht deserters, culminating in their legal rehabilitation in the Federal Republic in 2002 (Welch 2012).

Most absconders were more probably survivalists, not regime-changers. Occasionally, however, deserters became defectors, actively fighting alongside Allied troops. Most recorded cases involved desertions to partisan movements, including the later film director Falk Harnack, who crossed the lines in Greece in December 1943 (Paul 1995: 151). Only rarely, however, were deserters prepared to re-cross them and return to the Reich, such as Heinz Müller, parachuted in by the Red Air Force to reorganise communist resistance in Berlin. Indeed, most early literature celebrating collaboration came from East German quarters, where 'Allied' usually meant Soviet (Doernberg 1995). Conservative critics, on the other hand, seemed prepared to condone high treason conducted at a higher level and with more shattering consequences, simply because it was committed by Germans, for Germans.

Red connections and fears of a right-wing backlash dominated political discourse back in the early 1950s, as Germany's Cold War became entrenched. The young Federal Republic was facing the prospect of rearmament only five years after being 'demilitarised'. As Brian Etheridge has postulated, narratives of German postwar identity were at a tipping-point between Second World War narratives privileging anti-fascism and Cold War frameworks justifying anti-communism (Etheridge 2016: 55–72). Just weeks before *Decision*'s US premiere in December 1951, the Adenauer government had instituted banning proceedings against both Remer's far-right Socialist Reich Party and the West German Communist Party. The movie became caught in the cultural-political crossfire, touching raw nerves in a young Federal Republic transitioning from occupation to sovereignty. Naturally, Cold War paranoia was not a German monopoly; the movie appeared at the height of McCarthyism which also targeted Hollywood. Director Anatole Litvak, born in Kiev and culturally Russophile, claimed to be under FBI investigation during filming (Viertel 1992: 109–10). Would US audiences identify with a turncoat? As one executive warned Twentieth Century-Fox boss Darryl F. Zanuck, despite the twist of using a 'good German' as hero:

> are we, in fact, glorifying a traitor . . . who betrays his country, a man who helps cause the defeat of his own nation? Some people in the audience may find the similarity between Karl Maurer and the arch-heavy of American history, Benedict Arnold, a bit too close for comfort.[4]

Decision before Dawn, 1951

Decision before Dawn, like so many Hollywood productions, was based on a true story. Between autumn 1944 and spring 1945, America's Office of Strategic Services (OSS) – a proto-CIA – infiltrated some 200 German nationals into Nazi Germany (Heideking and Mauch 1996: 404–6). Most were labour movement exiles gathering political intelligence, but around thirty were POWs sent on so-called 'tourist missions', reporting Wehrmacht troop deployments and air-strike coordinates. A team of three OSS officers oversaw these missions: Peter Sichel, a British-educated, German-Jewish expatriate from a Rhineland winegrowing dynasty who later ran the CIA's West Berlin station; Peter Viertel, son of German-Jewish parents, who had immigrated to the States aged eight; and Carl Muecke, a New Yorker of German extraction who had the distinction of arresting Leni Riefenstahl in 1945. These three, supported by a dozen staff, scoured France's POW cages in late 1944 for likely Wehrmacht converts. Agent infiltration was extremely hazardous – half the 21 recruits in January and February 1945 were lost (Persico 1979: 114). Safer infiltration methods evolved: US troops would temporarily fall back while agents went to ground, or they were parachuted behind the lines. Armed with false leave papers, 'tourists' roved the German rear areas for a week to ten days before exfiltrating (Mauch 2003: 182).

Sichel recalled that motives ranged from careerism and pacifism, to a few convinced anti-Nazis, 'men willing to die for their ideals' (2016: 151–2). One such recruit, a twenty-three-year-old Berlin doctor's son named Stabreit (code name 'Jacques'), struck the OSS as unusually committed (Mauch 2003: 295). Parachuted into south-western Germany, Stabreit's transmissions eventually betrayed him to German radio detectors and in his bid to escape he apparently drowned swimming the Rhine. After the war, his fate caught the imagination of another OSS team member, George Howe, the unit's forged documents expert, who penned an imagined account of Stabreit's fateful mission in the novel *Call It Treason* (1949), which won the $15,000 Christopher Prize. (Howe's title derived from the Elizabethan courtier, Sir John Harington's, aphorism: 'Treason doth never prosper; what's the reason? Why, if it prosper, none dare call it treason.') The book was then optioned by Twentieth Century-Fox, before going into German translation in 1953.

The OSS connection did not end there. Peter Viertel, a former 'tourist mission' handler, had grown up in Hollywood, the son of émigré Weimar filmmaker Berthold Viertel, whose Santa Monica home became a salon for expatriate Austro-German antifascists, including Thomas Mann and Fred

Zinnemann. Viertel junior co-scripted Hitchcock's *Saboteur* in 1942, before serving in the Marines, then OSS. It was in fact he who had personally recruited Stabreit. After the war he returned to screenwriting when introduced by family friend John Huston to Litvak at his Malibu beach house, where the latter was considering filming Howe's novel. Viertel, who later criticised OSS's ruthless use of these 'poor little schnucks' from the POW cages (Scheingraber 2007) – all strictly against the Geneva Convention – agreed to adapt Howe's novel (Viertel 1992: 67–9). If *Decision* has an autobiographical character, it is American case officer Lt Dick Rennick, played by Richard Basehart, who moves from despising to revering the sacrificial German pawns in the not-so-great game. 'A traitor's always a traitor', argues his superior, consoling him after Happy's failure to return; 'just another Kraut', shrugs his jeep driver. As Rennick stares back steely-eyed across the Rhine, viewers know better (Heeb 1997: 52).

Call It Treason depicts an agent who never came back from the cold, narrated by an OSS man seeking the 'key to the Meanings of Treason . . . because it has more than one' (Howe 1949: 8) – lines echoed in the film. 'Riches and risk and faith' (ibid.: 16) are the three motivations explored in Howe's novel. Maurer/Happy is a believer, a friend of the Stauffenberg circle, invoking Americanised ideals: 'I want to work for freedom, sir . . . that's all. Für die Freiheit!' (ibid.: 66). Liberation came, of course, from outside, but he hopes that 'our freedom would come from inside the country before the destruction spread too far' (ibid.: 89). His American superiors are more cynical: 'if it makes him happier to think he's doing it for Germany rather than America', muses one, 'it's all the same to me' (ibid.: 92). As in the film, Maurer is contrasted with another line-crosser, Rudolf Barth or 'Tiger' (Hans Christian Blech), amoral and self-seeking, who survives the mission in a Mannheim cellar selling civilian clothing to Wehrmacht deserters. In the novel, Tiger is a disillusioned communist, but not in the film. The final member of the troika – completely absent from the movie (replaced by Basehart) – is a Russian, Paluka, who may or may not be a communist, but acts as an 'advance guard of the revolution: Hands across the continent, so to speak' (ibid.: 44). Happy's political convictions are never spelt out, although his fraternal internationalism may make him a fellow traveller. In the inquisitorial atmosphere of 1950, however, any such sympathies were written out of the screenplay. As Zanuck insisted: 'Under no circumstances can we have Karl expounding a political philosophy.'[5] The hero's motivation was to be strictly 'moral'.

Like most Hollywood adaptations, the base novel was altered significantly by Viertel, often at Zanuck's behest. Viertel recalled how in the first story conference he was under orders from Litvak to agree to everything

Zanuck suggested, however clichéd (Viertel 1992: 71). Zanuck pushed for dramatic content over historical authenticity. In the book, Maurer is shot as he crosses the sights of a startled German sentry, almost by accident, and not by firing squad; in the initial film treatment, and truer to life, he simply founders in the Rhine. This was not enough for Zanuck who did 'not know why Karl is such a hero':

> I believe that at the end we have to show that he has earned the right to have his story told. I think we have to show that he voluntarily gives up his life to save Rennick, so that Rennick can get back to the Americans with vital information. Karl is convinced that his beliefs are right; he believes he is not a traitor, and he gives up his life to back up this belief.[6]

Thus Zanuck suggested the opening device of a firing squad followed by a flashback to 1944. Indeed, Maurer is not a deserter as such; the novel highlights his efforts to evade capture. Asked in the film if he has qualms about fighting against his own people, he argues for a future greater good: 'I believe fighting against them now *is* fighting for them.' But the film personalises his choices: in one scene he has the opportunity to warn his father that his hospital abuts a prime Allied air target. Rather than compromise the mission, or explain his change of loyalty, Happy hangs up the phone instead, in a fit of self-doubt which revisits him moments before his own unhappy ending.

Figure 6.1 Karl Maurer/Happy (Oskar Werner) sacrificing himself to save the mission. Still from *Decision before Dawn* (1951).

To keep Happy 'moral', he could not become amorously involved with leading lady Hildegard Knef, although Zanuck later worried this might cast doubt on his virility. Oskar Werner's Vienna choirboy looks certainly suggest the *verträumter Schwärmer*, the dreamy idealist, of Germanic national stereotype. Kaleidoscopic sound montages of the day's conversations, played over close-ups of Werner's dark, melancholic eyes, occur at liminal moments between waking and sleeping. Happy's filmic self-sacrifice also follows subtle Christian motifs: OSS is concealed within a convent; he wears the sign of the (red) cross on his medic's brassard; the trio undergo a Gethsemane-like near betrayal in a ruined church; at the moment the spy is shot in the opening sequence, a church bell tolls; and his memory is 'resurrected' as Rennick vows not to let him be 'killed by forgetfulness', while standing beside a wayside crucifix. Nor did it harm Fox's publicity that Werner's own backstory echoed Maurer's: as an unwilling Wehrmacht conscript, he had been almost buried alive in a US air raid, before going AWOL in late 1944 with his 'half-Jewish' wife and baby. Hiding out in the Vienna Woods, they then re-crossed the lines under Russian fire in April 1945 (Dachs 1988: 34–5).

For authenticity and economy, *Decision* was shot entirely on location in Germany, filming indoor sequences at Munich's Geiselgasteig studios. Fox producer Frank McCarthy, briefly assistant Secretary of State in 1945, pulled strings with current Secretary Dean Acheson, to facilitate filming in sixteen towns across the former US and French zones.[7] Both the Department of Defense and CIA were sent draft scripts, but neither raised security objections, only requesting the mild subterfuge that OSS become 'SSS'.[8] The studio received GI extras, Air Force fighter-bombers and mothballed Wehrmacht equipment. Unable to take up French offers of Tiger tanks for insurance reasons, Fox persuaded the US Army to lend its own tanks instead, suitably mocked up. So realistic was the effect in one town that 'a startled and obviously absent-minded spectator responded with a Hitler salute as a column of ostensibly Nazi tanks ground through the cobbled streets.'[9] Location shooting had other hazards. McCarthy's diplomatic skills were tested in autumn 1950 when Würzburg's mayor got wind of Fox's 'anti-German' plot-device of a vital chemicals plant in the city, rendering it a legitimate bombing target. (Würzburg had suffered one of the RAF's worst firestorm raids on 16–17 March 1945, incinerating its centre and 5,000 civilians; there was no chemicals plant.) Matters escalated to the Bavarian state chancellery and Minister-President Hans Ehard, who lobbied a sympathetic US *Land* commissioner George Shuster. 'Negotiations' between *Regierungsrat* Kellner and *Regierungsdirektor* von Gumppenberg for Bavaria and McCarthy for Fox broke down when the studio refused sight of the script. Munich subsequently withdrew shooting rights, shutting down filming at 100,000 Deutschmarks (DM) a day. Litvak then launched his own charm offensive, pleading for international understanding: 'Naturally I will show good and bad Germans, black, white and grey, if you want. But I believe I am doing something good for Germany.' Hollywood would be exposing Americans to a German resistance, he argued: 'We will show the destroyed cities, the bloody wounded, the starving children, the desperate women, we will show a people that is suffering – a suffering people garners sympathy' (in Kempski 1950: n.p.). Filming resumed. But both sides could claim victory: in the English-language print the plant remains; in the German it quietly disappears.

Fox cast only two Hollywood stars, Richard Basehart and Gary Merrill. It was effectively a co-production, so large was the Austro-German contingent, witnessing US breakthroughs for Oskar Werner, Hildegard Knef and Hans Christian Blech. Wilfried Seyferth, normally associated with wartime Ufa comedies, appeared as an SS man. O.E Hasse was perhaps the highest profile pre-1945 supporting actor, known for, *inter alia*, *Stukas* (Karl Ritter, 1941) and later starring in the resistance biopic *Canaris* (Alfred Weidenmann, 1954). Other Germans played uncredited cameo roles, such as Helene Thimig, widow of theatre director Max Reinhardt, as a head nurse; Werner Fuetterer, a silent film veteran, as an army officer; and Munich stage actress Maria Wimmer, a mother caught in the curfew. The Germans were coached to deliver their lines in English, before redubbing them in German. Tellingly, none belonged to the wartime diaspora supplying Hollywood with 'good' and 'bad Germans', most of whom remained stateside.

Decision explores various iterations of the 'good German', who had become such a stock type that the term almost invariably appeared in inverted commas, suggesting both fixity and irony (Schönfeld 2013). Happy himself is prompted into volunteering by the fate of fellow prisoner Paul Richter. The wounded Richter, played by Swiss actor Robert Freitag, is treated with compassion by his American captors, but arouses suspicion among his die-hard compatriots. When challenged, he responds that his only crime is passivity: 'Like most of us, I talk but I do nothing.' Yet his defeatist comments still provoke his fatal defenestration by a self-appointed kangaroo camp court. Other would-be OSS recruits file past the camera, only to be rejected: the well-meaning coward who will not risk the life just handed back to him, or Klaus Kinski's unctuous Nazi party careerist who has 'never been interested in politics'. One successful recruit is Sgt Rudolf Barth, a former petty criminal turned circus animal-trainer, nicknamed 'Tiger'. Barth, played by Hans Christian Blech who went on to prominent 'good German' roles in *The Longest Day* (Ken Annakin, Andrew Marton, Gerd Oswald, Darryl F. Zanuck, Bernhard Wicki, 1962) and *Battle of the*

Bulge (Ken Annakin, 1965), is part loveable rogue, a ladies' man with a profit motive, part *Realpolitiker*, volunteering because 'you're winning the war'. Zanuck insisted on turning Barth into a more unpleasant character than the novel, sowing suspicions that he may have betrayed one fellow agent, and might act again. OSS values Barth's cunning, but he is a conditional 'good German'. When the film reaches its climax, he reverts to type, complaining: 'when I took this job, I wanted to live a little better, not to get killed.' The recidivist Barth is duly expended, unlike the novel, when he makes a last-minute run for it, only to be gunned down by Rennick.

The film is ambivalent in its negative stereotypes of 'bad Germans' too. Arno Assmann's Gestapo agent Ernst Brandenbacher squints through sinister, gold-rimmed spectacles straight from Nazi central casting. Gestapo authority is symbolically mocked, however, when a Wehrmacht officer removes the myopic, Himmleresque 'jam-jars', querying if he will be able to shoot straight in them. Worried at too much disparagement, Hollywood's Production Code Administration wanted changes to an early script version of Brandenbacher's demise, 'to omit the present indication that Happy deliberately murders an unarmed, wounded soldier'.[10] Maurer thus dispatches his Gestapo pursuer in self-defence. Yet *Decision* establishes the black and field grey compartmentalisation of guilt between SS and Wehrmacht which would characterise so many war films. Wilfried Seyferth's sweaty and pudgy Waffen-SS corporal Heinz Scholtz confounds superman stereotypes. Happy looks more 'Aryan', but Scholtz is not a figure of fun. Showing off his looted jewellery (in the film's only allusion to the fate of the Jews), he is a nationalist proud of giving the world twelve unforgettable years ('they'll never get us out of their system'), enraged at suggestions that Alsace might belong to France. A long sequence in both book and film occurs when Happy is detailed to care for heartsick panzer commander Colonel von Ecker, played by O. E. Hasse. Ecker is considerate towards the young medic, and his love of fine wine and classical music place him in the venerable trope of the 'split' German *Kulturträger* who appreciates Mozart, while remaining capable of barbarous acts. Happy overhears him sentencing a deserter to death, despite pleas from the accused that he had only absconded to help his bombed-out family. When Ecker suffers a coronary attack, Happy momentarily hesitates before injecting the antidote, unable to take one life to save another, though the death warrant remains unsigned. Granted a wish for saving the colonel's life, he pleads for commutation, but is cynically told that the man must die to preserve the illusion of discipline and final victory. After Ecker and Maurer raise a glass 'to our country' – a toast with a deliberately double-edged ring – Happy moves on, past the sergeant's dangling corpse, a reminder that this is not his country anymore.

Figure 6.2 'So die all TRAITORS TO THE FATHERLAND!' Wehrmacht drumhead justice. Still from *Decision before Dawn*.

Another position on the 'good/bad German' spectrum is represented by von Schirmeck (Peter Lühr), a Wehrmacht officer parlaying with the OSS for a local surrender on the Rhine. Nevertheless, he will not short-circuit his chain of command when his superior is put out of action. Despite OSS encouragement that it might still be a risk worth taking, to save American and German lives, Schirmeck demurs. Rennick then lets rip: 'They're right to call you traitors because you've betrayed yourselves.' 'It's all very easy for you to say', replies the officer, 'but you were never in our shoes.' 'That's true', responds Rennick. 'And I hope we never will be.' This exchange encapsulates the dilemma of any film seeking transnational identification; to borrow from the German rendering of the shoe metaphor, could one national public ever inhabit the 'skin' of another? The espionage device allows Happy to inhabit two skins simultaneously in a picaresque series of insider/outsider confrontations. Hildegard Knef plays Hilde, a prostitute in a Wehrmacht *Tingeltangel* nightclub (inspired by Litvak's nostalgic memories of his 'adoption' as a teenage cadet by a bordello in revolutionary Russia). Viertel avoids whore-with-a-heart-of-gold clichés. Hilde's corruption is explained by the horrors of war: a fallen fiancé and a child killed in an air raid. She becomes a sympathetic identification figure for female viewers, as Knef

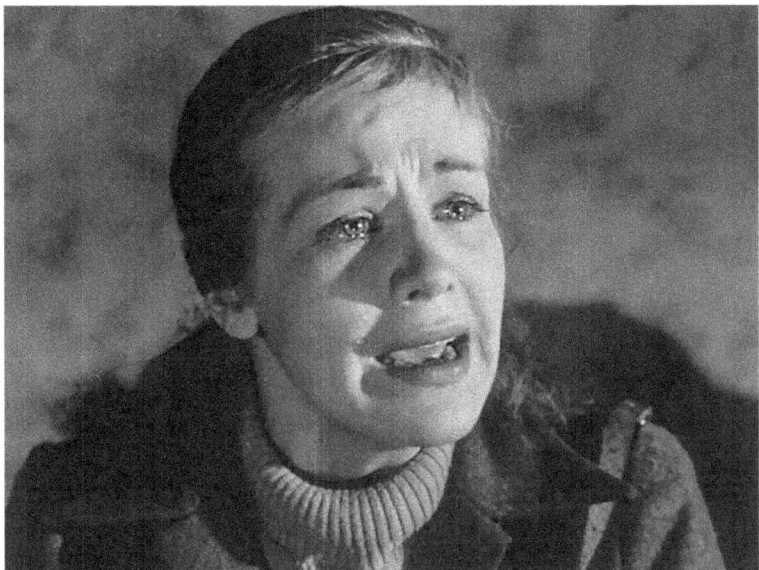

Figure 6.3 Hilde (Hildegard Knef): 'there are thousands and thousands like me'. Still from *Decision before Dawn*.

sobs in self-pity: 'dirty, miserable and alone – there are thousands and thousands like me'. Although accusing Happy of bourgeois priggishness, she is an incipient 'good German', protecting him from the SS's watchful eye and symbolically offering her redundant engagement ring to sell for money. For Hilde, Happy is a catalyst who 'for the first time . . . made me realise what was happening to me'.

The last 'bad/good German' is Tiger's nephew, Kurt, played by twelve-year-old Adi Lödel. The brainwashed Hitler Youth initially seems ready to turn in even family members to the pursuing patrols. Yet in a noirish encounter in a bombed-out church, chiaroscuro-lit by Austro-German cinematographer Franz Planer, he cannot bring himself to betray the cornered Rennick. In the film's most charged scene, beneath a Virgin Mary cradling the deposed Christ, Litvak employs no fewer than nine point of view and reverse point of view close-ups in a wordless exchange between Rennick, sinking into shadow, and Kurt, dissolving in tears. Kurt battles a lifetime's indoctrination, reverting from soldier of tomorrow to frightened child. But reality had no such happy ending for a boy actor typecast in other 'lost generation' roles: in what resembled a real-life *Germany, Year Zero* (Roberto Rossellini, 1948), supporting an impoverished family in a ruined Hamburg, Lödel was to hang himself four years later, aged just seventeen.

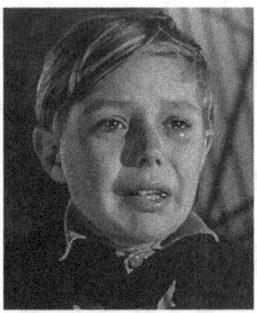 

Figure 6.4 Hitler Youth Kurt (Adi Lödel). Still from *Decision before Dawn*.

Figure 6.5 Lt Rennick (Richard Basehart). Still from *Decision before Dawn*).

Entscheidung vor Morgengrauen, 1952

Decision before Dawn's US reception was solid, but not sensational. It received Academy Award nominations for Best Picture and Best Editing, winning neither. The *New York Times* chief film critic, Bosley Crowther, had already lambasted Fox's 1951 sister film, *The Desert Fox* (Henry Hathaway), as too revisionist. *Decision*, on the other hand, 'considers treason as a pragmatic act and nothing more. No coloring, no character distortions, no eyewash of romantic tears are used here to make a turncoat action appear a display of gallantry' (Crowther 1952: n.p.). *Life* magazine made it its movie of the week, describing a country 'where the good citizens who go on doing their daily duty are only making the disaster worse and the only true patriots are the traitors'.[11] The film's export to Germany was integral to Fox's plans. Decartelised Hollywood was haemorrhaging domestic audience share to television. A successful foreign export could make a film. Whereas *Decision* had cost $2m, *Desert Fox* had cost only $1.4m, and had virtually recouped its costs from German rentals alone (Solomon 1988: 246). But *Decision* was released during a fraught West German rearmament debate and its counter-currents, the so-called 'Ohne mich!' or 'Count me out!' movement against the draft. Cold War demands for a German defence contingent reversed the Potsdam Agreement's calls for demilitarisation. Dealing with the Nazi past by a third party such as Hollywood would test German *amour propre*. For antifascists, cultural diplomacy encouraging forgive-and-forget attitudes would be sweeping the past under the carpet; at the other extreme, neo-Nazis à la Remer bridled at sympathetic traitors. Reconciliation films risked pleasing no one in a polarised, post-fascist society.

In 1951–2 a key player in the still semi-sovereign FRG was the Allied High Commission for Germany, HICOG, consisting of Franco-British-US commissioners, including America's John J. McCloy. His director of Public Affairs, Shepard Stone, had already ruled both *Desert Fox* and *Decision* 'unsuitable for Germany at this time . . . because they would damage the interests of the United States in Germany and the cause of German democracy'.[12] The studio then engaged in direct cultural diplomacy to reverse this decision, sending its president, Spyros P. Skouras, to Bonn on 9 November 1951, where HICOG screened *Decision* to sixteen West German government officials. Only two found it acceptable, with fourteen 'emphatically opposed', since:

A. It would further 'ohne mich' attitude in Germany by recalling wartime horrors of Allied bombings and general horror of war; both neo-Nazis and Communists would welcome it as support for their arguments.
B. Subject of treason in Germany today is very much alive, and right thinking Germans are only now convincing others that twentieth of July participants were patriots. Twentieth of July situation involved Germans against Germans. In case of DECISION BEFORE DAWN, however, treason is that of German who goes over to Americans. This, it was felt by Germans present, would serve only to confuse issue of treason versus patriotism and weaken case of twentieth of July action.
C. German participation in defense of Europe would not be furthered by such a film, but would, on the contrary, be retarded.
D. Picture revived civilian nightmares of war. Women present were particularly vehement on this point. (Ibid.)

Along with *Desert Fox*, a German release of *Decision* was put on ice until, as McCloy stipulated, 'such time as my office would give the word'.[13] Skouras's attempt to go over his head to Washington in January 1952 achieved nothing during a forty-five-minute interview with Acheson, despite the studio's promise to 'make pictures which would further the aims of US foreign policy abroad and support that policy at home'.[14] HICOG even pulled the movie from the second Berlin film festival in June 1952, much to the studio's embarrassment.[15]

As with *Desert Fox*, one way around was to work 'between the lines' of the script, in the dubbing and editing process (Major 2019: 222–3). Fox hired renowned Weimar playwright Carl Zuckmayer to translate the screenplay. Screenwriter for *Der blaue Engel/ The Blue Angel* (Josef von Sternberg 1930) and author of the anti-authoritarian play *Der Hauptmann von Köpenick/ Captain of Köpenick* (1931), as a naturalised American he had won renewed fame for the play *Des Teufels General/The Devil's General* in 1946 which set the post-war 'good German' archetype, of the chivalrous but self-destructive Luftwaffe 'man of honour'. Unbeknownst at the time, however, Zuckmayer had an OSS connection too. In 1943–4 he had drafted a secret report on the political leanings of the Third Reich's literary and artistic elite (Zuckmayer 2002). In 1946 he officially toured the US Zone, including Geiselgasteig, concluding to Washington 'that we would be making a big mistake if we neglected the themes of German internal resistance to Hitler'. This did not mean 'horror stories', but material for a new idealism, such as the story of Sophie Scholl and the Weiße Rose/White Rose: 'Youngsters must know and remember that Germans lived and died for the idea of freedom, for a free, decent, democratic way of life' (Zuckmayer 2004: 201).

The German script is generally true to the American, but Zuckmayer added a trailer message which faced potential criticisms head on. Despite conventional wisdom that the spy was 'probably the most despicable and infamous criminal', worthy of execution, he still asked, 'Can there be an "extraordinary" spy? Is high treason always a crime?' Zuckmayer highlighted the protagonist's 'deep moral seriousness'; treachery was not glorified. This was a film made 'without hate' and where 'one people was not sitting in judgement over another': 'do not judge!' This credo and Zuckmayer's blessing punctuated all the studio's publicity. Fox also undertook several cuts and re-dubs to avoid offending German audiences. Shots of French orphans (presumably 'made in Germany') at the OSS's convent headquarters were cut from the German release. The dub explains that Rennick was 'of German descent' (hence his flawless German, voiced by Curd Jürgens). His early line in the Hollywood original, that he regards Germans as 'all a bunch of lice', ended on the cutting-room floor (thus destroying his own conversion story arc; in *Entscheidung* Rennick *is* to all intents and purposes German). An American bombardier turned parachute dispatcher, when asked if he hated Germans, no longer replies: 'I haven't felt sorry when I've seen a string of 100-pounders leave that bomb-rack.' The German print even features extra footage of Lale Andersen's sentimental wartime hit 'Es geht alles vorüber' ('Everything Passes'), with added subversive anti-Nazi lyrics not shown in the US release, thus merging nostalgia and *Vergangenheitsbewältigung* (John 2005–6). The song provides a constant non-diegetic refrain in the film. And in the final scene, the handover of the mission's crucial military information is edited out as OSS start marking up their maps for countermeasures. German audiences experienced espionage without consequences.

The ultimate arbiter of the film's German fate was the Freiwillige Selbstkontrolle der Filmwirtschaft, the FRG's censor. By the time Fox submitted *Entscheidung vor Morgengrauen*, the geopolitical roller-coaster which had seen West Germany go from disarmed pariah to bloc member, had ended in May 1952 with entry into the European Defence Community (against considerable domestic opposition!). In June 1952, unlike the screenings seven months earlier to Bonn officialdom, the FSK unanimously passed a film which 'portrays in almost documentary style the conditions in Germany shortly before the collapse and will cause no offence to German sensibilities'. Any 'over-excitement' of adolescents (presumably by Hildegard Knef) was overridden by the 'film's high ethical value'.[16] Treason was no longer taboo and *Entscheidung* was finally released in the FRG in November 1952, many months after other European countries. German reviewers were cautiously positive, often commenting on the realism of wartime sights and sounds, as well as the constant police checkpoints, which had been repressed in the psyche ever since: 'a Stuka attack on our softly slumbering memory!'[17] For some, it was a brave venture by outsiders into a market overrun with escapist 'tear-jerkers' and 'restoration films that act as if nothing had happened' (Schaarwächter 1952: n.p.). One endorsed Litvak's description of Happy's mission as a 'patrol of the conscience'.[18] Indeed, subjective ethicality was often invoked in mitigation of treachery. 'For the formal thinker espionage for the enemy is always *Landesverrat*', conceded columnist Gerhard Daub, 'but does that answer the desperate questions of a burning conscience?' (1952: n.p.). Many reviewers were at pains *not* to draw wider conclusions for social behaviour from the film; it was an 'individual case' (Groll 1952: n.p.).

Some were more political. Robert Held at the *Frankfurter Allgemeine* noted the discrepancy between elite resistance and that of the little man: 'if a lance corporal ventured in that direction, it became treason, base treason, and the fact that he was crushed and forgotten, completes his tragedy' (1952: n.p.). But what the film had omitted was the sheer dread of the advancing Red Army which had kept Germans in line. Other analogies were drawn, for instance with German special forces executed by US troops in the Ardennes in 1944.[19] Only some echoed Fritz Bauer's arguments that the NS leadership had forfeited obedience: 'There will be a lot of talk of honour and oath-breaking', warned commentator Günter Ebert, 'but in the mouths of people who made themselves tools of a criminal regime flouting ethical laws, these great words are empty babble' (1952: n.p.). Others equivocated with arguments from the Cold War present: 'Do you call it treason if an eastern zone people's policeman defects to us to serve his true fatherland?'[20]

In one longer debate, legal, theological and military commentators crossed swords, including Fabian von Schlabrendorff, a 20 July survivor, who could not imagine a German-made *Decision*: 'Not yet. Something like this can only be done at a distance of 5,000km or 50 years.' Would historical defectors in the wars of national liberation, such as Baron vom Stein or General Yorck von Wartenburg, who had pre-empted Prussia's break with Napoleon, be judged so harshly? Marion Gräfin Yorck von Wartenburg, a Kreisau Circle resister and Yorck's direct descendant, challenged the basis of any *ad hominem* Führer oath, praising instead Happy's new-found loyalty to Rennick. Author Hans Werner Richter, himself an antifascist POW convert, warned that anyone accusing Happy must also condemn the Scholls and Stauffenbergs, and possibly 'millions of people now living in the East'. For Richter, Happy was 'tomorrow's hero', an internationalist transcending yesterday's last-ditch nationalism. Ex-army major Herbert Busse, while conceding Happy's good intentions, still regarded his action as a 'deadly mistake', hitting not state nerve-centres, but comrades-in-arms. Theologian Hans Köhler conceded that a moral imperative might trump temporal legality, but only if the state had breached God's laws. For Wilhelm Silgradt, a Berlin conservative, Happy was simply an 'evil fool' fumbling with 'anarchistic dynamite'. Only journalist Erich Kuby, who had himself spent nine months in a Wehrmacht stockade, reminded readers that they had watched a 'watered-down' version, designed for the 'forward bulwark of an empire directly threatened by communism'. If anything, it had not been provocative enough, and the feared 'white mice and stink bombs', which had disrupted *All Quiet on the Western Front* (Lewis Milestone) in 1930, had not materialised. Box office was slow. 'The film met with that famous German silence', observed Kuby, 'the silence of an exhausted people after twelve years of being shouted at and five years of re-education.'[21] *Entscheidung vor Morgengrauen*'s takings were indeed modest, making only a tenth of *Desert Fox*'s German revenue; 'a big disappointment', wrote Zanuck: 'We expected big things from it in Germany and yet it is an out and out flop' (Solomon 1988: 78). At the bottom line, treason never pays.

Contrary to Harington's aphorism, many West Germans *did* still dare call it treason, clinging to etatist definitions of *Landesverrat*. But things were changing, slowly. In 1953 the nascent Bundeswehr adopted the concept of 'inner leadership', which placed natural justice above positive law and hence empowered troops to disobey criminal orders for reasons of conscience. Nonetheless, Bonn's memory guardians regarded *Landesverrat* as the unacceptable face of treason, explicitly threatening their 20 July rehabilitation project. What is surprising is the level of coordination between US and

Federal German agencies over the cultural representation of antifascism. Germans were still not trusted to see quite the same movie as global audiences; spectatorship was not yet truly transnational. Just as the Department of Defense was prepared to intervene in 1950s Hollywood productions to uphold America's 'good war' (Haak 2013: 172–84), the State Department was capable, if not of stopping, at least of keeping 'good German' collaborators off West German screens at the height of rearmament controversies. Such censorship had been conducted with one eye on the pacifist left, championed by a rival East German state, and another on a resurgent right, but had failed to predict the hostile reception closest to home, on location, forcing the studio into its own small 'Munich Agreement'. Whatever its shortcomings, battling the elements and Bavarian red tape, *Decision/ Entscheidung* had nevertheless broken the taboo of not mentioning the war, daring to present home-front realism, not *Heimatfilm* escapism – a Hollywood film, despite its hero's name, without a happy ending.

Notes

1. The author thanks the British Academy for funding research trips for this piece. All translations from the German are the author's own. Archival resources are listed in endnotes rather than via in-text citation, for ease of reading; some newspaper articles from the archives are listed in this way where the full name of an author cannot be identified.
2. Twentieth Century-Fox Film Corp., 'Vital Statistics on *Decision before Dawn*', New York Public Library for the Performing Arts (NYPLPA), clippings collection.
3. Motion Picture Association of America brochure in: NYPLPA, clippings collection.
4. Michael Abel to Zanuck, 19 September 1950, University of Southern California–Cinema and Television Library (USC-CTL), *Decision before Dawn* (*DbD*) files. Arnold defected from the American revolutionary army to the British in 1780.
5. 'Conference with Mr. Zanuck', 2 May 1950, USC-CTL, *DbD* files (5).
6. Ibid.
7. Acheson to HICOG, 3 January 1950, National Archives and Records Administration (NARA), RG 59/CDF 1950–54/5251.
8. Towne (DoD Motion Picture Section) to Muto, 12 October 1950 and Lawrence Houston (CIA Strategic Services Unit), 10 October 1950, NARA, RG 330/140/681. For more on OSS and Hollywood see Willmetts 2017: 77–114.
9. 'Movie Realism Opens Old Wounds in Germany', *New York Times*, 10 December 1950.
10. Joseph Breen to Jason Joy, 15 September 1950, USC-CTL, *DbD* files (3).
11. 'The story of a traitor and patriot', *Life*, 17 December 1951, p. 118.

12. HICOG to State Dept, 21 November 1951, NARA, RG 59/CDF-1950–54/5251.
13. CINCEUR to Bonn, 28 November 1951, NARA, RG 59/5323/9.
14. State Dept memorandum, 22 January 1952, NARA, RG 59/CDF-1950–54/5251.
15. A.M.S., 'Nicht für Deutsche?', *Die Welt*, 21 June 1952.
16. FSK, 'Protokoll der Prüfungssitzung des Arbeitsausschusses vom 19.6.1952'; my thanks to Eva Diaz of the FSK for making this available.
17. Ba., 'Seine Kommandostelle: das eigene Gewissen', *Der Abend*, 21 November 1952.
18. R. Keller for 'Filmeinführung auf der Bundestagung 1960 Flensburg', Filmuniversität Babelsberg Konrad Wolf (FUBKW) clippings collection.
19. E.S., 'Der Überläufer', *Deutsche Wirtschaftszeitung*, 29 November 1952.
20. D.A., 'Ein Film fragt: WAR ES VERRAT?', *Der Abend*, 20 November 1952.
21. 'Entscheidung vor Morgengrauen: Diskussion um einen politischen Film', FUBKW clippings collection.

Works Cited

Balzer, Karl (1967) *Der 20. Juli und der Landesverrat: Eine Dokumentation über Verratshandlungen im deutschen Widerstand*. Göttingen: K. W. Schütz.
Crowther, Bosley (1952) 'If This Be Treason: "Decision before Dawn" Has Thrills and Thought', *New York Times*, 13 January, n.p.
Dachs, Robert (1988) *Oskar Werner: Ein Nachklang*. Vienna: Kremayr & Scheriau.
Daub, Gerhard (1952) 'Patriot oder Verräter?', *Deutscher Kurier*, 22 November.
Doernberg, Stefan (ed.) (1995) *Im Bunde mit dem Feind: Deutsche auf alliierter Seite*. Berlin: Dietz.
Ebert, Günter (1952) '"Nenn" es nicht Verrat!', *Das Freie Wort*, 13 December, n.p.
Entscheidung vor Morgengrauen viewed at: <https://www.youtube.com/watch?v=IZbb-6LbLR4> (last accessed 1 April 2019).
Etheridge, Brian C. (2016) *Enemies to Allies: Cold War Germany and American Memory*. Lexington KY: University Press of Kentucky.
Groll, Gunter (1952) 'Zeitbild und Zündstoff', *Süddeutsche Zeitung*, 20 November, n.p.
Haak, Sebastian (2013) *The Making of the Good War: Hollywood, das Pentagon und die amerikanische Deutung des Zweiten Weltkriegs 1945–1962*. Paderborn: Schöningh.
Hake, Sabine (2012) *Screen Nazis: Cinema, History, and Democracy*. Madison, WI: University of Wisconsin Press.
Heeb, Inken (1997) *Deutschlandbilder im amerikanischen Spielfilm, 1946 bis 1993*. Stuttgart: ibidem.
Heideking, Jürgen and Mauch, Christof (eds) (1996) *American Intelligence and the Resistance to Hitler*. Boulder, CO: Westview.

Held, Robert (1952) '"Nenn" es Verrat', *Frankfurter Allgemeine Zeitung*, 12 November 1952, n.p.
Howe, George (1949) *Call It Treason*. New York: Viking.
John, Eckhard (2005–6) '"Es geht alles vorüber, es geht alles vorbei": Geschichte eines "Durchhalteschlagers"', *Lied und populäre Kultur*, 50 (1), pp. 163–222.
Keller, Sven (2013) *Volksgemeinschaft am Ende: Gesellschaft und Gewalt 1944/45*. Munich: Oldenbourg.
Kempski, Hans Ulrich (1950) '"Legion der Verdammten" unter falschem Verdacht', *Süddeutsche Zeitung*, 8 November, n.p.
Kleine, Nils (2016) 'Der geschichtspolitische Ort des 20. Juli 1944 in der Frühphase der Bundesrepublik Deutschland: Fallbeispiel Remer-Prozess', in Nils Kleine and Christoph Studt (eds), *'Das Vermächtnis ist noch in Wirksamkeit, die Verpflichtung noch nicht eingelöst': Der Widerstand gegen das 'Dritte Reich' in Öffentlichkeit und Forschung seit 1945*. Augsburg: Wißner.
Major, Patrick (2019) 'Shooting Rommel: *The Desert Fox* (1951) and Hollywood's Public-Private Diplomacy', *Historical Journal of Film, Radio and Television*, 39 (2), pp. 209–32.
Mauch, Christof (2003) *The Shadow War against Hitler: The Covert Operations of America's Wartime Secret Intelligence Service*. New York: Columbia University Press.
Paul, Gerhard (1995) '"Die verschwanden einfach nachts": Überläufer zu den Alliierten und den europäischen Befreiungsbewegungen', in Norbert Haase and Gerhard Paul (eds), *Die anderen Soldaten: Wehrkraftzersetzung, Gehorsamsverweigerung und Fahnenflucht im Zweiten Weltkrieg*, Frankfurt am Main: Fischer, pp. 139–56.
Persico, Joseph E. (1979) *Piercing the Reich: The Penetration of Nazi Germany by American Secret Agents during World War II*. New York: Viking.
Schaarwächter, Hans (1952) 'Kein Makel ist an diesem "Happy"', *Der Mittag*, 4 December, n.p.
Scheingraber, Michael (2007) Interview with Peter Viertel, May, available at <http://www.peterviertel.com/between-the-lines-peter-viertel.php> (last accessed 12 May 2019).
Schönfeld, Christiane (2013) 'Being Human: Good Germans in Postwar German Cinema', in Pól Ó Dochartaigh and Christiane Schönfeld (eds), *Representing the 'Good German' in Literature and Culture after 1945: Altruism and Moral Ambiguity*. Rochester, NY: Camden House, pp. 111–37.
Sichel, Peter M. F. (2016) *The Secrets of My Life: Vintner, Prisoner, Soldier, Spy*. Bloomington, IN: Archway.
Solomon, Aubrey (1988) *Twentieth Century-Fox: A Corporate and Financial History*. Metuchen, NJ and London: Scarecrow.
Steinbach, Peter (2000) *Widerstand im Widerstreit: Der Widerstand gegen den Nationalsozialismus in der Erinnerung der Deutschen*, 2nd edn. Paderborn: Schöningh.

Viertel, Peter (1992) *Dangerous Friends: Hemingway, Huston and Others*. London: Viking.
Welch, Steven R. (2012) 'Commemorating "Heroes of a Special Kind": Deserter Monuments in Germany', *Journal of Contemporary History*, 47 (2), pp. 370–401.
Willmetts, Simon (2017) *In Secrecy's Shadow: The OSS and CIA in Hollywood Cinema, 1941–1979*. Edinburgh: Edinburgh University Press.
Wölfel, Ute (2015) 'At the Front: Common Traitors in West German War Films of the 1950s', *Modern Language Review*, 110 (3), pp. 739–58.
Zuckmayer, Carl (2002) *Geheimreport*, eds Gunther Nickel and Johanna Schrön. Göttingen: Wallstein.
Zuckmayer, Carl (2004) *Deutschlandbericht für das Kriegsministerium der Vereinigten Staaten von Amerika*, eds Gunther Nickel, Johanna Schrön and Hans Wagener (eds). Göttingen: Wallstein.

CHAPTER 7

Religious Pacifism and the Hollywood War Film: From *Sergeant York* (1941) to *Hacksaw Ridge* (2017)

Guy Westwell

Introduction

This chapter seeks to examine how the Hollywood war film finds ways to accommodate religious pacifism's principled objection to war. The chapter considers two war films which have religious pacifists as their central characters: Howard Hawks's *Sergeant York* (1941), which focuses on the story of Alvin York (Gary Cooper), a conscientious objector who fought in the First World War, and Mel Gibson's *Hacksaw Ridge* (2016), which tells the story of Desmond Doss (Andrew Garfield), a religious pacifist who became a US Army medic during the Second World War. In both films religious pacifists are shown to be transgressive of society's common-sense assumptions about war and because of this they are subjected to a range of containment strategies that seek to recuperate their radical anti-war beliefs. This process of containment, whereby religious pacifists are shown to take up arms or serve with the military, constitutes the primary ideological work of both films and will be carefully profiled here. However, I also want to draw attention to the precise ways in which these two films let loose the ideas of religious pacifism. I will argue that the films establish a strong sympathetic relationship between the audience and the transgressive beliefs initially held by their central characters, and that this relationship testifies to a widely held cultural suspicion of the dominant pro-war narrative and even to the possibility of desire for a different, more pacific view of the world.

War Cinema

Considerable scholarship attests that popular culture, including the cinema, upholds the view that war, though bloody and difficult, is necessary and positive (Westwell 2006; Turse 2008; Der Derian 2009; Stahl 2009; Bourke 2016). In my book *War Cinema*, I argue that the Hollywood war film's general tendency is to make an argument *for* war based on a number of elements that recur from film to film, and which bind into a coherent world view that audiences are invited to accept and adopt. These elements include an endorsement of jingoistic nationalism based on a prejudicial depiction of the enemy, the abnegation of individual differences and desires to the collective goals of the nation, the use of a rite-of-passage narrative structure in which boys become men and in doing so confirm and define conventional masculine identity and, related to this, the need for strong leadership (with potentially fascistic overtones), the depiction of a process of regeneration through violence, whereby inherited value systems are shocked and tested but are shown to be permanent and resilient, an acknowledgement of the 'price' of war but the justification of the need to pay this 'price', and the construction of a severely restricted point of view leading to a reduction of political and cultural horizons (Westwell 2006: 109–55). Even in the most bloody and gruesome war films (including those widely considered to be anti-war), these central elements largely come together to show war as a 'progressive' activity, entered into reluctantly but ultimately necessary, useful and productive (Westwell 2006: 114–15). Jeanine Basinger uses the Second World War propaganda film *Bataan* (1943) to exemplify this systematic cultural endorsement of war but the same elements, in varying combinations and patterns, can be seen in a range of contemporary war films from *Saving Private Ryan* (1999) through *Lone Survivor* (2013) to *Dunkirk* (2017) (Basinger 1986: 52).

Pacifism as a Transgressive Idea

Religious pacifism rejects military logic and confounds the common-sense view that war, and violence more generally, is necessary, useful and productive.[1] Writing in his journal after converting to Quakerism in 1959, and seeking to articulate this core belief, peace activist Adam Curle observed that:

> There is only one central idea: that there is an element of the divine in everyone. But from that follow a lot of things: that everyone is worthy of equal care and respect, that the violence of war, of any sort, is an affront to the essential goodness of the other; and that the idea of racism and racial superiority must be opposed. (Quoted in Lederach and Woodhouse 2016: 26)

Although varied across faiths and in different historical and cultural contexts, this belief confounds the logic of war and, by extension, the war film.[2] Here, religious faith, held unyieldingly and with conviction, constitutes a transgressive act precisely because it goes against a deeply seated cultural norm, that is that war is a progressive and necessary tool. Indeed, where military service is mandated by law, as was the case in the United States during the Second World War and the Vietnam War, refusing to fight meant breaking the law and led to lengthy prison terms for many. The transgressive challenge religious pacifism presents to the status quo is multifold. For instance, the view that every individual is made in the image of God and contains an element of the divine leads to a strong sense of the moral equality of all persons and this runs counter to the prejudicial construction of the enemy commonly found in the war film; in addition, the commandment not to kill simply and categorically refuses a core requirement of war. The importance of prayer, self-reflection and adherence to the teachings of God and the Church present an alternative to the governing logic and morality of the nation state, which (at times of war and through the effects of the mass media and the production of propaganda) demands obedience, servitude and conformity. The deferral to strong military or governmental leadership will inevitably be challenged via the greater moral authority of God; similarly, the restricted point of view (designated the task of blinkering those involved in war from wider historical and political frameworks) is, via religious belief, brought into contact with a trans-historical, universal viewpoint that demands events are placed within an open, and potentially more radical, perspective.

Ultimately, a religious emphasis on peace, love and mercy identifies all violence as destructive, and the violence of war particularly so due to its scale and reach. This is not to say that religion has never been turned to war; there are myriad examples of that, from the Crusades to the use of Christian imagery to legitimise the sacrifices made by soldiers during the First World War. However, where religious pacifist principles such as those articulated by Curle are adhered to – and the steadfast refusal of nationalism and racism is key here – the belief system has the potential to be genuinely transgressive and confound the positive formulation of war enshrined in the war film. This type of transgression is not one of breaking apart, rebelling against or seeking to upturn; it is more the adherence of an unyielding faith in a principled position in ways that are irreconcilable with the dominant social and cultural conventions of the wider culture. It is a form of transgression that has been at the heart of progressive movements for change, including South African anti-Apartheid protest, the US civil rights movement and the environmental activism of Extinction Rebellion. This kind of transgression is not a form of 'acting out', it is measured, controlled and resolute in its insistence that another way is possible, and as a consequence – and as this chapter will indicate – it has the capacity to retain the sympathy of a great many people looking on.

The Containment of Pacifism

Considering this radical potential, it is perhaps suprising that religious pacifist characters do appear in war films. To understand how these characters are treated by the genre it is helpful to consider the depiction of pacifism in Hollywood film more generally. Rick Clifton Moore notes that

> the relationship between the dominant American ideology and pacifism seems to be played out in two ways – through exclusion, that is, the scarcity of presentation of pacifism as a film subject, and through containment, the presentation of predictable formulas [sic] that frame arguments and lead to acceptable conclusions. (Moore 1996: 103)

It is certainly fair to say that pacifism is not an often treated subject in Hollywood films in general, and in the war film in particular. And when it does appear, as Michael Anderegg notes, 'Hollywood's traditional depiction [of] a pacifist is someone who refuses to fight or kill as long as he is not faced with any reason to do so, but who gives up his principles whenever a good, compelling, immediate and personal motive presents itself' (Anderegg 1979: 190). The western genre in the 1950s is an exemplar of the way pacifist ideas are, to use Clifton Moore's term, 'contained'. For instance, in *High Noon* (1952) Marshall Will Kane (Gary Cooper) is married to Amy Fowler Kane (Grace Kelly), a devout Quaker, who inspires her husband to seek a peaceful life. However, by the film's close, Amy has used violence to protect her husband and he has killed to protect the town. Clifton Moore notes other films with similar strategies such as *Shane* (1953), *Fastest Gun Alive* (1956) and *The Peacemaker* (1956) and argues that these form a distinct 1950s cycle that depicts religious pacifists only in order to display how their anti-war convictions are undone.[3] In the final instance, these films show violence to be inevitable, ineluctable and, ultimately, righteous, and are governed by the logic of what Jacques Ellul calls the 'necessity' of violence whereby violence is framed as the only given rational and moral option available to otherwise peaceful people (Ellul 1969: 122–4). This is, of course, a position regularly articulated by politicians and leaders rallying nations to war.

In relation to the war film, as Richard Slotkin and Jeanine Basinger argue, a similar pattern can be found. This is, perhaps, unsurprising considering the war film displays a strong imprint of the western (Basinger 1986: 4; Slotkin 1992: 321). In *Bataan*, for example, the patrol's medic, Pvt. Matthew Hardy (Philip Terry), is a conscientious objector. Hardy is a quiet, introspective former school teacher who cares deeply for the men, listening to their dying confessions and carefully tending their graves. He even gifts them his own dose of quinine and as a consequence contracts malaria. As the situation worsens, he snaps and in a delirious rage attacks the Japanese with grenades, and is shot and killed. The film appears to show that even the most measured and principled anti-war position will fold in the face of Japanese atrocity. Although Basinger doesn't discuss Hardy directly she argues this process of 'conversion' (which she describes via other members of the group) is indicative of the way war films show the necessity to

> work together as a group, to set aside individual needs, and to bring our melting pot tradition together to function as a true democracy since, after all, that is what we are fighting for: the Democratic way of life. (Basinger 1986: 27)

Here we see the containment strategy at work: pacifism is recognised as a principle that has value – Hardy's position is respected by the men – but this idea is subsumed by the film's promotion of the wider value system of liberal democracy, which is set in stark terms against Japanese militarism and fanaticism. For many scholars this staging of religious pacifism as a way of validating the wider system and condoning war is an act of bad faith (Moore 1996; Anderegg 1979). However, my analysis will show that the pacifist ideas retain their ability to persuade: they do not always accede to their own undoing. In *Bataan*, Hardy 'converts' only as a result of the unbearable pressure of the situation and the deleterious effect of malaria; his 'attack' on the Japanese positions is deranged, ineffectual and suicidal. It is hard to read his actions as some kind of considered and productive advance from principled pacifism to necessary belligerence. The film's treatment of Hardy's dilemma, indeed the dangerously transgressive nature of his commitments, is indicative of how pacifism, or at least some kind of alternative to war, is never fully sequestered, leaving moments of uncertainty and contradiction that are indicative of a latent anti-war sensibility in the wider society.

From Delinquency to Religious Faith

Sergeant York and *Hacksaw Ridge* are based on the experience of real-life figures Alvin C. York and Desmond Doss. As a member of the Church of Christ in Christian Union in rural Tennessee, York was a pacifist and conscientious objector but was conscripted into the US Army and in 1918, during the Meuse-Argonne offensive, was involved in fighting that resulted in the surrender of 132 Germans soldiers. York received a Congressional Medal of Honor for his actions and was widely lauded as a war hero. Doss was born in Lynchburg, Virginia and attended a Seventh Day Adventist church. He was a pacifist but volunteered for the US military and served as a medic in Guam, the Philippines and Okinawa, where he rescued seventy-five wounded men under heavy fire. He also received a Congressional Medal of Honor. Both men have featured (often reluctantly) in public life as well as appearing in novels, television specials, documentaries and websites, in celebration of their wartime actions.[4] These biographical accounts of their lives show them to be remarkable and brave, but also complex and contradictory (Herndon 2004; Mastriano 2014). However, it is not the aim of this chapter to set the films against historical fact. The films are offered here as a measured sample of how religious pacifism is treated by US popular culture, with genre as a determining factor. Indeed, in addition to their clear status as war films already noted, both *Sergeant York* and *Hacksaw Ridge* contain elements common to the biopic. In particular a chronological approach to their life stories, in which their early lives, and especially their conversion to Christian faith, are shown by way of contextualising and explaining the characters' later heroic actions in battle.

The early sequences of *Sergeant York* show York as a delinquent alcoholic, carousing with his friends and behaving immaturely. In one scene he disrupts a church service, showing his indifference to religion by shooting his initials in a nearby tree. Poverty is shown as an extenuating factor here, with Mother York (Margaret Wycherly) observing her son's travails, and by way of explanation for his drunkenness, stating 'Patchin' and scratchin' at the hard land. It's mighty hard work getting corn out of rocks.' After York meets a spirited Gracie Williams (Joan Leslie) he determines to marry her and sets out to reform himself and earn the money to purchase some land. As he works towards this goal York discusses religion with Pastor Rosier Pile (Walter Brennan) who tries to persuade York that 'A fella has gotta have roots in something beyond himself.' York secures the funds but discovers the land has been sold to someone else, which he considers a betrayal. In this moment of crisis, and drunk on whiskey, York sets out to violently settle the matter with the man he feels has betrayed him. In a heavy thunderstorm, York is struck by lightning and his gun is destroyed. He is unharmed and staggers to the church, finding the congregation enthusiastically singing, 'Give Me That Old Time Religion'. The lyric, 'makes me love everybody', punctuates a coming together of the community, with York tentatively entering the church and being encircled and embraced by the congregation, including Mother York and Gracie.

Reformed under this Christian faith York forgives the man who bamboozled him and makes a start on settling down and marrying Gracie.

These schematic but heartfelt scenes, lifted by clever performances from Cooper and Brennan in particular, show religion as grounded in community, something heartfelt and genuine. The viewer is encouraged to commend York's new life direction and the tenor of the classical Hollywood style presents all this with life, humour and directness, celebrating some simple tenets in ways commensurate with Curle's claim that pacifism be founded on the principle that 'everyone is worthy of equal care and respect' (quoted in Lederach and Woodhouse 2016: 26). These scenes, including York's conversion (Figure 7.1), rehearse a way of life in which religious principle originates in personal experience and community in ways that are stable enough to empower individuals to speak their own truth to power, and thereby question modern society's commitment to the waging of war.[5] As we shall see, York does choose to fight in the film's close, but in contrast to the usual operation of the classical Hollywood film style there is no immanence in these scenes: his conversion is sincere and complete and the audience are invited to find this right and satisfying. This binding of character, viewer and the religious pacifist position is, I wish to argue, the grounds on which the claim can be made that the film (like York) constitutes a transgressive object that wittingly endorses pacifism.

Figure 7.1 York joins the religious community and embraces pacifism. Still from *Sergeant York* (1941).

The depiction of Doss's early life in *Hacksaw Ridge* has some broad correspondences with those shown in *Sergeant York*. Like York, Doss is animated, rebellious and displays an anti-authoritarian attitude, especially to his father Tom Doss (Hugo Weaving). The film gathers a number of incidents that together shape his pacifist world view and show his conversion to Christian faith to be less abrupt than that of York. After a fight with his brother, in which Doss hits him with a brick and nearly kills him, Doss views a tapestry sampler showing the Ten Commandments, with the camera lingering on the sixth: thou shalt not kill.[6] In slowly revealed scenes (including flashbacks from the later battle sequences) we learn that as a child Doss witnessed his alcoholic father beat their mother and that, as a young man, Doss restrained his father and threatened him with a gun. Recounting this in battle, a fellow soldier reassures, 'But you didn't kill him', to which Doss replies: 'In my heart I did'. Frightened by his own capacity for violence, Doss makes a promise to God that he will never touch a gun again. In addition, war is also shown to be destructive via the negative impact it has had on Doss's father, who is traumatised by his experience of the First World War. A key feature of these scenes is the attempt to convey Doss's introspection, thoughtfulness and ensuing resolve. His father notes how, before making any decision, his son will 'sit and think and pray about everything'. David Sims writes that 'Garfield captures this by projecting an almost alien (or perhaps divine) quality in Doss's baleful smiles' (2016). Ultimately, Doss's refusal of violence is shown to be a reaction to his own capacity for violence, the violence of his father towards his mother and an awareness of the violent legacy of war that, in part, extenuates his father's behaviour.

In contrast to York's religious epiphany, Doss's is shown to be organic and individual, coming from within rather than dovetailing with the wider community organisation of the Church. Now reformed, Doss meets nurse Dorothy Schutte (Teresa Palmer) and falls in love. The hospital and his affair with Dorothy become a place of sanctuary: Doss's gentleness (he is a vegetarian) and sensitive knowledge of nature woos her (he places a feather of a rare bird in her ornithology book) and they walk together in the mountains. As with York's relationship with Gracie, the romantic bind is used to hold together the wider value system presented in the film. Both men will fight (or not) partly in order to defend and return to their women, with the women as proxies for a certain stable and peaceful way of life.

Both films, then, present religious pacifism in very positive terms. Each film shows a young man uncertain in the world and torn between two possibilities: on the one hand, selfishness, violence and disorder and, on the other, family, community, work, order and faith. In both cases, Christian belief and a religious pacifism stemming from that belief is shown to tip the balance in the right direction. This tipping towards order is shown, via association with individual spiritedness, community and romance, to be natural, organic, morally right and, importantly, specifically American. Relevant here is the class identity of the two protagonists: they are poor, meek, humble, disempowered, and this is indicative of their ability to see clearly, unencumbered by convention and social mores. In taking the time to draw the early lives of the two men, the films provide substance to their respective beliefs. As a consequence, their principled stances cannot be discounted in the viewer's mind as something other-wordly, fragile or contingent; their beliefs are hard won and originate in an everyday and recognisable context. This measured setting out of their beliefs has the effect of eliciting viewer sympathy for their religious pacifism and, crucially, for their subsequent transgressive acts.

The Pacifist's Dilemma

With York's and Doss's religious convictions carefully detailed, the films' attentions turn to war. In *Sergeant York*, the onset of the First World War sees York conscripted. He at first applies for an exemption from the draft board but is refused on the grounds that his denomination is not a recognised pacifist Christian faith (such as the Quakers). He is persuaded by Pastor Pile to attend basic training from where he might be able to plead his case directly to the Army. During basic training he proves to be a formidable marksman and the Army are keen to retain his services but he announces his pacifist beliefs and is called to meet Commanding Officer, Major Buxton (Stanley Ridges) and Second-in-Command, Captain Danforth (Harvey Stephens).

In a remarkably conciliatory, cogent and carefully staged scene, Buxton and Danforth seek to persuade York that his principles, though important, don't exempt him from the duty to fight. York is humble, polite and deferential but also strongly principled. Danforth debates different passages of the Bible with York, seeking to show how violence is merited. In response, York reasons out his pacifist position convincingly. Into this exchange, Buxton interrupts, handing York a book detailing the history of the United States and stating, 'That's the story of a whole people's struggle for freedom'. He continues:

> You're a religious man, York. You want to worship God in your own way? You're a farmer. You want to plough your fields as you see fit? To raise your own family according to your own lights? And that's your heritage. And mine, and every American's. But the cost of that heritage is high. Sometimes it takes all we've got to preserve it – even our lives.

Figure 7.2 York determines to reconcile his pacifism with the need to defend his country. Still from *Sergeant York*.

York is granted ten days' furlough to think things through and uses the time to travel home. As he walks into the mountains he passes a tree carved with the initials of American folk hero, Daniel Boone (a key figure in the book he has been given). Later, seated on a rocky ledge, contemplating the surrounding farms and landscape (Figure 7.2) and following Buxton's cue, York learns from the book that radical democracy (a government of the people, by the people, for the people) is rare, precious and must be defended at all costs, and with violence if necessary. York hears Pastor Pile's voice say 'pray your God' and Major Buxton's, 'defend for Country', and as he faces this dilemma the film cuts away to his mother cooking a meal in a simple homestead, neatly activating a sense of humble religious faith and family to ground the loftier themes. Providentially the Bible falls open at a passage – 'Render unto Caesar' – that appears to endorse some kind of accommodation of the two positions.[7] The staging of the action here calls on a landscape associated with Manifest Destiny (via Daniel Boone) and combines a deep nationalist commitment ('America [My Country Tis of Thee]' plays in the background) with divine ordainment (the falling open of the Bible, a shaft of near celestial light breaking through the clouds). The scene seeks visual form for what Birdwell describes as 'the symbolic essence of America – the myth of its unique history as the new Eden and the last bastion of Judeo-Christian ethics in the world' (Birdwell 1999: 120). Framed in this deeply symbolic way, York settles on rapprochement, accepting his promotion to corporal and deciding to travel to France.

In comparison, Doss's experience is less genteel. Doss volunteers to join the Army, reasoning that he can work as a medic and help people. He is shipped out to Fort Jackson, South Carolina, where he proves himself an extremely capable recruit, excelling at physical challenges and showing resolve and determination. However, during rifle practice he refuses to pick up a weapon and is revealed to be a religious pacifist. As a consequence, his squad turns against him and under the direction of drill Sergeant Howell (Vince Vaughn), and with the tacit blessing of Captain Glover (Sam Worthington), he is subject to violent bullying and harassment. In discussion with Glover, Doss describes himself as a 'conscientious collaborator' and in conversation with an over-reaching Army psychologist, who asks: 'Does God talk to you?' Doss replies that he is not insane but that 'God says not to kill. That's one of his most important commandments.'

Things reach a head when Doss is refused furlough on the weekend of his wedding for refusing to carry a rifle. Awaiting his court martial in jail, Doss prays and meditates and it is here we see the flashback to him disarming his father, which, as already noted, was crucial to the formation of his pacifist beliefs. Doss is found guilty but is rescued by a last-minute intervention by his father, who appeals to his former commanding officer from the First World War, now a general, who overrules the court and claims Doss's religious pacifism is protected by the constitution. In a more pronounced way than in *Sergeant York*, the film's reconciliation of pacifist belief with military service remains undone. The court martial is fudged as a result of nepotism and a relaying of soldierly duty and sacrifice from an earlier war licensing the accommodation of religious pacifism in a later war.

No Pacifists in Foxholes

As might be expected of two war films, this careful staging of religious pacifism comes to a head in scenes of battle. In France, York enters the fray during the Meuse-Argonne offensive. In a thunderstorm, a tracking shot shows US and British soldiers being shelled as they await the order to advance, with one of York's friends killed by shrapnel. Once underway the battle is ambitiously staged and shown to be difficult and dangerous. The American forces are pinned down by machine gun fire and suffer heavy casualties; a strangulated version of 'Yankee Doodle Dandy' on the soundtrack seeks to convey how the naive Americans succumb to the horrors of the battlefield. As the fighting proceeds York assumes command and is calm and certain, following intuition gained through hunting, and single-handedly storming a machine-gun post, flanking an enemy position, killing numerous German soldiers, and forcing the surrender of more than one hundred more. In contrast to *Hacksaw Ridge* (as we shall see) there is a commitment here to clear lines of action and strategy (an early scene has explained how to shoot turkeys on the wing, a tactic used by York in the battle), and this is consonant with the classical Hollywood style. York's composure combined with the film's intelligibility pull together to show the necessity and effectiveness of placing pacifism on hold to deal with the current emergency; all are needed to prevail over such a powerful threat.

After the battle, as York receives battlefield commendations, including the Congressional Medal of Honor, he observes that 'The Lord sure does move in mysterious ways' and reasons that by killing the machine gunners he saved more lives than he took, adding a utilitarian perspective to the 'Render unto Caesar' rationale. The remainder of the film shows York receiving accolades and a ticker tape parade in New York (the montage sequence includes actual footage of York's return), as well as refusing lucrative but potentially compromising business opportunities. He returns home, where he is welcomed back into the community and taken by Gracie to a large farm and homestead purchased with public money to celebrate his actions. The film's resolution, with romance and family the threads that tie the liberal democratic ideological knot firmly in place, confirms York's decision to compromise was the right one.

In the later film, Doss is involved in fighting on Okinawa in the Pacific in 1945. His unit heads to an area known as Hacksaw Ridge where Japanese troops have repelled a number of US advances. As they enter the battlefield they witness an infernal scene: body parts, intestines, heads eaten by maggots, as well as flies and rats, all shrouded in smoke. As the troops advance the Japanese open fire: the film stages the action in ways similar to *Saving Private Ryan* (Steven Spielberg, 1998): bodies are torn to tattered shreds, viscera spill, and men fall like pins in the face of Japanese machine gunners. Here the horror of the battlefield is used to set in stark relief the stoicism, selflessness and courage of the American troops. Yet the film also departs from the disciplined 'reality effect' of *Saving Private Ryan*, blending it with even more extreme elements – an injured man sits up and screams, he is shot in the back of the head which also kills the man he scares, then both are riddled by machine-gun bullets – and adding more conventionally generic heroic vignettes; in a feat of superhuman strength, a soldier fires a heavy machinegun with one hand while carrying half a Japanese corpse as a shield with the other. Unlike *Saving Private Ryan*, where the Normandy beaches are shown to be a great churning war machine and survival a matter of chance, *Hacksaw Ridge* retains a residual sense (found in older war films) that masculine capability and good soldiering can mitigate war's chaos. In this balance, Doss is exposed to the carnage (and has his principles tested and proven) but, in the final instance, is also able to exert his will.

In contrast to York, who is a model of conviction and clarity during battle, Doss suffers. The fighting is ferocious and attritional and he begins to doubt himself. As the ridge is evacuated after the first failed offensive, Doss has a moment of profound doubt, shouting to God, 'I can't hear you'. Nevertheless, Doss stays on the battlefield to rescue wounded soldiers left behind, re-entering the inferno and working through the night. Exhausted, his hands and face bloodied, he repeats the phrase, 'Please Lord help me get one more'. And with each soldier rescued the film indicates divine providence at work, with Doss's actions shown to be nothing short of miraculous.[8]

The ordeal is not yet over, for Doss or the viewer. The next day, washed clean of blood, Doss prays for the troops and the men return to battle. In this second advance, Doss rescues injured soldiers as an integral part of the fighting, with members of his patrol, including those previously suspicious and hostile towards him, protecting him by killing Japanese troops. Where one might expect Doss's role in the battle to create contradiction he here becomes a facilitator, heroically servicing the war machine and ensuring it prevails. Pacifism becomes concerted military action with objectives, resolve, agency and heroism. This is a clear demonstration of what 'conscientious collaboration' looks like. Indeed, in this second attack US forces prevail and the scenes of the Japanese being defeated play as revenge, mirroring Second World War propaganda films such as *Bataan* in their depiction of the Japanese as faceless, insane and animal-like, and subject to the cleansing power of the flamethrower (Dower 1986: 9).

As the battle draws to a close, Doss is injured and lowered onto a litter, his wounds stigmata-like, a Bible clutched in one arm (Figure 7.3). Floating in space, body relaxed, the sun breaking through the clouds, a visual connection is made to Christ's passion. The sanctification of Doss also enfolds that of the other men, and the US Army in the Pacific theatre (and beyond), underwriting the myth of the 'greatest generation' view of Second World War in which citizen soldiers fought to protect democracy and freedom. The film ends with a sequence showing news photographs of Doss receiving the Congressional Medal of Honor and excerpts from news and documentary interviews with Doss and other figures from the film.

Figure 7.3 Doss's pacifism sanctifies military violence. Still from *Hacksaw Ridge* (2016).

Conclusion

As Clayton R. Koppes and Gregory D. Black note, *Sergeant York* was one of a cycle of films that took Hollywood 'from being fearful of political subjects to being aggressively interventionist' (1990: 39). Similarly, Thomas Schatz labels the films in this cycle 'conversion narratives' designed to move, or 'convert', their audiences from an anti-war or neutral position to one in support of the Allies in their war against Nazi Germany (1998: 96). In short, religious pacifism is co-opted into the articulation of a pro-war ideology in a process that converts pacifism into belligerence. Even though *Hacksaw Ridge* doesn't have its central character pick up a weapon, the film does show Doss integrated effectively into the military unit. As such, Koppes and Black's and Schatz's point can also be made about *Hacksaw Ridge*.

However, in this chapter I have sought to demonstrate how the operation of ideology is not as straightforward as claimed: pacifism is not solely, or straightforwardly, depicted to simply activate its other. In short, *Sergeant York* and *Hacksaw Ridge* blend two broad constituting value systems, a religious one containing the belief in peace, love and pacifism and a secular liberal democratic one which values (among other things) war, nationalism and military action. Both are shown to be principled, valuable and credible. This results in a transgressive religious pacifism being valued and endorsed even in anticipation of it being refused and contained.

An explanation of sorts is found in US society's relation with Christianity, which in the American context tends to be supportive and co-constitutive. A broadly sympathetic view of religion licenses the inclusion of a transgressive figure (and their attendant radical belief system) who challenges society's norms and conventions; the films do seek to contain this radical difference but this difference is drawn accurately and with sympathy. And there may be more specific factors bearing on the way in which the films are drawn, almost instinctively, to the positive peaceful formulations of pacifism. First, the film's creators – producers, writers, directors, cinematographers – may well have genuine affiliations with the religious pacifist position they describe in their films. Second, the classical Hollywood style and the storytelling function of commercial cinema requires agency and purpose, and attendant to this, dramatic tension and disequilibrium. What better way to create this narrative flux in a war film than introduce a character who opposes war? This formal motivation also points to the way film serves as a mechanism for examining points of tension and contradiction at large in society at any given moment. Third, the presence of religious pacifist characters might be understood as an act of commercial opportunism designed to draw in as diverse an audience as possible to the war film, including potentially anti-war viewers; of course, this commercial decision unwittingly acknowledges that support for war is never total nor unquestioning. Hollywood's careful handling of the conversion theme suggest audiences are suspicious, hostile and wary of war, and indicates in the population at large some measure of support for pacifist positions. And, fourth, following Basinger (as well as Clifton Moore), there is truth in the view that airing just enough of an alternative point of view before showing it to be misguided is an effective containment strategy and serves to broker political consensus.[9]

So, perhaps it is enough to say that the representation of religious pacifism is overdetermined, and in the final instance the transgressive potential of pacifism is made safe. But I would argue that the films have articulated that the religious pacifist position taken by their central characters is morally right; indeed, it is preordained and sanctified. Audiences, whether religious or not, gravitate to this position and seem willing (indeed, this is the films' preferred reading) to entertain and adopt it, even if temporarily. This is not only a faith position; audiences reflecting on the experience of the First World War in the case of *Sergeant York*, or wars in Afghanistan, Iraq and Syria in the case of *Heartbreak Ridge*, might rationally refuse to endorse the view that war is necessary and productive. And in this, the films are at least partly on their side. This surprising outcome is a measure of how a faithful representation of a transgressive position, even as it is recuperated, has the potential to seed an alternative world. This surplus meaning, fully realised in mainstream commercial cinema, is grounds for cautious optimism; there remain in the culture at large purposefully transgressive designs that advocate for a less violent society.

Notes

1. The etymology of the word pacifism is distinctly modern. According to Howlett, the term was coined in the 1890s (1991: xvii) and its meaning was stabilised during the First World War when it narrowed to mean an individual's total renunciation of war and social violence. Religious pacifism is a descriptor for those individuals who renounce war as a result of their religious faith. This article focuses on Christian religious pacifism. Secular pacifist characters, for example, appear rarely in Hollywood films and are not treated as sympathetically.
2. For a nuanced and comprehensive account of the histories of different pacifist faith groups in the US see Brock (1968) and Brock and (Young 1999).
3. I have produced a detailed analysis of an outlier film in this cycle, *Friendly Persuasion* (William Wyler, US, 1956), in which I claim the film to be a bona fide peace film due to its sympathetic depiction and accommodation of Quaker pacifism (Westwell 2019).
4. For example, York's story is told in Robert Penn Warren's Pulitzer Prize-winning novel, *At Heaven's Gate* (1943).
5. In this the film is kin to a cycle of progressive New Deal-era classical Hollywood films which Richard Rushton argues are typified by 'dissensus', that is films with narratives that rehearse how characters with seemingly incompatible identities might accommodate one another (Rushton 2013: 148–53).
6. In an early draft of the script for *Sergeant York*, York's pacifism was rooted in his accidental killing of a friend (Birdwell 1999: 112).
7. The passage is Matthew 22: 21 and reads in full 'Render unto Caesar the things that are Caesar's, and unto God the things that are God's'. The words are attributed to Jesus who is commenting on whether the Jews must pay taxes to the Roman empire. The meaning of the passage is much debated: it can be taken to acknowledge that Christians must respect the authority of the state (which is, in any case, God given); or it can be understood to encourage a pragmatic separation of the affairs of the state and religious belief, with both to be respected; others have read it as dictating respect for authority but only if this does not contradict religious principle. Many pacifist religious Christian sects, including the Quakers and Mennonites, have resisted paying tax to be used for military purposes and this passage of the Bible is often called upon and debated in relation to this.
8. The film shows Doss rescuing a number of wounded Japanese troops from the battlefield, in keeping with his belief that all humans are made in God's image. And, as he enters the Japanese cave complex, he comes across an injured Japanese soldier and helps him with a bandage. Though shown, these inconvenient facts are mitigated by a casual aside which implies that the rescued prisoners were summarily executed ('He even lowered a couple of Japs. [Pause] They didn't make it').

9. Richard Maltby talks of the 'commercial aesthetic' that results from these processes and which overdetermines any mainstream entertainment film (Maltby 2003: 35).

Works Cited

Anderegg, Michael A. (1979) *William Wyler*. Boston, MA: Twayne.
Basinger, Jeanine (1986) *The World War II Combat Film: Anatomy of a Genre*. New York: Columbia University Press.
Birdwell, Michael E. (1999) *Celluloid Soldiers: The Warner Bros. Campaign against Nazism*. New York: New York University Press.
Bourke, Joanna (2016) *Wounding the World: How Military Violence and War-Play Invade Our Lives*. London: Virago.
Brock, Peter (1968) *Pacifism in the United States from the Colonial Era to the First World War*. Princeton, NJ: Princeton University Press.
Brock, Peter and Young, Nigel (1999) *Pacifism in the Twentieth Century*. Syracuse, NY: Syracuse University Press.
Der Derian, James (2009) *Virtuous War: Mapping the Military-Industrial-Media-Entertainment Network*. London: Routledge.
Dower, John W. (1986) *War Without Mercy: Race and Power in the Pacific War*. New York: Pantheon.
Ellul, Jacques (1969) *Violence: Reflections from a Christian Perspective*. New York: Seabury.
Herndon, Booton (2004) *The Unlikeliest Hero: The Story of Desmond T. Doss, Conscientious Objector*. Nampa, ID: Pacific Press Publishing Association.
Howlett, Charles F. (1991) *The American Peace Movement: References and Resources*. Boston: G. K. Hall.
Koppes, Clayton R. and Black, Gregory D. (1990) *Hollywood Goes to War: How Politics, Profits, and Propaganda Shaped World War Two Movies*. Berkeley, CA: University of California Press.
Lederach, John Paul and Woodhouse, Tom (2016) *Adam Curle: Radical Peacemaker*. Stroud: Hawthorn Press.
Maltby, Richard (2003) *Hollywood Cinema*. London: Blackwell.
Mastriano, Douglas V. (2014) *Alvin York: A New Biography of the Hero of the Argonne*. Lexington, KY: University Press of Kentucky.
Moore, Rick Clifton (1996) 'Pacifism in Film: Exclusion and Containment as Hegemonic Processes', in Paul Loukides and Linda K. Fuller (eds), *Themes and Ideologies in American Popular Film*. Bowling Green, OH: Bowling Green State University Popular Press, pp. 103–21.
Rushton, Richard (2013) *The Politics of Hollywood Cinema: Popular Film and Contemporary Political Theory*. London: Palgrave Macmillan.
Schatz, Thomas (1998) 'World War II and the Hollywood "War Film"', in Nick Browne (ed.), *Refiguring American Film Genres: History and Theory*. Berkeley, CA: University of California Press, pp. 89–128.

Sims, David (2016) 'In Hacksaw Ridge, Faith Is a Bloody Business', *The Atlantic.com*, 2 November <https://www.theatlantic.com/entertainment/archive/2016/11/mel-gibson-blends-faith-and-violence-again-in-hacksaw-ridge/506264/> (last accessed 6 August 2019).

Slotkin, Richard (1992) *Gunfighter Nation: The Myth of the Frontier in Twentieth-Century America*. New York: Maxwell Macmillan International.

Stahl, Roger (2009) *Militainment, Inc.* London: Routledge.

Turse, Nick (2008) *The Complex: How the Military Invades Our Everyday Lives*. New York: Metropolitan Books.

Westwell, Guy (2006) *War Cinema: Hollywood on the Front Line*. London: Wallflower.

Westwell, Guy (2019) 'Peace Cinema: Religious Pacifism and Anti-War Sensibility in *Friendly Persuasion* (1956)', *Open Screens*, 2 (1) <https://openscreensjournal.com/articles/10.16995/os.11/> (last accessed 6 August 2019).

CHAPTER 8

Military Masculinity and the Deserting Soldier in *Stop-Loss* (2008)

Thomas Ærvold Bjerre

This article will focus on the transgressive figure of the deserting (or AWOL) soldier in American culture. The figure of the deserting soldier runs like a controversial leitmotif through American literature as well as several important Hollywood films. Given the central role of the military hero in the cultural imaginary (Connell 2005: 213), I am interested in exploring how the deserting soldier is depicted, especially in relation to the transgression of essential norms of masculinity and nationality. Within the larger context of the deserter in American culture, I will examine the deserter trope as it is represented in Kimberly Peirce's Iraq War film *Stop-Loss* (2008). The film tells the story of US Army Staff Sergeant Brad King, a squad leader who has served two tours, Afghanistan and Iraq. He returns to the US, only to find that he is being sent back, he is being stop-lossed.[1] He then goes AWOL, and the film becomes a road movie, whose plot centres on King and his best friend's fiancé plotting an escape to Mexico, but whose overall theme explores the question of transgression – both of traditional understandings of gender and of nation.

Julian Wolfreys has defined transgression as 'the act of breaking a law, committing a crime or sin, doing something illegal', and 'to cross a line, to step across some boundary or move beyond convention' (2008: 3). As will become clear below, the deserting soldier transgresses several distinct boundaries. As an institution, the military is defined by disciplinary control, by a long list of rules and regulations, including how to be (and not to be) a man. As R. W. Connell argues, the imagery of masculine heroism is essential in gluing the army together

> or at least enough in line for the organization to produce its violent effects. Part of the struggle for hegemony in the gender order is the use of culture for such disciplinary purposes: setting standards, claiming popular assent and discrediting those who fall short. (Connell 2005: 214)

As Jon Robert Adams concludes, 'men who exhibit traditional masculine behaviours are soldier-heroes', while those who 'fail to exhibit actions commonly associated with' traditional masculinity 'transgress, moving closer to the elements in gendered binaries describing what men are not' (2008: 9, 12). This transgression can take many forms, and Adams lists 'homosexuality, race, cowardice, bodily coherence, and sexual or heroic performance' (2008: 13). In my discussion of *Stop-Loss*, I will be particularly interested in the notion of cowardice as transgression, especially as it relates to notions of heroic performance. Examining transgressive images and content in films is important, as Joel Gwynne has noted, 'since it exposes the mechanisms of censorship and regulation and the limits and conventions of media forms; how they are challenged and overturned' (2016: 1). Additionally, Gwynne points to the importance of genre and its conventions as an example of boundaries that can be breached (2016: 2). The war film genre, which *Stop-Loss* inscribes itself into, is itself regulated by certain conventions regarding masculinity, heroism and national identity, conventions that director Peirce both challenges and, to a certain extent, sustains.

War and Masculinities

Numerous scholars have pointed to the link between war and masculinity: the military has been called the most 'prototypically masculine of all institutions' (Segal 1995: 758) and is seen as playing 'a primary role in shaping images of masculinity in the larger society' (Barrett 2001: 77). This 'nexus linking war, militarism, and masculinities' (Higate and Hopton 2005: 432) has been referred to as 'military masculinities' (Higate and Hopton 2005; Basham 2016) or 'soldierly masculinity' (Adams 2008). Most scholars agree that one type of military masculinity is clearly dominant: summing up the various scholarly characterisations of the term military masculinities, Kimberley Hutchings points to 'risk taking and rationality, as well as discipline, endurance, and absence of emotion' (2008: 393). These traits correlate with Adams's definition of what he calls 'soldierly masculinity', which refers to 'the particular brand of traditional male function associated with heroism – courage, suppressed emotion, strength, and clear-headed decisiveness' (2008: 9). Importantly, these traits fit into Connell's definition of hegemonic masculinity (2005: 213), the current idea of which in Western culture is 'a man who is independent, risk-taking, aggressive, heterosexual and rational' (Barrett 2001: 79). As will become important to my discussion of *Stop-Loss*, these traits that define military/soldierly masculinities also correlate with the most universally recognised heroic qualities, which, according to Brian Wansink et al., are leadership, loyalty and risk taking (2008: 547).

One of Adams's main points is that 'war provides society with definitions of manhood, while, simultaneously, men experience war as the antithesis of society's definition' (2008: 2). While Adams uses American war literature from the First World War to Desert Storm to support his thesis, the paradoxes at the heart of the so-called civil-military gap have been pointed out by many scholars. American culture is steeped in particular military traditions and expectations to such an extent that, as Andrew Bacevich claims, the 'global military supremacy that the United States presently enjoys . . . has become central to our national identity' (2013: 1). Yet with 'less than 1 percent' of the US population 'deploying in Iraq and Afghanistan between 2001 and 2011' (Dao 2011), the civil-military gap has perhaps never been broader (Goldich 2013: 79). Where does all this leave the soldier who deserts? What happens when traditional male gender role behaviours – in this case the male warrior type – are suddenly charged with allegations of disloyalty, dishonesty, disrespect, selfishness, dishonour, lack of integrity and cowardice? These are all terms that are the antithesis to traditional military masculinity, as well as to hegemonic masculinity.

The many ways in which soldiers can transgress from traditional masculinity have created an 'induced gender fear in men' in relation to the military and war, which has ultimately compelled many men to go 'to war to prove they were not "sissies"', according to Kathy J. Phillips (2006: 3). Discussing British and American war literature, Phillips argues that the reason 'gendered fears work to propel men to war is that societies place the label *womanly* on widespread *human* traits, which men are sure to detect in themselves, rendering them insecure' (2006: 191–2, italics in original). Phillips quotes from Evan Wright's Iraq War reportage *Generation Kill* (2004), in which he records how 'the most dreaded derision still labels a man with feminine terms' (Phillips 2006: 192): 'fucking pussy wimp', and 'a scared little bitch' (Wright 2004: 57). Or, even more elaborately, 'pussy faggot' or 'pussy faggot leftie' (ibid.: 37), two examples of what Phillips sees as reactions to the threat of 'a category of men specially constructed to mean womanly' (Phillips 2006: 194). In a filmic context, the most famous example of this naming tendency is probably the drill instructor Gunnery Sergeant Hartman from Kubrick's *Full Metal Jacket* (1987), whose insults and derisions are often rooted in induced gender fear. However, parallel with this dominant narrative of hypermasculinity built on gendered fears, a counter-narrative has existed, one that has deflated the binary moral categories dominating war narratives. As Sarah Cole notes, 'Considering people in their relation to war is, almost inevitably, to think in categorical and binary terms', such as 'combatant and civilian', 'men and women', and 'enemy and friend' (2009: 25). But war writing, she argues, follows a 'deconstructive pattern', a trope of which is the disintegration of these categories: 'war creates distinct types only to miscegenate them' (ibid.: 26).

Desertion

Desertion is certainly one such transgression that destabilises and fractures 'the dichotomizing categories that underpin the structure of war' (Cole 2009: 26). Using Chris Jenks's definition of transgression as the 'unstable principle by which any status either sustains or transforms' (2003: 80), the trope of desertion deflates binary categories such as 'us and them', 'enemy and friend', 'hero and coward'. Deserting soldiers have existed as long as there have been soldiers and a military to desert from.[2] Numbers show that while US desertion rates have fluctuated since their 5 per cent peak during the Vietnam War (NBC 2007), the numbers dropped in the first years after 9/11 (Nichols 2007). However, in 2007, Associated Press reported an 80 per cent increase in Army deserters since the US invasion of Iraq in 2003. The article noted that 'the increase comes as the Army continues to bear the brunt of the war demands with many soldiers serving repeated, lengthy tours in Iraq and Afghanistan' ('Army Desertion' 2007). A 2016 *Vice* article puts the total number of Army deserters from 2001 to 2004 at 36,195. Of these, only 1,932 have been prosecuted. But 'when it comes to those who deserted and left the country', the prosecution rate 'jumps to 50' (Khandaker 2016). Additional numbers from the Army show that 'from 2001 to 2014, more than 3,500 people were convicted of being AWOL, and 980 of those were convicted of desertion. Most of those happened . . . in the US' (Koenig 'Present' 2016).

Notions of masculinity play an inherent role in the entire rhetoric surrounding deserters. While it is common to equate desertion with labels such as cowardice and treason, there is an element of boldness, perhaps bravery, inherent in the act. As Maria Fritsche observes, 'To flee one's unit or to hide away was a bold act, but in the eyes of the military and political authorities it was "unmanly". Deserters were publicly denigrated as cowards so as to dishonour them' (2012: 36). Alluding to the gendered regulatory system that Connell, Phillips and Adams also highlight, Fritsche notes how 'characterization as "weak", "fearful" or "soft" demasculinized deserters who became designated as an "Other" who had no place in the male community' (ibid.: 36). Aligning with Connell's assertion that 'the imagery of masculine heroism' is essential in gluing the army together (Connell 2005: 214),

Fritsche asserts that 'The goal was to create a distance between the majority of "manly" soldiers and the "unmanly" deserter, and thus to strengthen the cohesion of the military unit and affirm the dominant masculine ideal' (2012: 36).

While the 'deconstructive pattern' of war narratives serves as a counter-narrative in the larger culture, it dominates American war literature (Cole 2009: 26), taking the form of what we could call an AWOL or deserter narrative. An early central text is Stephen Crane's Civil War novel *The Red Badge of Courage* (1895), in which the protagonist Henry Fleming struggles with the clear demarcation between manhood and cowardice. He was raised to believe that 'a man became another thing in a battle' and is eager to overcome his doubts and fears, to 'go into a battle and discover that he had been a fool in his doubts, and was, in truth, a man of traditional courage' (Crane 1991: 73). But once in battle, Fleming finds himself in the middle of a retreat and, consumed by guilt, he flees 'like a proverbial chicken' (1991: 93). When fellow soldiers admire his head wound – the red badge of courage – Fleming is acutely aware that it is a result not of 'his courage but his cowardice and confusion' (Gray 2004: 304). The red badge of the title, according to Richard Gray, 'measures the gap between false courage, heroic illusion and reality' (2004: 305). Ernest Hemingway's First World War novel *A Farewell to Arms* (1929) continues the general deconstructive pattern of war literature. In an often-quoted scene, the protagonist Lieutenant Frederic Henry observes, 'I was always embarrassed by the words sacred, glorious, and sacrifice . . . Abstract words such as glory, honor, courage, or hallow were obscene' (Hemingway 1994: 165). Later in the novel, Henry deserts his post in the Italian Army at the prospect of certain death. And while he feels like 'a masquerader' in civilian clothes, Henry is adamant: 'I was going to forget the war. I had made a separate peace' (ibid.: 217).

In a larger American cultural context, the Second World War is perhaps the most triumphant war narrative. Guy Westwell talks of a '"greatest generation" interpretation of the Second World War in which the war is seen in relation to the individual experience of dignified, honourable men, and through a nostalgic lens' (2006: 99). But before the term 'greatest generation' gained traction, some of the men who fought in and wrote about the Second World War constructed narratives that questioned the binary categories mentioned above. In his historical survey of the term cowardice, Chris Walsh connects Crane's novel with James Jones' Second World War novel *The Thin Red Line* (1962). Jones wished to show, as he said, that 'bravery and cowardice' have 'no human reference anymore' (Aldrich, Jr 1967: 247). David Boulting has shown how '[t]he conventions, norms, fantasies, and taboos associated with appropriate soldierly conduct function in the novel as a restrictive or destructive agency rather than one that is empowering or socially cohesive' (2010: 111–12). And Walsh highlights a central scene in the novel, where Jones problematizes the dichotomy between cowardice and courage by 'associating some of the archetypal features of cowardice with an act that seems to be the very epitome of courage: victory in hand-to-hand, one-on-one combat' (2014: 72–3). While Private Bead is 'squatting with his pants down, his behind still dirty' (Jones 1998: 171) to defecate in the woods, he is attacked by a Japanese soldier: after Bead has 'kicked him, choked him, clawed him, bayoneted him, shot him' (ibid.: 172), all the while trying to keep his pants from falling down, he 'fell down on his hands and knees and began to vomit' (ibid.: 173). As Walsh summarises, 'in associating paradigmatically courageous behavior with a reviled symptom of cowardice, Jones deflates, even denatures, these moral categories' (2014: 74).

Joseph Heller's Second World War novel *Catch-22* (1961) not only deflates moral categories, it is a central work in the deserter narrative, one that, in Adams's words, 'imagines an AWOL masculinity' (2008: 63). Adams reads the novel as a 'bridge' to Vietnam. Even though it is a Second World War novel, in Heller's own words, *Catch-22* 'wasn't really *about* World War II. It was really about American society during the Cold War, during the Korean War, and about the possibility of a Vietnam' (Merrill 1975: 68, original emphasis). Adams sees central protagonist Yossarian as a transgressive figure, 'a nonheroic hero who would become a trope of war representations for the remainder of the twentieth century', thereby redefining 'heroic masculinity as a dereliction of duty – as AWOL masculinity' (2008: 63, 65). The ending of the novel in which Yossarian escapes 'effectively rescripts Second World War heroic masculinity as a dereliction of military duty and establishes a trope of unheroic soldierly masculinity ...' (ibid.: 63). Adams argues that Heller constructs the narrative in a way that 'enables the reader to view [AWOL protagonist Yossarian] as heroic instead of a whining soldier who shirks his duty'. Furthermore, 'Yossarian's escape at the novel's end, despite any questions about loyalty or duty that may arise, emerges as the *only* appropriate response to his catch-22' (ibid.: 69, original emphasis). Adams traces the trope in later representations of war, 'such as Tim O'Brien's Vietnam War novel *The Things They Carried* (1990) and David O. Russell's Desert Storm film *Three Kings* (1999), among others' (ibid.: 69–70). One can add Charles Frazier's Civil War novel *Cold Mountain* (1997) and its 2003 cinema adaptation to the list.

The most recent desertion controversy in the US is the case of former POW Bowe Bergdahl, who was held captive by the Taliban for almost five years. In 2014, Bergdahl became a figure of transgression: overnight he went from hero to traitor when it was disclosed that he was AWOL at the time of his kidnapping. Bergdahl was the target of vitriolic assaults, especially from right-wing groups, whose response, as Robert K. Musil argues, was 'to immediately attack Bergdahl and resort to old stereotypes that he is a deserter, the worst thing you could possibly be' (quoted in Kreitner 2014). Musil also points to the jingoism inherent in anti-desertion rhetoric, where the term 'deserter' functions as 'a classic stereotype' that is 'wildly derogatory' (quoted in Kreitner 2014). As historian Brian K. Feltman asserts, echoing Adams's point about the soldier-civilian gap: 'The debate surrounding Bowe Bergdahl is part of our continued struggle to balance idealized expectations of soldierly virtue against the psychological strains of modern warfare' (2015).

The Bergdahl case received renewed (and much more nuanced) attention in late 2015, when it became the focus of season 2 of the highly popular *Serial* podcast. Sarah Koenig, host and executive producer of *Serial*, listed several points of interest in the Bergdahl case: 'what it means to be loyal, to be resilient, to be used, to be punished' (Koenig, 'Welcome' 2015). It is not a stretch to see season 2 of *Serial* as a continuation of the deserter narrative. It breaks down binary categories and asks complex questions just as Crane, Hemingway and Heller did, although the form is different. The podcast gives a voice to both defenders and detractors of Bergdahl's actions – and it gives a voice to Bergdahl himself.

Serial plays an interview with Bergdahl, in which he likens himself to Hollywood action hero Jason Bourne: 'Doing what I did was me saying "I am like . . . Jason Bourne"', Bergdahl says. 'I had this fantastic idea that I was going to prove to the world that I was the real thing . . . You know, that I could be what it is that all those guys out there that go to the movies and watch those movies, they all want to be that, but I wanted to prove that I was that' (Koenig, 'Dustwun' 2015).[3] Here Bergdahl unwittingly stresses one of Connell's points about hegemonic masculinity: that the 'most visible bearers of hegemonic masculinity' need not be real people. 'Instead, they may be prototypes, such as film actors, or they can even be fantasy figures, such as film characters' (2005: 77). But as the podcast shows, Bergdahl's story becomes yet another recognisable story of initial glorious ideas about war (and manhood) followed by disillusion. Pushing back against the jingoistic charges of cowardice and treason that dominated the public response, *Serial* treats Bergdahl's action not as a transgression but as something normal – which in itself becomes a transgressive act. By insisting that Bowe's action does not designate him as an Other, *Serial* transgresses the strict gendered regulatory system of the military, and of our culture in general: 'Bowe is also normal in war', says retired US Army officer Paul Edgar, who was part of the team searching for Sergeant Bowe Bergdahl. He stresses that 'as a society we treat Bowe as some aberration, when really, his case is simply a very normal part of war' (Koenig, 'Present' 2016). The eleven-episode season concludes with Koenig paraphrasing Edgar:

> When we signed up [for war], we were also signing up for all the things we tend to forget but that nevertheless attend war: mistakes, accidents, people dying for avoidable or even ridiculous reasons. An Army recruiting system that lowers its standards when it needs more bodies. Twenty-something-year-olds who quickly become disillusioned and do something rash, or criminal. It's all, unfortunately, normal. (Koenig, 'Present', 2016)

Stop-Loss

Released in 2008, years before the Bergdahl debacle, Kimberly Peirce's *Stop-Loss* was part of the first wave of Iraq War films. Taken as a whole, this first wave was a transgression from American war films: they generally dismissed both the mythic heroism that pervades Second World War films and the disillusionment of many Vietnam War films (Bjerre 2011: 223). And while some of these early representations of the Iraq War also focused on the disillusionment and anger felt by returning veterans, *Stop-Loss* is the only one of these to tackle the issue of desertion head-on.

Figure 8.1 Ryan Phillippe as Staff Sergeant Brandon King in charge of roadblock duty in Tikrit, Iraq. Still from *Stop-Loss* (2008).

The film's protagonist Staff Sergeant Brad King (Ryan Phillippe) is constructed as an archetypal soldier hero, a natural-born leader who looks out for his men both on the battlefield and back home. He lives up to the most universally recognised heroic qualities: leadership, loyalty and risk-taking (Wansink et al. 2008: 547). These traits are also typically used to define hegemonic masculinity, and they echo the traits of 'military masculinities' and 'soldierly masculinity'. According to the film's production notes, 'For the key role of the heroic, conflicted Sgt. Brandon King, Peirce was looking for someone who could express the strength and masculinity to lead men into and through battle and also possess the warmth and humor that is necessary to be at the center of these men's lives' ('*Stop-Loss*. Full Production Notes' 2008). David Denby sees King as 'both violent and highly moral (a classic American combination)', and he posits that 'Brandon may represent some essence for [director Peirce], as if all American manhood were poured into a pair of Army fatigues. Brandon King is a strong guy with his head screwed on right' (Denby 2008).

Denby calls Phillippe's performance 'intelligent and physically dynamic' and notes how Phillippe 'squares his jaw, mostly hides his handsome smile, and throws his body into everything, as if he felt invulnerable' (2008). Likewise, pointing to the film's emphasis on 'the killer abs of both Phillippe and co-star Channing Tatum', Molly Friedman asked, tongue-in cheek: 'Are Ryan Phillippe's abs enough to convince audiences to see an Iraq-themed movie?' (2008). Joking aside, there is, of course, a correlation between the male body and notions of essential, unchanging manhood, the idea that over centuries, 'the hard, distinct male [body] remain[s] inflexibly the same' (Braudy 2003: 10). This is important because Phillippe's fit body and masculine good looks are used to support the film's initial image of him as an embodiment of dominant soldierly/military masculinity. He not only acts like a moral hero; he looks like one. This connection was made by Robert Warshow in his 1954 discussion of the masculine values inherent in the iconographic Western hero – an icon that has served to shape the popular ideal of the American soldier in general: 'A hero is one who looks like a hero. Whatever the limitations of such an idea in experience, it has always been valid in art' (1998: 47). Brandon King's Texas background and Stetson hat only further cement the connection between the mythic western hero and 'soldierly masculinity'.

The film builds up King as a heroic leader from the outset as King and his unit man a roadblock in Tikrit. When insurgents attack, we see King as clear-headed as well as morally and ethically 'correct', ordering his men not to shoot because 'there are too many civilians'. King leads his men in pursuit, but they wind up in an ambush in which one of his men dies and another is severely wounded. Even here, King is depicted as brave and clear-headed. John Markert refers to King as an 'action hero' and points out his 'dead-eye accuracy' in shooting insurgents (2011: 255), while Terence McSweeney calls him 'intensely patriotic' (2014: 62). In the battle following the ambush, King risks his life in order to save another of his men, his childhood friend Sgt Shriver, in the process killing Iraqi civilians. So the moral complications of war are introduced early in the film, suggesting 'the heavy baggage of war' that Feltman refers to in his discussion of Bowe Bergdahl (2015). The next scene sees the soldiers returning to a welcome home parade in King's and Shriver's home town of Brazos, Texas, where King receives the Purple Heart and the Bronze Star with valour. The state senator attending the ceremony points out that King and Shriver were 'high school football heroes' and now they are 'war heroes'. But asked to say a few words, King is unable to deliver the patriotic jingoism expected of him, and the first signs of transgression emerge. His friend Shriver steps in, yelling, 'We're over there killing them in Iraq so we ain't got to kill them in Texas!' As expected, the crowd goes wild.

Before the parade and the speeches, on the bus riding into town, Lt Col Miller goes through a long list of what the soldiers cannot do while on leave: 'You will not drink and drive. You pick up a young lady, let her drive. Let her get the DUI. You will not beat up civilians! You will not fuck anyone underage. I say again, you will not fuck anyone underage. You will not beat your wife, you will not beat your kids. You will not kick your dog. Am I understood?' Drinking, picking up girls, fucking, fighting: all markers of hypermasculine behaviour. The Lt Col's orders are met with laughs, suggesting the division between the rules of the civilian world and the military system. In the latter, it is suggested, hypermasculine behaviour is called for, even necessary, while it takes on transgressive traits in the civilian world. As it turns out, some of the soldiers will do exactly what they have been ordered not to. At a dance after the parade, Tommy punches a civilian who hits on his wife, only to have King break up the fight. And later that night, King once again comes to the rescue when a drunk Shriver has lost it and is digging a foxhole in his front yard. King also learns that Shriver has hit his fiancé, King's childhood friend Michelle, after they had been 'fooling around' and 'he couldn't' get an erection.

As a true leader, King does not indulge in the excessive drinking and violence. Compared to the men surrounding him, King is restrained. Shriver is an interesting contrast to King. Played by Channing Tatum, his muscular physique and big square jaw are literal embodiments of traditional notions of hegemonic masculinity. On top of that, he seems to be a natural killer and is urged to pursue sniper school.[4] But Peirce makes it clear that Shriver's

Figure 8.2 Staff Sergeant Brandon King and Channing Tatum as Sgt Steve Shriver. Still from *Stop-Loss*.

and Tommy's hypermasculine behaviour is exactly that: hyper, thereby too much. Dobie points to the combination of '[p]hysical aggression and mental docility' as the key to fitting in the military and sums up the kind of person most likely to 'succeeded in the military as an alpha male type who can take orders real well' (2005: 35). Compared to the tall, muscular, square-jawed Tatum, Sgt King comes off as less 'hyper', but his 'soldierly masculinity' remains intact.

When King complains to Lt Col Miller about being stop-lossed, the officer falls back on the strategy of gendered fears, as described by Phillips: 'You have extenuating circumstances? You gay or pregnant?' he asks King, while the lieutenant next to him smirks. Brandon's reply confirms the image of him established in the first thirty minutes of the film: 'Sir, you know me. I'm a squared-away soldier.' And to prove his claim, King adds: 'I volunteered to fight in [the war]. I ran over 150 combat missions for you, no complaint . . . But after doing right by this Army, I'm getting burned by some fine print in a contract.' So, when King goes AWOL in protest of being stop-lossed, it is clear to us that he does so not because he is a coward, a traitor or otherwise afraid, despite this being the common cultural understanding of deserters. In fact, King can be said to hold on to his heroic traits. Rather than following ranks and obeying orders blindly, his transgressive act is a moral one, and his action can be read as an employment of the above-mentioned heroic traits, albeit on a strictly personal level: taking leadership of his own life, being loyal to his moral compass and taking a great risk (of prison or a life on the run). In this way, the transgression that his desertion creates opens up a space in the film that makes it possible for Peirce to engage in an indirect dialogue with the viewer that problematises heteronormative perspectives in relation to the army and the US in general. In this way, King's transgression forms the base of a counter-narrative, one that Peirce partly grounds in the deserter narrative outlined above.

In *Stop-Loss*, the viewer is clearly meant to sympathise with Sgt King, just as the reader is meant to sympathizse with Yossarian in *Catch-22*. But the two texts are crucially different in their approach. While *Catch-22* was marked by 'pastiche, [a] postmodern feel and . . . indecipherability,' (Adams 2008: 65), *Stop-Loss* is marked by a painstaking attempt at authenticity and realism, one that characterises the new Iraq War films (Bjerre 2011). But despite Peirce's liberal tendencies, the film seems cautious not to offend 'our troops'. King's narrative trajectory proposes that his status as a born leader makes him unable to remove himself from that position. Even while AWOL, King visits the family of his fallen soldier and his maimed soldier at a VA hospital. Not even the soldier's family has visited him. It is clear that King cannot leave behind him his position as leader.

The man in New York who provides King with a new identity before his planned escape across the border tells him: 'Do you understand what I do? I strip away who you are.' As viewers, we understand by now that this cannot be done. And immediately after, when King learns that Tommy has killed himself, it becomes clear that he cannot refuse his own position as the leader of the squad. He goes back to Tommy's funeral in Texas, where he makes up with the slighted Shriver after a tumultuous fistfight. Where Yossarian escapes at the end of *Catch-22*, in *Stop-Loss* we see Sgt Brandon King poised at yet another point of transgression: the border between the US and Mexico. Throughout the film, the viewer has been inundated with monologues and dialogues summing up the justifications and reasonings for Brandon's choice to get out. But perched at the threshold of his nation, Brandon realises that he cannot pull through with his plan. His mother, who supports his desertion, tries to plead with him. But he has made his decision: His final lines in the movie are: 'This war ain't never gonna be behind me. I'm sorry, Mom.'

The next and final scene shows Sgt King back on the bus, next to his friend Sgt Shriver, on their way to Iraq. Several critics have argued that the film fails to provide an understanding for King's last-minute change. He even repeats his reason for going AWOL at the end of the film: 'I'm done with killing. And I ain't leading any more men into a slaughter.' So why does he change his mind? McSweeney asserts that

Figure 8.3 Staff Sergeant Brandon King and Sgt Steve Shriver on their way back to Iraq. Still from *Stop-Loss*.

it is a combination of King's 'post-traumatic stress disorder' and his realisation that 'it is impossible to live as a fugitive, which sees him labelled as unpatriotic and a coward' (2014: 62). But a reason can also be found in the connection between (masculine) identity and nationality. When King's says, 'Across that border, that ain't gonna be me coming up the other side . . . It's gonna be the ghost of me,' we see how the film ties his identity as a soldier and as a natural-born leader to his men and to his national identity. If he deserts, he deserts not just the war but also his men and his nation. All that will be left of the exemplary 'squared-away' leader will be a ghost. That is a transgression that he is ultimately not able to make, which perhaps should not surprise us, given the way these traits have been stressed throughout the film. Could Peirce suggest that King acquiesces to society's expectations and definitions of the soldier hero? If so, the film is a damning condemnation of the corrosive effects of hegemonic masculinity – in the military and in the culture as a whole. The film's recurring contrast between the squared-away Brandon and the military culture of hypermasculinity – especially Tommy and Shriver's hypermasculine acts and misdeeds – would seem to suggest this reading.

While King's transgression is ultimately checked and he ends up back in the ranks, his actions have opened up a space that enables director Peirce to criticise the political implications of the stop-loss policy and the corrosive effects they have on the young men fighting America's new wars.

And she is able to address issues of AWOL/desertion without resorting to the tired, unnuanced clichés that link cowardice with effeminacy. On the other hand, the construction of King still relies on gendered binaries and affirmative notions of 'nation'. He emerges as a figure of transgression who retains the masculine traits connoted by soldierly masculinity. While some of his men crumble around him, victims not just of the heavy baggage of war but of their own apparent need to perform hypermasculinity, Brandon King seeks to remain in control of his own destiny.

Given the jingoistic atmosphere surrounding the war on terror as well as the emerging scepticism about the war at the time of production, *Stop-Loss*'s transgressive stance works to destabilise established notions of masculinity and national identity tied to ideas about what it means to be a soldier. But Peirce's transgressive representation of the deserting soldier is ultimately checked by the culturally powerful trope of the ideal male soldier that, in the end, cannot turn his back on his men and his country. Even at the start of the twenty-first century, the perceived causality between the American soldier and the nation is so culturally potent that even an independent filmmaker like Kimberly Peirce can only suggest ways of transgressing or challenging that convention; she is never able to overturn or transgress it fully.

Notes

1. Stop Loss is 'a force management program that involuntarily extends or retains active duty enlisted service members beyond their established separation date' (Henning 2009: 1).
2. Desertion and AWOL (Absence Without Leave) are often used interchangeably. But while AWOL refers to a temporary absence, desertion refers to an intended permanent absence. For the official definitions, see the Uniform Code of Military Justice, § 885. Art. 85. Desertion and § 886. Art. 86. Absence without leave.
3. Bergdahl was interviewed by Mark Boal, the screenwriter on *The Hurt Locker* (Kathryn Bigelow, 2008) and *Zero Dark Thirty* (2012).
4. With the Texas setting, Tatum's character would make an interesting comparison to Chris Kyle, the 'American Sniper' made famous in his memoir and later in Clint Eastwood's 2014 blockbuster adaptation: a film that serves as the pinnacle of the second wave of Iraq War films' return to a familiar heroic narrative.

Works Cited

Adams, Jon Robert (2008) *Male Armor: The Soldier-Hero in Contemporary American Culture*. Charlottesville, VA: University of Virginia Press.

Aldrich Jr, Nelson W. (1967) 'James Jones', in George Plimpton (ed.), *Writers at Work: The 'Paris Review' Interviews*, 3rd series. New York: Viking, pp. 231–50.

Bacevich, Andrew (2013) *The New American Militarism: How Americans Are Seduced by War*, updated edn. Oxford: Oxford University Press.

Barrett, Frank J. (2001) 'The Organizational Construction of Hegemonic Masculinity: The Case of the US Navy', in Stephen M. Whitehead and Frank J. Barrett (eds), *The Masculinities Reader*. Malden, MA: Polity, pp. 77–99.

Basham, Victoria M. (2016) 'Gender and Militaries: The Importance of Military Masculinities for the Conduct of State Sanctioned Violence', in Simona Sharoni et al. (eds), *Handbook on Gender and War*. Cheltenham: Edward Elgar, pp. 29–46.

Bjerre, Thomas Ærvold (2011) 'Authenticity and War Junkies: Making the Iraq War Real in Films and TV Series', *Journal of War & Culture Studies*, 4 (2), pp. 223–34.

Boulting, David (2010) 'Lethal Enclosure: Masculinity under Fire in James Jones's *The Thin Red Line*', in Rainer Emig and Antony Rowland (eds), *Performing Masculinity*. New York: Palgrave Macmillan, pp. 110–29.

Braudy, Leo (2003) *From Chivalry to Terrorism: War and the Changing Nature of Masculinity*. New York: Alfred A. Knopf.

Cole, Sarah (2009) 'People in War', in Kate McLoughlin (ed.), *The Cambridge Companion to War Writing*. Cambridge: Cambridge University Press, pp. 25–37.

Connell, R. W. (2005) [1995], *Masculinities*, 2nd edn. Berkeley, CA: University of California Press.

Crane, Stephen (1991) [1895] *The Red Badge of Courage*, in *The Red Badge of Courage and Other Stories*, 1895. New York: Penguin Classics, pp. 43–212.

Dao, James (2001) 'They Signed Up to Fight', *New York Times*, 6 September <https://www.nytimes.com/2011/09/06/us/sept-11-reckoning/troops.html> (last accessed 16 January 2019).

Denby, David (2008) 'When Soldiers Return', *New Yorker*, 7 April <https://www.newyorker.com/magazine/2008/04/07/when-soldiers-return> (last accessed 16 January 2019).

Dobie, Kathy (2005) 'AWOL in America', *Harper's*, March, pp. 33–44.

Edgar, Paul (2014) 'Sergeant Bowe Bergdahl, Disillusioned Youth and the Heavy Baggage of War', *Foreign Policy*, 21 November <https://foreignpolicy.com/2015/07/21/sergeant-bowe-bergdahl-disillusioned-youth-and-the-heavy-baggage-of-war-2/> (last accessed 16 January 2019).

Ehrenreich, Barbara (1997) *Blood Rites: Origins and History of the Passions of War*. New York: Henry Holt.

Feltman, Brian K. (2015) 'Blurred Lines: Prisoners of War, Deserters, and Bowe Bergdahl', *UNC Press Blog*, 21 January <http://uncpressblog.com/2015/01/21/brian-k-feltman-blurred-lines-prisoners-of-war-deserters-and-bowe-bergdahl/> (last accessed 16 January 2019).

Friedman, Molly (2008) 'Are Ryan Phillippe's Abs Enough to Convince Audiences to See an Iraq-Themed Movie?' *Gawker*, 14 March <http://gawker.com/368206/are-ryan-phillippes-abs-enough-to-convince-audiences-to-see-an-iraq-themed-movie> (last accessed 16 January 2019).

Fritsche, Maria (2012) 'Proving One's Manliness: Masculine Self-perceptions of Austrian Deserters in the Second World War', *Gender and History*, 24 (1), pp. 35–55.

Goldich, Robert L. (2013) 'American Military Culture from Colony to Empire', in David M. Kennedy (ed.), *The Modern American Military*. Oxford: Oxford University Press, pp. 79–109.

Gray, Richard (2004) *A History of American Literature*. Malden, MA: Blackwell.

Gwynne, Joel (2016) *Transgression in Anglo-American Cinema: Gender, Sex, and the Deviant Body*. New York: Wallflower Press.

Hemingway, Ernest (1994) [1929] *A Farewell to Arms*. London: Arrow Books.

Henning, Charles A. (2009) 'U.S. Military Stop Loss Program: Key Questions and Answers', *Congressional Research Service*, 10 July <https://fas.org/sgp/crs/natsec/R40121.pdf> (last accessed 16 January 2019).

Higate, Paul and Hopton, John (2005) 'War, Militarism, and Masculinities', in Kimmel et al. (ed.), *Handbook of Studies on Men and Masculinities*. Thousand Oaks, CA: Sage, pp. 432–47.

Hutchings, Kimberly (2008) 'Making Sense of Masculinity and War', *Men and Masculinities* 10 (4), pp. 389–404.

Jenks, Chris (2003) *Transgression*. London: Routledge.

Jones, James (1998) [1962] *The Thin Red Line*. New York: Dell.

Khandaker, Tamara (2016) 'These American Deserters from the Iraq War May Finally Get Refuge in Canada, *Vice*, 17 August <https://news.vice.com/article/these-american-deserters-from-the-iraq-war-may-finally-get-refuge-in-canada> (last accessed 16 January 2019).

Koenig, Sarah, host (2015) 'Dustwun', *Serial*, season 2, episode 1, 10 December <https://serialpodcast.org/season-two/1/dustwun> (last accessed 16 January 2019).

Koenig, Sarah, host (2015) 'Welcome', *Serial*, 10 December <https://serialpodcast.org/2015/12/season-two-welcome> (last accessed 16 January 2019).

Koenig, Sarah, host (2016) 'Present for Duty', *Serial*, season 2, episode 11, 31 March <https://serialpodcast.org/season-two/11/present-for-duty> (last accessed 16 January 2019).

Kreitner, Richard (2014) 'Bowe Bergdahl and the Honorable History of War Deserters', *The Nation*, 5 June <http://www.thenation.com/blog/180144/bowe-bergdahl-and-honorable-history-war-deserters> (last accessed 16 January 2019).

McSweeney, Terence (2014) *The 'War on Terror' and American Film: 9/11 Frames per Second*. Edinburgh: Edinburgh University Press.

Markert, John (2011) *Post-9/11 Cinema: Through a Lens Darkly*. Lanham, MD: Scarecrow Press.

Merrill, Sam (1975) 'Interview with Joseph Heller', *Playboy*, June, pp. 59–76.

NBC/Associated Press staff writer (2007) 'Army Desertion Up 80 Percent since Iraq War', *NBC/Associated Press*, 16 November <http://www.nbcnews.com/id/21836566/ns/us_news-military/t/army-desertion-percent-iraq-war/> (last accessed 16 January 2019).

Nichols, Bill (2007) '8,000 Desert during Iraq War', *USA Today*, 7 March <https://usatoday30.usatoday.com/news/washington/2006-03-07-deserters_x.htm> (last accessed 16 January 2019).
Paramount Pictures (2008) '*Stop-Loss*. Full Production Notes', available at <http://madeinatlantis.com/movies_central/2008/stop_loss_production_details.htm> (last accessed 16 January 2019).
Phillips, Kathy J. (2006) *Manipulating Masculinity: War and Gender in Modern British and American Literature*. New York: Palgrave Macmillan.
Segal, Mady Wechsler (1995) 'Women's Military Roles Cross-Nationally: Past, Present, and Future', *Gender and Society*, 9 (6), pp. 757–75.
Uniform Code of Military Justice (2006). United States Code, 2006 edition, supplement 5, Title 10 – Armed Forces. Subtitle A – General Military Law. Part II – Personnel. Chapter 47 – Uniform Code of Military Justice. Subchapter X – Punitive Articles. Section 885 – Art. 85. 'Desertion' and Art. 86. 'Absence without leave'. Available at <https://www.gpo.gov/fdsys/pkg/USCODE-2011-title10/pdf/USCODE-2011-title10-subtitleA-partII-chap47-subchapX-sec885.pdf> (last accessed 16 January 2019).
Walsh, Ben (2014) *Cowardice: A Brief History*. Princeton, NJ: Princeton University Press.
Wansink, Brian, Payne, Collin R. and van Ittersum, Koert (2008) 'Profiling the Heroic Leader: Empirical Lessons from Combat-Decorated Veterans of World War II', *Leadership Quarterly*, 19 (5), pp. 547–55.
Warshow, Robert (1998) [1954], 'Movie Chronicle: The Western', in Jim Kitses and Gregg Rickman (eds), *The Western Reader*. New York: Limelight Editions, pp. 35–47.
Westwell, Guy (2006) *War Cinema: Hollywood on the Front Line*. London: Wallflower Press.
Wolfreys, Julian (2008) *Transgression: Identity, Space, Time*. Basingstoke: Palgrave Macmillan.
Wright, Evan (2004) *Generation Kill: Devil Dogs, Iceman, Captain America, and the New Face of American War*. New York: Berkley Caliber.

CHAPTER 9

Activist, Mother, Filmmaker: Competing Transgressions in the Syrian War Documentary

Lisa Purse

Introduction

As the war emerging from the Syrian government's crackdown on the 2011 protest movement has become increasingly destructive, the number of documentaries on the conflict has proliferated. The films that have succeeded in finding an audience on the festival circuit, in movie theatres and on television, are those focused on the protestors fighting to overthrow Syrian President Bashar al-Assad's regime, and fighting to survive bombings, sniper attacks, homelessness, resource depletion and human loss, in besieged cities such as Aleppo and Homs. This article examines the importance of political and personal figures of transgression to the types of images and reflections offered by these documentaries, as they seek to encourage North American and European spectators to take action to address the worsening crisis on the ground. The plight of children in the conflict zone is an important frame through which these notions of political and personal transgression are articulated, and it produces the activist parent as a potentially transgressive figure, too, in this fraught context. To examine these issues further, the chapter's second half will focus on two case study documentaries which feature an activist mother: *A Syrian Love Story* (Sean McAllister, UK,[1] 2015), which focuses on the family of political prisoner Raghda Hasan as they negotiate living under Bashar al-Assad's regime and eventually flee it; and *For Sama* (Waad al-Kateab and Edward Watts, UK/Syria, 2019), a first-person account of an activist journalist, Waad, who gives birth to and raises her child during the siege of Aleppo.

Against the backdrop of the Arab Spring in countries like Egypt and Tunisia, and people's frustration at the al-Assad regime's failure to address corruption, increasing poverty and inequality, drought and the continuation of state brutality, the Syrian uprising was sparked off in 2011 in the southern city of Deraa (Yassin-Kassab and Al-Shami 2016: 32–9).

Children who had painted revolutionary slogans on city walls were detained and tortured, their parents told by a local security chief 'Forget your children. Go sleep with your wives and make new ones, or send them to me and I'll do it' (ibid.: 38). Local peaceful demonstrations by outraged citizens were violently supressed, with many protestors killed or abducted by the army or police; the resulting protests 'grew rapidly in numbers and geographical spread' (ibid.: 39). The government's armed response to mass demonstrations included besieging key cities like Homs and Hama in the west and Aleppo and eventually Idlib in the north. Some anti-regime protestors organised themselves into an armed resistance, to protect citizens, rebel territory and supply routes. Al-Assad's forces and their allies have used tanks, snipers and aerial bombardment including incendiary devices (HRW 2019: n.p.) and chemical weapons (OPCW 2019: 32) on besieged cities, killing civilians indiscriminately, restricting access to humanitarian aid, and bombing hospitals and volunteer rescue teams (HRW 2019: n.p.). As of March 2018, the death toll since the start of the conflict was estimated by the UK-based Syrian Observatory for Human Rights to be 511,000 (McDowall and Roche 2018), and as of January 2020 an estimated 6.6 million Syrians have been displaced internally and 5.6 million internationally, out of a population of 22.5 million.[2] While the twin forces of political dissent and state oppression have a long history in Syria, this period heralded conflict on an unprecedented scale, which continues at the time of this writing.

Citizen Filmmakers

The Syrian protests, regime responses and the emerging civil war have been documented widely in videos recorded by local journalists, activists and private citizens on mobile phones or video cameras, often at great personal risk. The filming of protests was banned and could not only lead to the confiscation of cameras but also detention and worse. To circumnavigate a regime-sympathetic state press, this 'citizen filmmaker' footage is circulated through social media, producing what has been called 'the most socially mediated civil conflict in history' (Lynch et al. 2014: 5). The desire is to bring global attention to these events in a call for international compassion and intervention. For example, filmmaker Waad al-Kateab, in her narration for *For Sama*, says, 'The regime denied there were protests. Filming on mobiles was the only way to show the world we were fighting for our freedom.' Collated by anti-regime Local Coordinating Committees, such footage was passed to Syrian diaspora activist networks that curated them for a wider international public (ibid.: 8–9; Andén-Papadopoulos and

Pantti 2013; Asha 2013). Assisted by exiled Syrian supporters who were familiar with Western conventions of television news, activist journalists developed their craft with an eye on the international audience.[3]

North American and European mainstream news media were not able to physically access large parts of Syria as the conflict unfolded, but they also wanted to claim direct access to the war zone for their audiences. As a result, they relied heavily on video material captured by local activists, its unvarnished immediacy producing an impression of an unmediated window onto the conflict (Wall and el Zahed 2015: 725) despite the challenges of verifiability and clarification of discursive framing it presented (Mast and Hanegreefs 2015: 595).[4] So, too, do most of the documentaries that have emerged into North American and European distribution channels during the period since 2011. These documentaries focus on people navigating life under bombardment and siege. This includes activists and journalists in *The Return to Homs* (Talal Derki, Syria, 2013), *Red Lines* (Andrea Kalin, Oliver Lukacs, US/Turkey/Syria, 2014), *7 Days in Syria* (Robert Rippberger, USA/Syria, 2015), *A Syrian Love Story*, *The War Show* (Andreas Dalsgaard, Obaidah Zytoon, Denmark/Germany/Finland, 2016), *Cries from Syria* (Evgeny Afineevsky, US/Czech Republic, 2017) and *For Sama*; doctors in *Saving Syria's Children* (Darren Conway, UK, 2013), *50 Feet from Syria* (Skye Fitzgerald, Turkey/USA/Syria, 2015), *For Sama* and *The Cave* (Feras Fayyad, Syria/Denmark/Germany/Qatar/US, 2019); rebel fighters in *Cries from Syria* and *The Return to Homs*; and volunteer rescue workers the Syrian Civil Defence, nicknamed the 'White Helmets', in *Last Men in Aleppo* (Feras Fayyad, Steen Johannessen, Denmark/Syria, 2017) and *The White Helmets* (Orlando von Einsiedel, UK, 2018).

Framing the Conflict: Competing Transgressions

The activist footage taken up by mainstream news media and integrated into documentaries on the Syrian war (there is some crossover) echoed anti-regime discourse by articulating the conflict in terms of two opposed figures of transgression. On the one hand, the activists positioned themselves as political transgressors fighting for freedom, and frequently used the word 'revolution' in their videos and statements, with its connotations of transformational change and regime overthrow. This pointedly countered the al-Assad regime's historical use of the word 'revolution' to describe its own route to power and its continued tendency to claim its legitimacy through the suggestion that it was founded in a mass 'movement' of people (Asha 2013: 54, 56; McHugo 2014: 153; Yassin-Kassab and al-Shami 2016: 12). In reclaiming the word 'revolution', the activists situated themselves as political transgressors forged in Syria's long history of heroic dissent. On the other hand, the activists in their on-camera and voiceover statements, and in the type of footage they chose to film and circulate, frame the actions of Bashar al-Assad explicitly in terms of another kind of transgression: the transgression of human dignity and the human right to life enshrined in international law. This is further couched in terms of the betrayal of the nation and its people. In *Silvered Water*, for example, protestors are recorded shouting off camera (in different incidents) 'Traitors, traitors, traitors, the Syrian Army betray the people!' and 'He who kills his people is a traitor!' An important element of this framing is the circulation of images of children killed by the regime, a point I will return to later in the article. Thus competing figures of political transgression, the activist and the authoritarian leader shape the call to action initiated by such filmed material.

But there is another figure of transgression that emerges from this fraught zone of conflict. The revolution has offered women opportunities to step outside of normative social roles, at the same time as increasing anxieties in some sections of the community about this stepping outside. One Syrian activist, in an interview for the International Federation for Human Rights, noted how central women were to the revolution:

> In demonstrations in the universities, women protest side by side with men. In the streets of Damascus, women gather in the centre of processions and men surround them to protect them. In villages, men start the marches and women follow. When the security forces arrive to make arrests, women intervene to prevent them. When the security situation prevents women from participating in street demonstrations, women organise meetings inside their homes. They use social networks and online videos to let the outside world know what is happening. (Speaking in January 2012, quoted in Belhassen et al. 2013: 54–5)

While men tend to dominate the political opposition bodies and the Free Syrian Army, women dominate the civil resistance, 'which is made up of an extensive network of people largely women both from within and outside the country' (al-Om 2014 273). They risk the same punishments as their male counterparts, from arrest and detention to torture, rape and murder, to the detention and murder of family members (Belhassen et al. 2013: 54; Rice et al. 2011).

Activist Rajaa Altalli notes that women 'have been able to benefit from less stringent searches at regime checkpoints. They have thus been able to conceal cameras in their clothing and upload videos that provide evidence for the regime's crimes' (Asha 2013: 59). Wiam Bedirxan in *Silvered Water* smuggled in a camera; both she and al-Kateab in *For Sama* use their looser clothing to help them secretly film street scenes. In her voiceover narration, Bedirxan describes street filming thus: 'After a month of searching for a cameraman, I realized no one but I will do it! I folded my femininity and I walked. Searching for meaning in the images that flee into my small camera.'[5] Women have experienced their taking up of activism as an 'elevation in free expression and a genuine sense of liberation', with often respectful and supportive relations between male and female protestors, yet this positivity is not always shared by their families or spouses (Al-Om 2014: 278). The fact that female activists risk violent reprisals, rape and even death reframes them as figures of transgression, and not just as political transgressors but as transgressors of normative social and gender roles: they no longer occupy the idealised position of being protected and contained within marriage and the home. As Tamara Al-Om has pointed out, 'Syria is a socially conservative society where women are intrinsically restricted by familial obligations and expectations, both within rural and urban sectors of society and a common feature regardless of religion or class' (2015: 276).[6] Those who choose, despite fear of punishment and bodily harm, to become active in the protest movement, are open to being pilloried, and worse. A woman commented to Al-Jazeera news channel:

> While I'm only a civilian activist, I'm still stigmatised as a loose woman because I travel a lot from one place to the other to deliver food and medicine . . . Bashar al-Assad is giving me a hard time, but so are my parents and the whole neighbourhood. (Asha 2013: 62)

And the *United Nations Universal Periodic Review of The Syrian Arab Republic* makes clear that:

> Upon release from detention or checkpoints, and after house raids, women are often alienated from their families and viewed as 'unfit' for marriage, and in some instances divorced or killed, because family members believe they were raped. (HRGJC et al. 2016: 2)

The documentaries that have been made for North American and European markets do not directly replicate these negative responses to female activism, yet the tensions between domesticity and activism nonetheless inform these films' narratives in significant ways. In the second half of this essay, I want to examine how two films explicitly focused on activist mothers negotiate these issues of gender roles and their activist calling, in the context of the documentaries' function to make a case for intervening in Syria.

A Syrian Love Story

Sean McAllister's documentary film, *A Syrian Love Story*, places the principle of political transgression right at the heart of its initial introduction of its subjects. The film's opening shows a bemused McAllister on a government press tour of the region designed to present Syria as the 'next tourist hotspot'. McAllister is keen to claim his own political transgression – as the independent filmmaker explicitly sceptical of the regime – through his dialogue, voiceover and the editing together of various images that draw on orientalist stereotypes of the Middle East (camels, guides pointing to and fro, canted angle postcard shots of ancient buildings) to poke fun at the tour and its organisers. 'Knowing that Syria's jails were full of political prisoners, I wanted to find a real story', McAllister says in his voiceover narration. He finds it in Amer Daoud, drinking in a Damascus bar, and talking about his wife Raghda Hasan, who is a political prisoner. Amer is raising their two younger children, Bob and Kaka, on his own in their hometown of Tartus (a region sympathetic to the regime), while campaigning for Raghda's release. McAllister films the family from November 2010, in a briefly pre-revolutionary moment, to 2014, by which point they have moved from Tartus to the Yarmouk Palestinian camp on the outskirts of Damascus, to exile in Lebanon, and finally to asylum in France. The couple's history is defined by political activism; he is a former Palestinian freedom fighter with the PLO and she is a Syrian communist revolutionary (Ya Libnan News 2010: n.p.). Raghda has been incarcerated because she wrote a novel about her time in prison in the early 1990s (Khosrokhavar 2016: 201). The couple met and fell in love when they were both political prisoners in adjoining cells during that earlier period of incarceration. Amer tells McAllister that he first 'saw her from the hole in the door'; she was 'covered in blood, with a swollen face, and eyes'. In the present, she is once again under physical attack in prison, receiving extra beatings because she is from the same Alawite sect of Islam as al-Assad.

The film's opening moments celebrate Raghda as a heroic woman activist; Amer describes her approvingly as 'a very strong woman', and the film returns repeatedly to images of Raghda on Amer's mobile phone, on the laptop and in photographs, their visual repetition in close-up echoing the way in which these images are treasured by the family while they hope for her release. She is idealised in her absence, one half of the great love story Amer tells for McAllister, in which her political transgression finds common ground with his, and produces the family that McAllister now encounters. Raghda is freed in a fleeting gesture of amelioration by the al-Assad regime in the early stages of the 2011 Syrian revolution. Her love story with Amer, picked up by the film's title, seems to have its happy ending, but the notion acquires an undertow of pathos when their relationship begins to fall apart in the face of Raghda's traumatisation. Additionally, they are forced to flee to Lebanon after McAllister is caught and briefly imprisoned with footage of Amer and Raghda on his camera. In Lebanon Raghda becomes depressed, she explains, because 'I don't have any possibility to do anything. I'm just a prisoner.' Amer and she become estranged: she leaves the family for a period of time. The Syrian revolution has turned into a war which has destroyed their old neighbourhood in Tartus and is killing many of their friends, but Raghda longs to return to fight the regime. Amer wants to take the family to Europe, but as a Palestinian he needs her to join him in order to be given asylum as a Syrian refugee family. They do succeed in reaching France, but while the children flourish in their new surroundings, Raghda and Amer's relationship worsens. He is angry with her for leaving, she is angry because he has had an affair, but also crucially because she can no longer answer what she feels is her calling as a political activist. She attempts suicide and subsequently leaves for good, moving to Turkey, close to the border with Syria, and taking up a position as cultural and political advisor to the leader of the Syrian opposition government.

The nature of the film's engagement with Raghda and her activism shifts as *A Syrian Love Story* progresses. A heroic political prisoner at the start, once back in the domestic sphere Raghda's continued desire to participate in the burgeoning revolution becomes problematic for the family,

Figure 9.1 Raghda in a moment of introspection, silently contemplating her youngest child. Still from *A Syrian Love Story* (2015).

but also for the film. Amer is frustrated that she would put her activism above her duties as a wife and mother: 'She thinks if she's out of Syria she's nothing . . . she feels she cannot be special like she was in Syria', he complains. But Raghda later reveals what has been so difficult – juggling her trauma-related mental health difficulties and her desire for self-expression through activism while having to take on the demands of all members of the family at once has been too much: 'Nobody take care for me', she says, in an emphatic close-up. 'Because all the family need to take . . . But I want [care too].' It is a poignant moment but what is striking is how little time the film chooses to spend engaging with Raghda, given that it is her prisoner status that prompted Amer and McAllister to connect in the first place. This seems partly a result of the filmmaker's decision to eschew translators in his sojourns with the family; Amer and the children's English is much more fluent, and thus they are easier for McAllister to interact with on the ground. But it also seems connected to what the film wants to value more in this milieu. The children, and Amer's attempts to keep the family together, are the dominant focus. Raghda's pain, manifesting in forms of interpersonal withdrawal, seems less cinematically engaging for the filmmaker, while without a translator she is not able to express the full complexity of her thinking (see Figure 9.1). Raghda has transgressed gendered norms because of her continued commitment to political transgression, and is subsequently sidelined by the film in order to focus on her husband and children. At the end of *A Syrian Love Story*, the last glimpse of Raghda is fleeting in comparison with the more extended visit McAllister makes to Amer in France. There is just a brief conversation with Raghda in a Turkish café, in which she reveals she feels she is beginning life again more positively: 'I cannot change . . . But inside me still, I have this hope, for humanity, for freedom, for my country.' She is happy her children are safe, in good schools, with good lives, but her activism is about 'build[ing] a future' for them. 'You are walking the right street now', she says about herself, with a smile. In this way, Raghda finally finds a way to reconcile her motherhood, her trauma and her activism, even though the film appears reluctant to fully embrace this in its presentation of her choices.

Framing the Conflict: Children

A Syrian Love Story followed a family out of Syria before the revolution became a militarised conflict and makes its case for a humanitarian response to Syrian refugees through its focus on the family at the expense of the estranged activist mother. In the other Syrian war documentaries, the focus on protestors and civilians who stayed in Syria, many in the besieged cities, produces a heightened nexus of concern around the plight of the child and the quandary of the parent, posing anew the question Raghda also struggled with: to stay or to go. 'It's not about us, the dilemma is our children', says Khaled Omar Harrah in *Last Men in Aleppo*. Khaled is a volunteer rescue worker, one of the eponymous 'White Helmets' of the Syrian Civil Defence, who risks his life every day in the besieged city, pulling the dead from the rubble of bombed-out buildings. He has two young children and a wife at home, but feels he can't leave. His daughter is showing signs of malnutrition and he is considering taking them to safety in Turkey, but sadly he doesn't manage to do this before he is himself killed by a bomb that lands as he is mid-rescue, in August 2016. Khaled's story is indicative of the challenges facing those living under regime bombardment. Parents who choose to remain for activist or humanitarian reasons (or a combination of the two) are at risk, but so too are their children.

A recurrent preoccupation of the activist footage shared on news media is children suffering trauma and death in increasing numbers. Child victims were early catalysts of the expanding protests, from the schoolboys detained and beaten for painting slogans, to Hamza al-Khateeb, a thirteen-year-old tortured and then killed after being arrested at a peaceful protest (Verma 2011: n.p.; MacLeod and Flamand 2011, n.p.). Subsequently, children have been injured, raped or killed in military detention, in school and hospital bombings and in chemical weapons attacks, and have suffered malnutrition and psychological trauma as well as displacement in enormous numbers (UNICEF 2019). Scholars have rightly noted that images of suffering children have particular currency for news networks, 'as if societies' moral and political stances only take shape in reaction to images and voices of children's suffering' (Al-Ghazzi 2019, n.p.; see also Moeller 2002; Malkki 2010). The presence of children in news media footage of war and its devastation lend such images an affective immediacy that has been desirable for news channels and also for those feeding them footage. Children were used by news media to frame the Syrian conflict for North American and European audiences, in line with the foreign policy emphases of their respective national contexts. So, particular children became synecdoches of the innocent victims of al-Assad's legal and humanitarian transgressions: as a collective of deceased children in the coverage of chemical weapons attacks in 2013 (McHugo 2014: 25–6); as an individual child lost in the process of displacement, as three-year-old Alan Kurdi was in 2014 – the image of his body on the beach circulated around the world (Adler-Nissen et al. 2020); or as an individual child shell-shocked in the rubble of bombardment, as five-year-old Omran Daqneesh was in 2016, his image, too, reaching across traditional and newer news media networks (Barnard 2016). Children were also used in social media campaigns by opposition groups, as Omar Al-Ghazzi has noted (2019: n.p.). In this way, Al-Ghazzi argues, the 'distant witnessing of the plight of children in Syria . . . has been shaped by mutually reinforcing trends of, on the one hand, the quest for and assumption of the possibility of unmediated witnessing, and on the other hand, the politicization of witness accounts' (ibid.: n.p.).

Drawing on work by Luc Boltanski (1999), Susan Sontag (2003) and Lilie Chouliaraki (2008), Libby Saxton has noted that mainstream news coverage tends to work to 'dissimulate and discourage reflection on the unequal relation between protected Western viewer and vulnerable non-Western other, for instance by fostering a narcissistic pity which masquerades as altruism' (Saxton 2010: 67). Certainly the activist filmmakers and their protestor colleagues in the Syrian war documentaries are very aware of the lack of material action generated by such 'narcissistic pity'. In *Return to Homs* the director, Talal Derki, notes ruefully in voiceover, 'I thought that these images would shake the world to its core', yet North American and European countries declined to intervene directly, backing off just as al-Assad was suspected of using chemical weapons, because Islamist groups were increasing their presence in the region (McHugo 2014: 228, 230–1). The documentaries made during this period sought more effective ways to prompt the attention and action of international spectators, rendering in stark audiovisual detail the material horror of the circumstances in which they found themselves. The documentaries return again and again to images of suffering and death: scores of dead children wrapped in sheets and children severely malnourished, their bones protruding from their skin, in *Cries from Syria*; dead babies and children being pulled from the rubble in *The Last Men in Aleppo* and *The White Helmets*; boys being beaten and tortured in military detention in *Silvered Water*; babies and children brought in unresponsive or dying on gurneys and operating tables in *For Sama*.

They are a cumulative testament to the scale of the devastation wrought on children and their parents, designed to force the geographically distant spectator to act, by purposefully and persistently transgressing norms around visual access to the dead or dying body. Specifically, they purposefully transgress European and North American news media industry codes of practice for communicating death and violence, and the 'informal norms of decency and propriety' that inform them (Campbell 2004: 59). David Campbell has noted the traditional reticence of such news media to show dead bodies, contributing to a 'disappearance of the dead' that Campbell argues elides war horrors and their contributing contexts (ibid.: 71). The fact that these are documentary films rather than rolling television news media coverage permits the dead body to be included in the visual field, to connote the horrors of war in a more direct way. Channel 4 News had declined to show some of Waad al-Kateab's Aleppo hospital footage because its graphic nature was 'not suitable for television' (De Pear, in Frontline Club Q&A 2019), but in the feature documentary *For Sama*, al-Kateab is able to reinsert the dead into her visual testimony on the conflict. In the final section of this article, I will suggest that *For Sama* differentiates itself from the other Syrian war documentaries in the way it integrates images of the dead as a call to action, precisely because it does so through a meditation on whether motherhood and political transgression can be compatible in a worsening war zone.

For Sama

For Sama draws on footage recorded by activist and journalist Waad al-Kateab on her own camera,[7] as she traces the evolution of the Syrian uprising from her personal perspective in the city of Aleppo over five years.[8] The film is co-directed with British filmmaker Edward Watts, who directs 'in the edit', constructing a narrative from al-Kateab's footage (with editors Chloe Lambourne and Simon McMahon), with al-Kateab's input and her voiceover narration. The result is a first-person documentary that combines the political – the revelation of the violence of the al-Assad regime and its destruction of the city and the lives within it – and the personal – as al-Kateab's own personal life evolves in ways that pose the dilemma of parenting versus activism in the sharpest ways. The film cuts in particular between two moments in time: 2012, when al-Kateab was a fourth-year economics student at the University of Aleppo, protesting and dodging the security services with her friends; and 2016, when Aleppo is struggling under siege and daily bombardment, and al-Kateab is raising her baby daughter, Sama, in a single room in a makeshift hospital run by her new husband Hamza. The footage comprises first person camerawork in the thick of bombardments, life and death crises in the hospital, and lighter moments with Hamza and Sama and their friends. Throughout, al-Kateab's voiceover narration dictates a long-form message to Sama, seeking to explain to her child why her parents decided to bring her into the world in Aleppo and decided to stay there (and indeed return there at one point) for her first year of life. 'I need you to understand why your father and I made the choices we did,' she says, and 'Will you blame me for staying here or blame me for leaving?' This visual and aural personal testimony foregrounds the parental quandary that al-Kateab and her medic husband, both activists, share with the protagonists of *Last Men in Aleppo* and the other documentaries mentioned above: to leave and survive, unmoored from home and from the fight against al-Assad, or to remain and live, under the threat of death.

In *For Sama*, the dilemma itself, and the affective force of its articulation through images of the dead, *is* the call to action. In her opening voiceover, al-Kateab sees the roots of her activism in her parents' assessment of her 18-year-old self: 'My parents told me to be careful,' she says. 'They always said I was headstrong, even reckless. I never knew what they meant until I had a daughter. You'. 'Be careful' is an instruction that implies al-Kateab should be careful with her politics (negotiating the security services was already an established problem for all Syrians (Gissi 2020: 17)), as much as it is a gendered warning to remain a 'respectable' woman. Yet the 'until I had a daughter' comment that ends this opening voiceover narration also points to what will become al-Kateab's overriding concern – is it 'reckless' to participate in and document the revolution instead of fleeing the conflict when she becomes a mother? (Her parents and parents-in-law clearly think so from their vantage point across the border in Turkey, where they encourage Hamza, al-Kateab and Sama to join them.) The remainder of the opening segment underscores the risk, as al-Kateab's handheld camera records her bundling Sama out of their room and along a hospital corridor filling rapidly with smoke as they seek shelter underground from the latest shelling incident. It is no coincidence that at the end of the sequence al-Kateab includes a snippet of banter from the hospital staff in which they pretend Sama is saying, 'Mum, why did you give birth to me? It's been nothing but war since the day I was born.' Through the rest of the film, al-Kateab moves between past and present, so that the happy evolution of al-Kateab's relationship with Hamza and the arrival of her child is counterposed with scenes of present-day devastation in the hospital treatment rooms that dramatise in horrific and heart-wrenching detail the consequences al-Kateab may soon face as a mother who does not leave Aleppo. A necessary part of this dramatisation of risk and consequence is the purposeful imaging of the dead in a series of pointed juxtapositions.

In one of these juxtapositions, the story of al-Kateab's wedding proposal is intimately tied to the failure to save a young boy in the operating room. Al-Kateab's camera carefully films the unresponsive child just slightly out of focus in the mid ground of the shot as he is treated, a doctor's arms obscuring his face as they reach across his body. Later, his face is similarly obscured, this time by the laying over of a shroud. Over these images, al-Kateab's voiceover reveals she cried in the treatment room at the boy's plight, and was told to leave by an angry Hamza. Hamza explains why later: because he is in love with her, and hates to see her upset. Will she marry him? The dead body shares its moment of revelation with a key milestone in al-Kateab's own happiness; the juxtaposition feels uncomfortable because it is meant to. This is Aleppo under siege, the dead alongside the living, the dissonances in the circumstances finding expression in the structure of the film itself. The film also regularly counterposes images of Sama – contemplating or at play – with children and babies who have died in the hospital treatment rooms. Here the tension between the drive to resist the regime, stay in Aleppo and save those affected by bombardment on the one hand, and on the other hand to leave Aleppo to guarantee the life and health of the family, the parents and the child, is most evidently and obviously conveyed. In one scene, Hamza is holding Sama as they playfully 'baby talk' to each other. In al-Kateab's voiceover she explains, 'Tonight, after the daily bombing, a friend brings you down to us.' Only in the next shot does the voiceover make it clear that they are in the emergency room. Sama is now in the background of the shot, sitting on the lap of someone in scrubs (perhaps Hamza). After a while, the camera tilts down slightly and refocuses to reveal a dead boy on the gurney in the foreground. The camera pans down the length of his body, white with brick dust, his face pale, eyes closed, his body, feet and hands bound for burial (see Figure 9.2). 'I hate to admit it', al-Kateab says in voiceover, 'but I envy this boy's mother. At least she died before she had to bury her child.' Living and dead share the same space and time, fear and its object existing simultaneously.

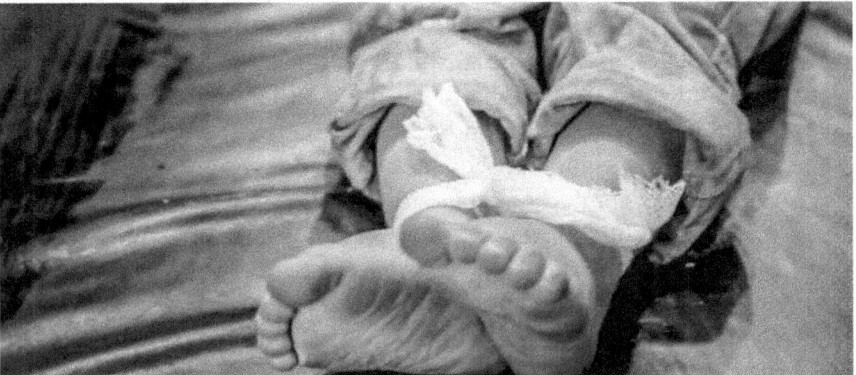

Figure 9.2 The bound feet of a toddler killed in the Syrian war. Still from *For Sama* (2019).

These long takes permit the spectator to spend time with the body of the dead child, to reflect on what has brought them to the hospital and the wider context of war and oppression, while the juxtaposition with al-Kateab's living child – and her ongoing dilemma – uncomfortably underscores what is still at stake, and could still be lost if no action is forthcoming. Elsewhere in the film, al-Kateab's footage emphasises this point further by asking the spectator to also spend time with the parents of these lost children, as their grief is witnessed in long takes that are challenging to experience. After Sama is passed to a babysitting colleague, al-Kateab films a boy rushed into the hospital treatment room, two distraught brothers looking on. He dies, and later his mother arrives, and sweeps him up into her arms. Hospital staff offer to help her carry him, but as she bears him out of the building and down the street, her protective parental instinct finds tragic expression amidst her loss: 'He is my son and I'll carry him. He is my son. This is my love. Why wouldn't I carry him?' (see Figure 9.3). Later in the film, a mother screams in horror over her dead toddler, asking al-Kateab, 'Are you filming? Why are they doing this to us? Film this, film this!' and, to her unresponsive son, 'It's mummy, I've got your milk! Wake up Alaa, I beg you.' And after a sniper attack floods the hospital with new victims, a father tries chest compressions on his teenage daughter. His wife stops him: 'Leave her, she's dead.' He cries out in grief and disbelief that they only tried to escape the city for her, for his daughter. 'We never made it, we never made it out!' his wife wails next to him. In such scenes, the emotional appeal to the spectator is rooted in the figure of the distraught parent who can no longer protect their child and is

Figure 9.3 A mother carries her dead child, Mohammad Ameen, from the hospital. Still from *For Sama*.

anchored in the durational mode of presentation. This is al-Kateab's fear, but it is also a recognisable fear to any parent. Thus the call to action relies on a relatability that is not easy, but instead deeply uncomfortable, since it depends on the emphatic transgression of the convention to image the dead briefly and from a distance.

Conclusion

In this article I have foregrounded the extent to which notions of political and personal transgression are at issue in the lived experience of the Syrian war, as mediated through the Syrian war documentary. These cultural representations, like the on-the-ground footage they rely on, are spaces across which the fight to live, to protest and to survive in spite of the regime are articulated in the service of seeking to prompt North American and European spectators into some form of ethical response. The tension between activism and domestic life, analogised by the collapsed, bombed-out dwellings of Syrian citizens in urban regions, finds its most grave and potent expression in the deployment of images of the dead. It is this tension that demonstrates to the distant observer what might still be lost in the conflict and why it is still important to act. The extent to which these documentaries have succeeded in overcoming the passivity of the West's 'narcissistic altruism' is, sadly, debatable, but the recent reception of *For Sama* and Feras Fayyad's *The Cave* (both award-winning and both nominated for Academy Awards in 2020) offers some small hope.

Notes

1. The countries involved in the production of each documentary will be listed alongside the director and year of release in the rest of the article, so that readers can get a sense of the types of co-production arrangements which have made these documentaries possible.
2. Figures visible on front page of UNHCR Syria emergency appeal <https://www.unhcr.org/uk/syria-emergency.html> (last accessed 24 January 2020).
3. For example, Hadi Al-Abdullah, a journalist and activist, presented his reports to camera holding a microphone in a conventional reporter style, as demonstrated in *Cries from Syria*.
4. This preference for activists' materials (rather than the regime's) also tacitly reflected their countries' foreign policy positions (Zhang and Luther 2019: 20). Lynch et al. note that Syrian opposition groups operated as gatekeepers to this at first glance unmediated flow of footage, prioritising that footage which would reinforce their narrative of peaceful protest and the effects of regime violence. They further note that as armed protest increased and anti-Assad

militias including Islamist groups became more prevalent, this complicated North American and European news narratives, which tended to focus more on the humanitarian consequences of the ongoing war (2014: 8–9).
5. These women filmmakers take their place in a longer history of female creatives' participation in Syrian dissent. She, alongside many others, including journalist Yara Badr (Halasa et al. 2014: xi) and novelist Samar Yazbek (Yazbek 2012), were forced into exile under threat of imprisonment or death in the current conflict.
6. Even before the revolution, legislation did not deal adequately with honour killings or rape within marriage, and the stigma of rape fell squarely on the victim.
7. First her own camera and then a camera provided to her by Channel 4 News.
8. Some of the material was previously communicated through Channel 4 News, who recruited her to offer on-the-ground access to the besieged Aleppo. Nina Grønlykke Mollerup and Mette Mortensen have noted the power imbalance that maintains Syrian filmmakers in bodily, professional and economic precarity while the receiving news media organisation benefits from the footage and its cultural currency (2018). Al-Kateab took huge risks to gather the footage, but unusually Channel 4 News awarded her a staff contract with insurance to recognise this, a perk not available to most of her peers (Mollerup and Mortensen 2018: 14). Al-Kateab has subsequently garnered professional recognition for her journalism and her filmmaking.

Works Cited

Adler-Nissen, Rebecca, Andersen, Katrine Emilie and Hansen, Lene (2020) 'Images, Emotions, and International Politics: The Death of Alan Kurdi', *Review of International Studies*, 46 (1), pp. 75–95.

Al-Ghazzi, Omar (2019) 'An Archetypal Digital Witness: The Child Figure and the Media Conflict over Syria', *International Journal of Communication*, 13, pp. 3225–43 <https://link.gale.com/apps/doc/A609924424/AONE?u=rdg&sid=AONE&xid=261ad376> (last accessed 26 January 2020).

Al-Om, Tamara (2014) 'Syria's "Arab Spring": Women and the Struggle to Live in Truth', in Larbi Sadiki (ed.), *Routledge Handbook of the Arab Spring: Rethinking Democratization*. London: Routledge, pp. 273–84.

Andén-Papadopoulos, Kari and Pantti, Mervi (2013) 'The Media Work of Syrian Diaspora Activists: Brokering between the Protest and Mainstream Media', *International Journal of Communication*, 7, pp. 2185–206 <https://ijoc.org/index.php/ijoc/article/view/1841/996> (last accessed 25 January 2020).

Asha, Karel (2013) '"Mothers at Home and Activists on the Street?" The Role of Women in the Syrian Revolution of 2011–2012', *McGill International Review*, 2 (3), pp. 50–65.

Aufderheide, Patriica (1997) 'Public Intimacy: The Development of First-person Documentary', *Afterimage*, 25 (1), pp. 16–18.

Barnard, Anne (2016) 'How Omran Daqneesh, 5, Became a Symbol of Aleppo's Suffering', *New York Times*, 18 August <https://www.nytimes.com/2016/08/19/world/middleeast/omran-daqneesh-syria-aleppo.html> (last accessed 25 January 2020).

Belhassen, Souhayr et al. (2013) 'Syria', in *Women and the Arab Spring: Taking Their Place?* Paris: International Federation for Human Rights, pp. 54–61.

Boltanski, Luc (1999) *Distant Suffering. Politics, Morality and the Media*. Cambridge: Cambridge University Press.

Campbell, David (2004) 'Horrific Blindness: Images of Death in Contemporary Media', *Journal for Cultural Research*, 8 (1), pp. 55–74.

Channel 4 Staff Writer (2017) 'Channel 4 News Wins International Emmy for News' (6 October) <https://www.channel4.com/news/channel-4-news-wins-international-emmy-for-news> (last accessed at 26 January 2020).

Chouliaraki, Lilie (2006) *The Spectatorship of Suffering*. London: Sage.

Frontline Club (2019) Screening of *For Sama* and Q&A with Waad al-Kateab and Ben de Pear (Channel 4 Head of News) on 21 October, video available at <https://www.frontlineclub.com/for-sama-qa/> (last accessed 10 February 2020).

Gissi, Angela (2020) 'Countering Depoliticized Representations of Syrian Women: Memories of Dictatorship from Pre-war Syria', *Gender, Place and Culture*, 20 January, pp. 1–21.

Halasa, Malu, Omareen, Zaher and Mahfoud, Nawara (eds) (2014) *Syria Speaks: Art and Culture From the Frontline*. London: Saqi Books.

Human Rights and Gender Justice Clinic, City University of New York School of Law, MADRE and the Women's International League for Peace and Freedom (2016), 'Human Rights Violations Against Women and Girls in Syria', Submission to the United Nations Universal Periodic Review of the Syrian Arab Republic, 26th Session of the UPR Working Group of the Human Rights Council (24 March), New York and Geneva <https://www.upr-info.org/sites/default/files/document/syrian_arab_republic/session_26_-_november_2016/js7_upr26_syr_e_main.pdf> (last accessed 27 May 2020).

Human Rights Watch (2019) 'Syria: Events of 2018', *World Report 2019* <https://www.hrw.org/world-report/2019/country-chapters/syria> (last accessed 25 January 2020).

Khosrokhavar, Farhad (2016) *The New Arab Revolutions That Shook the World*. Abingdon: Routledge.

Lynch, Marc, Freelon, Deen and Aday, Sean (2014) 'Syria's Socially Mediated Civil War', *Peaceworks*, 9 (January). United States Institute of Peace, pp. 1–33.

McDowall, Angus and Roche, Andrew (2018) 'Syrian Observatory Says War Has Killed More Than Half a Million', *Reuters* (12 March) <https://www.reuters.com/article/us-mideast-crisis-syria/syrian-observatory-says-war-has-killed-more-than-half-a-million-idUSKCN1GO13M> (last accessed 27 May 2020).

McHugo, John (2014), *Syria: A Recent History*. London: Saqi Books.

Macleod, Hugh and Flamand, Annasofie (2011) 'Tortured and Killed: Hamza al-Khateeb, Age 13', *Al Jazeera* news site, 31 May <https://www.aljazeera.com/indepth/features/2011/05/201153185927813389.html> (last accessed 20 January 2020).

Malkki, Liisa (2010) 'Children, Humanity, and the Infantilization of Peace', in Ilana Feldman and Miriam Ticktin (eds), *In the Name of Humanity: The Government of Threat and Care.* Durham, NC: Duke University Press, pp. 58–85.

Mast, Jelle and Hanegreefs, Samuel (2015) 'When News Media Turn To Citizen-Generated Images of War', *Digital Journalism*, 3 (4), pp. 594–614.

Moeller, Susan (2002) 'A Hierarchy of Innocence: The Media's Use of Children in the Telling of International News', *Harvard International Journal of Press/Politics*, 7 (1), pp. 36–56.

Mollerup, Nina Grønlykke and Mortensen, Mette (2018) 'Proximity and Distance in the Mediation of Suffering: Local Photographers in War-torn Aleppo and the International Media Circuit', *Journalism* (August), pp. 1–17.

Organisation for the Prohibition of Chemical Weapons (OPCW) (2019) 'Note by the Technical Secretariat: Report of the Fact-finding Mission Regarding the Incident of Alleged Use of Toxic Chemicals as a Weapon in Douma, Syrian Arab Republic, on 7 April 2018' (1 March) <https://www.opcw.org/sites/default/files/documents/2019/03/s-1731-2019%28e%29.pdf> (last accessed 25 January 2020).

Rice, Xan, Marsh, Katherine, Finn, Tom, Sherwood, Harriet, Chrisafis, Angelique and Booth, Robert (2011) 'Women Have Emerged as Key Players in the Arab Spring', *The Guardian*, 22 April <https://www.theguardian.com/world/2011/apr/22/women-arab-spring> (last accessed 26 January 2020).

Saxton, Libby (2010) 'Ethics, Spectatorship and the Spectacle of Suffering', in Lisa Downing and Libby Saxton (eds), *Film and Ethics: Foreclosed Encounters.* London and New York: Routledge, pp. 62–75.

Sontag, Susan (2003) *Regarding the Pain of Others.* London: Penguin Books.

UNICEF (2019) 'Whole of Syria Humanitarian Situation Report' (December) <https://www.unicef.org/appeals/files/UNICEF_Whole_of_Syria_Humanitarian_Situation_Report_Dec_2019.pdf> (last accessed 26 January 2020).

Verma, Sonia (2011) 'How a 13-year-old Became a Symbol of Syrian Revolution', *Toronto: The Globe and Mail*, 1 June <https://www.theglobeandmail.com/news/world/how-a-13-year-old-became-a-symbol-of-syrian-revolution/article4260803/> (last accessed 12 December 2019).

Wall, Melissa and el Zahed, Sahar (2015), 'Syrian Citizen Journalism: A Pop-up News Ecology in an Authoritarian Space', *Digital Journalism*, 3 (5), pp. 720–36.

Ya Libnan News Staff Writer (2010) 'Syrian Human Rights [*sic*] Demands Release of Raghda Hassan', *Ya Libnan News*, 16 February <https://yalibnan.com/2010/02/16/syrian-human-rights-demands-release-of-raghda-hassan/> (last accessed 10 January 2020).

Yassin-Kassab, Robin and Al-Shami, Leila (2016) *Burning Country: Syrians in Revolution and War.* London: Pluto Press.

Yazbek, Samar (2012) *A Woman in the Crossfire: Diaries of the Syrian Revolution*, trans. Max Weiss. London: Haus.

Zhang, Xu and Luther, Catherine A. (2019) 'Transnational News Media Coverage of Distant Suffering in the Syrian Civil War: An Analysis of CNN, Al-Jazeera English and Sputnik Online News', *Media, War and Conflict* (May), pp. 1–6.

CHAPTER 10

Marie Colvin – The War Hero and the 'Nasty Woman'

Agnieszka Piotrowska

Preliminary Remarks

There are many ways of beginning this chapter about the iconic war correspondent Marie Colvin, as it is about a number of things. First, I am writing it using different registers deliberately. It continues my persistent attempts in my work to push the boundaries of what might be acceptable in academic writing, here combining the biographical accounts of somebody's life with theoretical concepts. Because of the nature of the subject matter, my registers will include an autoethnographic mode too, and an almost journalistic register at times, next to a rigorous and appropriately referenced scholarly analysis. This chapter is therefore a piece of practice research too, and the research is about the writing and the combining of these different registers. This writing, which includes first-person narrative, is in itself a gesture of subversion in academia. That this piece is about Marie Colvin, a female figure who is both very powerful but also controversial, demands a particular kind of writing.

In my work (2014, 2017, 2019, 2020) I have heralded the importance of subjective accounts particularly for women. This is not a new way of thinking about knowledge and goes back to Donna Haraway's writings about 'situated knowledges' (1988: 581), particularly regarding challenging knowledge claims and female authorship. In the academy this kind of approach is gaining traction but it is still considered radical. Haraway argues for

> politics and epistemologies of location, positioning, and situating, where partiality and not universality is the condition of being heard to make rational knowledge claims. These are claims on people's lives. I am arguing for the view from a body, always a complex, contradictory, structuring, and structured body, versus the view from above, from nowhere, from simplicity. (Ibid.: 589)

In what follows I seek to deploy a 'view from a body' to challenge normative interpretations of Colvin's life. 'Autoethnography' and 'reflexivity' are but labels, attempting to make something fundamentally fluid, deeply subjective and even emotional at times, more than 'scientific', 'objective' or at least 'scholarly'. Tessa Muncey in the preface to her book *Creating Autoethnographies* (2010) states boldly the purpose of using autoethnography alongside other more established and more obviously scholarly research methods, which is 'to contribute to or *subvert the dominant discourses* that underpin much of our research, [for which] strategies and techniques need to be found for portraying experiences that don't rely on the affinity of shared assumptions' (Muncey 2010: xi, my emphasis). She goes on to identify the reader for her book: 'there may be those who want to include a personal story in their study or paper and want to find a theoretical justification to do so' (ibid.: xii). She says that this kind of register often offers a missing story in the otherwise predictable academic voice.

For Muncey, and others who will be evoked henceforth, 'autoethnography' is any account which uses the first-person narrative of the author, relying on the latter's memory, photographs, letters and, importantly, feelings. She argues for using 'the highly personal' alongside 'the highly scholarly' – in

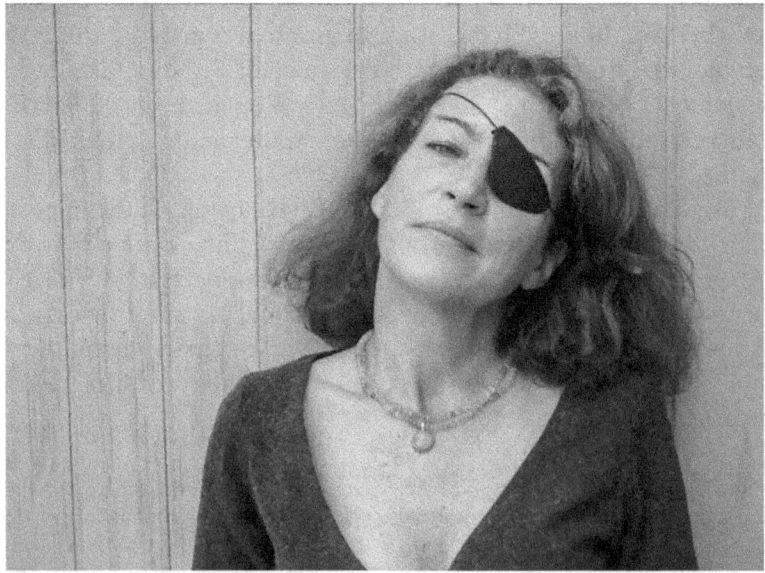

Figure 10.1 Marie Colvin on holiday in France in 2008. Image courtesy of Richard Flaye.

the interests of furthering 'knowledge' and indeed scholarship itself (ibid.: 44). In more recent scholarship Mary Harrod (2018), building on work on the importance of female autobiography (Young 1990; Smith 1993), details how the acknowledgement of the female embodied encounter with the world can translate itself into a particular creativity (in her essay this is about Lena Dunham but clearly it is relevant to female creativity as a whole). I am always fond of quoting Kaja Silverman (1988) who suggested more than thirty years ago that the issues of male and female subjectivity in cinema and elsewhere are deeply linked to the voice with which they speak – figuratively and literally. She notes that 'male subjectivity is most fully realised . . . when it is least visible [. . .] – female subjectivity is most fully achieved . . . when it is visible' (Silverman 1988: 164). She also adds: 'the crucial project with respect to the female voice is to find a place from which it can speak and be heard, not to strip it of discursive rights' (ibid.: 192). Writing which uses personal experience is almost always perceived as transgressive in some way. This chapter about this highly transgressive figure in a volume about transgression uses these transgressive writing methods advisedly.

The Myth and the Legend

On a basic level, ßmy chapter is about a powerful and brilliant war correspondent, Marie Colvin, who was murdered by the extreme patriarchal regime in Syria in February 2012, while on assignment in Homs. There are difficulties in discussing Marie Colvin for, in the few short years since her passing, a number of different narratives have emerged. I am very interested in how we lose control over our narratives – particular as women, and particularly when we die. By 2012 Marie was already a famous journalist and a transgressive figure, an impression which is conveyed in the fictional and documentary accounts of her life. She had already been injured and suffered while in the field covering war for *The Sunday Times*. She was single, sexually liberated and by her own account haunted by her demons which included PTSD and substance abuse, as presented in the documentaries about her life in which she took part when still alive (*Bearing Witness* (Bob Eisenhardt, Barbara Kopple and Marijana Wotton, 2005)), or those created after her killing (*Under The Wire* (Chris Martin, 2018)), or in the fiction in which her character was played by the Hollywood star Rosamund Pike (*A Private War* (Matthew Heineman (2018)). In these accounts she emerges as a powerful and brilliant figure who made her own rules, was ambitious in a man's world, who was bold, successful and driven, committed to the truth but also almost mentally ill towards the end. Her unmatched commitment to the stories she told and the people about whom she wrote should rightly be held up as a role model for any aspiring journalist, regardless of gender; clearly she constitutes a great role model for young women, and she earned the admiration, too, of her colleagues; photojournalist Paul Conroy in his account of her death calls her 'the Martha Gellhorn of our generation' and 'my Chechen queen' (2013: 222).

Lindsey Hilsum's biography *In Extremis: The Life of War Correspondent Marie Colvin* (2018) has a clear aim: to create a narrative which in some way is more than a sum of facts. It contributes to the legend of Marie Colvin which Hilsum aspires to create or at least contribute to – as a tribute to her friend Marie as much as an iconic war journalist. It is that biography in which I am most interested in this short chapter. Before I proceed any further, I need to say very clearly that I like Hilsum's book, my reservations notwithstanding. It is here where my own autobiographic mode will be deployed because I believe it contributes something to a discussion about the legend of Marie Colvin. Hilsum situates Colvin unapologetically in relation to the myth of the heroic war reporter: Colvin went further, endured more and took greater risks than any of the other reporters around her. Hilsum's statement, 'The fact that Marie was a woman just added to her allure' (ibid.: 220), is revealing, however. Some of the ways in which Hilsum frames Colvin's choices draw on normative ideas about so-called unruly women that are worth highlighting. I am here engaging in conversation with Hilsum's storytelling regarding what kind of narrative of Marie's final stretch and her final decision-making is being presented to the world, in order to highlight and challenge the gender politics of this myth-making, and highlight its links to the cultural framing of other female figures who undermine patriarchal systems: the 'nasty woman' and the femme fatale.

In my work on documentaries, I have observed how often the subjects of documentary films grow to dislike their representation on the screen. This is, I have suggested, not directly connected to whether that representation is positive or not. It is rather a sense of the uncanny, of the double that somebody else presents to the world on our behalf (see, for example, Piotrowska 2014: 171–91). It is the sense of losing control over one's narrative. As Marie Colvin is dead, the control over her narrative is now in the hands of historians, journalists and filmmakers. Because of the way she died and because of her glamorous persona, she lends herself not just to being mythologised, but in fact to becoming the heroine of a legend.

It is beyond the scope of this chapter to discuss the notion of a 'legend' in any great detail but the ground-breaking book of Hippolyte Delehaye (1907) on the lives and legends of the saints is useful to clarify the distinctiveness of the concept of the legend and its relevance to this writing. In terms of the

Figure 10.2 Marie Colvin on the Thames, on the old boat she shared with Richard Flaye. Image courtesy of Richard Flaye.

female saints, the notion of expiation through sacrifice has a time-honoured tradition in the Catholic church and the saint is often tortured by barbaric men. Delehaye makes an important distinction between the myth and the legend, the former being totally fantastical: 'The essence of the myth consists in the personification of a force or of an abstract idea; or, if you prefer it, the myth is simply an explanation of natural phenomena adapted to the capacity of a primitive people (ibid.: 12). The legend on the other hand is based on a true person but the interpretation of the events can lead to quite significant and sometimes fantastical differences (ibid.: 13). He explains further that a legend 'refers imaginary events to some real personage, or it localises romantic stories in some definite spot'.

> The development of the legend is, according to our definition, the outcome of an unconscious or unreflecting agent acting upon historical material. It is the introduction of the subjective element into the realm of fact. If, the day after a battle, we were to collect the narratives of eye-witnesses, we should find the action described in twenty different ways while identical details would be related from the most diverse points of view with the same accent of sincerity. (Ibid.: 15)

It is here that the personal knowledge of the person in question is important.

My Neighbour Marie Colvin

We were not close but we were neighbours and friends as she used to live five minutes from my house, and when her last lover and my good friend Richard Flaye moved into the area the friendship intensified. I had dinner with them both often; I had been to their parties. I accompanied them on their old boat up and down the Thames, so yes, I did know her quite well. This knowledge is a little more than acknowledging the position from which I speak, paraphrasing Antonio Gramsci (1982), a little more than making up an inventory, as Edward Said (2003) would have it.[1] This knowledge gives some an insight to the distance between the narratives presented – at least the one of the very last stretch of Marie Colvin's life – and the narrative I know and believe to be true, and in particular the way her last romantic relationship, with Richard Flaye, is refracted through these differing narratives. Hilsum's account, in which this last relationship is associated finally with betrayal, feeds into a bigger picture of what a woman who transgresses the rules of convention must expect in life and must be punished for even by those who ought to love and protect her. That narrative to my mind disempowers Marie Colvin and it is for that reason I want to offer a counter-narrative here through my own autobiographical account. A longer reflection about why the narrative of anybody's life is as important, at times as important or even more important than their work, demands a more thorough thinking through and there is not space for that within the constraints of this chapter. In Colvin's case it is possible that her way of reporting the war, her first-person narratives, have contributed to the interest in who the reporter was. Certainly we can see her as part of the tradition of feminist autobiographical writing that I have already invoked; in her case, operating in the context of war reporting, her narratives concerned the lived experience of the people – often women – she encountered in these conflict zones.

Marie Colvin's persona as a brilliant, multi award-winning and unassailably talented journalist who died defying the Assad regime and her own fear will stand shining no matter what I or anybody else will write now or in future. She was a unique and powerful individual and journalist. Her legacy, including the price she paid to follow through her desire, will no doubt live forever too; rightly so. She got to places that nobody else did including such war zones as Chechnya, Palestine, the Tamil territories where she lost her eye to a grenade, and of course Syria, where she went a few times and ended up losing her life. She occupies therefore a particular position in the collective psyche which already is beginning to be more legendary than her professional achievements alone. I am interested in thinking through further what that position might be. The most important facts of Marie Colvin's life and death are clear and, fairly recently, we discovered that her death was no war accident, that it was a planned assassination by the regime, as her stories went a long way in undermining that regime's credibility. One could further say, therefore, that the personal details of her last love relationships are in this context unimportant, as I wouldn't be writing about her if not for her professional successes and the manner of her death. And yet I argue that it is important to consider her final decisions and choices, and her relationship with Richard Flaye, as the narrative offered by Lindsey Hilsum in *In Extremis: The Life of War Correspondent Marie Colvin* (2018) casts Colvin as the victim of an allegedly unscrupulous man, speculating that this may even have contributed to her decision to go back to Syria. This seems at odds with the desire to capture Colvin as she was, and alongside my autobiographical reflections below, I suggest it is instead more productive to see Marie Colvin's final stretch as a triumphant march of a difficult woman – even a femme fatale at times – who pursued her destiny to the end no matter what, of not 'giving up on one's desire' – of which more later.

'The Nasty Woman'

In writing about Marie Colvin I have multiple motivations and reasons for doing so while at the same time I am anxious about the project. As a brilliant and unconventional journalist, Marie Colvin fits perfectly into my category of 'the nasty woman', which I have developed and written about (Piotrowska 2019). This 'nasty woman' is a good person, but she is 'nasty' in order to subvert convention so that she can and does fight patriarchal systems. There are two problems with framing Marie Colvin as a 'nasty woman' of the kind I describe in my book: first of all, my book focused on cinema and mostly (although not exclusively) on fictional characters. However, the concept of the 'nasty woman' is rooted in real historical figures: the whole concept stems from the famous exchange between Donald Trump and Hillary Clinton during the 2016 election campaign (Clinton 2017: 136). I also evoke other historical nasty women such as Artimesia Gileneschi (Bal 2006), and Sarah Polley and her documentary film *Stories We Tell* (2013), in which I suggest that both the filmmaker and her mother (which the film is about) are examples of 'the nasty woman'. The second issue has to do with Marie Colvin's attitude towards being a feminist – or at least her stated attitude towards feminism. At Yale, where she studied, she did not take the Gender Studies class and was even quoted as saying she despised the on-the-nose attitudes of feminism (Hilsum 2018: 40). Her attitude to fellow women was not always sisterly – although most if not all her best friends were women. Despite her bold life and her uncompromising attitude, it is a fact that she did not define herself as a feminist, perhaps either misunderstanding the term or just because she was fond of being a counter-proposition to almost everything.

However, the narrative of her life and work, her bravery and professional achievements notwithstanding, could be positioned almost exactly within the parameters of my nasty woman concept: even her attitude to men was often that of a femme fatale – beautiful, dangerous, sexually dangerous and ultimately dead before her time. In the next section, I will recall briefly some of my ideas pertaining to the archetype of the 'nasty woman', in particular Antigone's stance of 'not giving up one one's desire', and connect these with Marie Colvin (Lacan [1959–60] 1992: 305).

Don't Give Up on Your Desire

I have written extensively about Antigone elsewhere (Piotrowska 2014, 2019) and I will evoke her here again, even though she is problematic as a role model. Nonetheless, it is relevant to my discussion of Marie Colvin. Lacan interpreted Sophocles' Antigone in his Seminar VII (*The Ethics of Psychoanalysis*) (1986, 1992) My theorisation of the 'nasty woman' therefore begins with the Lacanian notion of the ethical act consisting of 'not giving up on one's desire' and, once the commitment is made, to be able to be faithful to it 'beyond the limit' as Lacan puts it (Lacan [1959–60] 1992: 305) or 'to the end' in Žižek's words (1989). Antigone is the protagonist of Sophocles' play written in 441 BC about the daughter of Oedipus who disobeys the current ruler of her kingdom, Creon, as she insists on performing several times the act of burial of her deceased brother Polyneices, knowing as she does that the act will evoke the fury of Creon and will result in her certain death. In the event, despite the repeated and increasingly desperate pleas of her family, including her sister Ismene and fiancée Haemon (who happens to be Creon's son) she carries on with the repeated attempts to bury her brother; her punishment is to be buried alive in a cave. When Creon changes his mind too late and breaks the entrance to the cave, Antigone is found already dead, having committed suicide, presumably choosing her agency again over a slow and painful death by starvation. As a direct result of her actions, her fiancée commits suicide too, as does his mother. Creon is a broken man and the whole kingdom is left in ruins.

Antigone, her dazzling beauty in her determination to do the thing she is committed to, has fascinated scholars, poets and writers for centuries. She has been appropriated by the feminist icon Luce Irigaray (1985, 1991, 1997) and the radical thinker Judith Butler (2003).[2] Bonnie Honig, in her fascinating book *Antigone Interrupted* (2013), offers both a review of the scholarly work to date on Antigone as well as her own interpretations of what she might mean in the history of ideas and defiant stances against male authority. Marie Colvin's determination to be faithful to her mission and her desire fits into this archetype well. But of course Marie Colvin is more than just Antigone-like – she has a connection to another archetypal figure: the femme fatale.

Figure 10.3 Marie Colvin and Richard Flaye at a family party in 2008. Image courtesy of Richard Flaye.

The Femme Fatale as a Transgressive Figure

One of the iterations of 'the nasty woman' I argue in my book (2019) is the cinematic figure of the femme fatale. A femme fatale does not choose sacrifice most of the time, not the one that would involve her in any event. She appears to like sex and at times uses her sexuality to achieve her goals. The femme fatale has been the subject of some disagreements as to whether she is but a male fantasy or whether she might be relevant to contemporary feminism (see, for example, Doane 1991; Copjec 1993; Cowie 1997; Bronfen 2004, and many others). She is usually immoral and beautiful. Both as a male fantasy and as a representation of female power, she holds endless appeal which, I would argue, originates not only from her sexuality and beauty, but because she offers a way out of the rigid patriarchal systems of power and authority – which are also tediously restricting even for those who benefit from these conservative patterns – namely men.

In the heyday of femmes fatales in the 1940s (in films such as, for example, *Double Indemnity* (Billy Wilder, 1944) or *The Postman Always Rings Twice* (Tay Garnett, 1946)), she might have been the sole figure fracturing male dominance in Hollywood narratives – but she was allowed to do so briefly – for the spectator's fun, before being disempowered. Traditionally, this transient fantasy is immediately exposed as 'nasty' – it is far too dangerous to let a character who manipulates men live her independent life – and so she is usually killed off (a trope very familiar from the Gothic novels and operas), or perhaps occasionally gets domesticated. The difference between the story of Antigone and the narratives of these contemporary films and the neo-femmes fatales created by female writers and directors is that they do not perish. A sacrifice is often called for and delivered – but not the final one. Here sadly Marie Colvin of course differs and does sacrifice her life. It is because of this tragic ending that it is even more important to be very careful how one constructs the final narrative leading to her death.

Not a Broken Heart

In literature and popular perception the 'nasty woman' who becomes nasty after traumatic love experiences, sexual violations and disappointments, and who is driven to madness by men, is a trope that becomes a very popular and familiar one in Gothic novels, including those written by women in the late eighteenth, nineteenth and early twentieth centuries. The notion of insanity or hysteria, which might appear a way out of the patriarchal system, has been prevalent throughout the nineteenth and twentieth centuries with works such as Horace Walpole's *The Castle of Otranto* (1764), Walter Scott's *The Bride of Lammermoor* (1819), Ann Radcliffe's *The Mysteries of Udolpho* (1794), Jane Austen's *Northanger Abbey* (1817) and Emily Brontë's *Wuthering Heights* (1847). The heroines in these novels are usually stripped of their agency in the main narrative of the story and their nastiness becomes a desperate gesture that usually leads to their death – not as a conscious sacrifice but rather as an inevitable consequence of their madness. The message conveyed by these works is clear: any gesture against the hetero-normative ideals is a highly risky affair and will leave the one who attempts it totally disempowered and probably dead before long.

One could interpret Marie Colvin's assassination as a continuation of the line of these women except for one huge difference: Marie Colvin is more akin to Antigone as she has her agency intact to the end. Lindsey Hilsum in her *Guardian* article quotes the judgement of the US court: '"She was specifically targeted because of her profession, for the purpose of silencing those reporting on the growing opposition movement in the country," wrote Judge Amy Berman Jackson of the US District Court in Washington DC' (Hilsum 2019). Colvin chooses to stay in order to fight on, in order to get at the truth as she saw it and not to succumb to the evil dictator. It is the moment of her decision to go back to Syria, the rationale for it, the clarity of her vision that I believe is important here. It is clear to me that Lindsey Hilsum's book and the *Vanity Fair* article on which the fictionalised film is based (Brenner 2012) do not intend on a conscious level to diminish Marie Colvin's ability to decide clearly and rationally for herself whether she wanted to continue her work as a war correspondent or not. Nonetheless, it is almost impossible to throw off the cultural heritage of the perception that only a mad woman would want to go back to the danger again. The Richard Flaye narrative (of which more later) also feeds into the archetype of the sexually free woman always needing to be punished.

Culturally, there are stories and indeed operas in which the nasty and sexually unconventional woman moves away from her position of some power over men (be it through her sexuality) to a position of sacrifice and a necessary death (to atone for her nastiness) – the famous and influential novella by Alexandre Dumas *The Lady of Camellias* (*La Dame aux Camélias*) (1848), then made into numerous theatre adaptations and then the famous opera by Verdi, *La Traviata* (1852), are but some examples. It was also the subject of multiple film and television adaptations; the public taste for a tale of a fallen woman redeemed by love but still having to be punished is quite remarkable. Puccini's *La Bohème* (1896) has a nasty fallen woman too who is redeemed in her sacrifice for the man she loves. The death of the woman, nasty and tainted despite her newly attained purity, is obviously a necessary quality of this work. This trope was very popular in early cinema too, in films starring Pola Negri such as *Mania* (1918), *Madam Dubarry* (1919), *Das Martyrium* (1921) and others. Another fantasy of a nasty woman who tries to defy the patriarchal order only to be killed by a betrayed lover is George Bizet's *Carmen* (1875) (based on a story of the same name written by Prosper Mérimée, which indeed became one of Pola Negri's great roles in 1920). We love Carmen stating boldly to Don Jose, who at this point is her husband and not just a lover any more: 'I don't want to be harassed and above all I don't want anyone telling me what to do. I want to be free and do what I like' (Mérimée 1980: 95). But, it is very clear that her (sexual) freedom cannot last and her way of living is doomed: Don Jose begs her to give it up but she, Antigone-like, refuses and so has to die: nastiness does not pay in the patriarchal world. The extraordinary thing about Marie Colvin's life and death is that she did embody the fantasy of freedom and made it her own, being so much more than any of these characters. She could and did say many a time: 'I don't want anyone telling me what to do. I want to be free and do what I like.'

It is here, then, that the war journalist Marie Colvin fits in, even if it feels blasphemous to suggest that Marie Colvin inhabits the archetype of 'the nasty woman' and the neo-femme fatale. It is important to state that her often personal reporting set new standards for the female voice in war journalism. Her unconventionality did create a dent in the expectation of what a woman journalist was capable of doing and the stories she was able to write about, acknowledging at times her position as a woman. In that way, Marie Colvin arguably surpassed her great journalist heroine Martha Gellhorn. The boldness in her personal life translated directly into her approach to her journalism: unconventional, uncompromising and finally demanding the ultimate sacrifice.

In Extremis

Lindsey Hilsum, in *In Extremis: The Life of War Correspondent Marie Colvin* (2018), does meticulous work piecing together the narrative of Marie's life and work based on a variety of sources, including interviews with her friends, lovers, husbands and collaborators, and archive materials of various kinds, which provide valuable data. However, the book's unique feature is the author's access to Marie's diaries and journals, which she kept over decades and from which Hilsum quotes extensively and which therefore become a guiding light to her investigations.

From Hilsum's book some things become clear early on. In the late 1970s, Marie felt the pressure of her family and friends, and that which she put on herself too: 'everyone around me expects me to succeed' (ibid.: 48), and then: 'how was she to satisfy her ambition without negating her femininity?' (ibid.: 49). She was writing these words as a student at Yale and then a very young journalist: she was very clear very early on that she wanted to be successful on her own terms. Her feminine sense of beauty and the power that comes with it in a patriarchal system was something she wanted to hold onto. At the age of twenty-four she actually states in her diary she wants to be a 'bad girl' and she wants to be a great iconic professional success at the same time – but also interestingly and controversially that she wants something sexual in her rebellion. She did in fact want to be a *femme fatale* of sorts, but also she wanted recognition for her intellectual and journalist talents, and later for her bravery and skill. Here is one of her entries:

22nd May 1980: For those of us who want to break out, be a bad girl, there are no role models, nor the chance of earning recognition a la Norman Mailer, James Dean, Marlon Brando. Something sexual, desirable in their rebellion. (Ibid.: 49)

As the years went by and she was learning and doing her various apprenticeships at local newspapers Colvin was reflecting on what kind of journalist she wanted to be, and that was to follow the traditions of John Hersey and Martha Gellhorn, telling individual stories of the victims and the survivors of war. She also wanted to build on the traditions of the famous Italian writer and thinker Orlana Fallaci, who specialised in in-depth interviews with world leaders. That Colvin did do, in due course, in particular with her interviews with Muammar Gaddafi and PLO chairman Yasser Arafat (Ibid.:114)

As Hilsum's account of her diaries attests, the tension between her ambitions to become a journalistic star and her desires for love and affection became a feature of her whole life, alternately falling in love with men who then were incapable of being faithful to her and then Marie herself hurting various men who loved her. There has been a certain repetitiveness about these experiences which one can only see perhaps from the distance of time. She married a fellow journalist, Patrick Bishop, in 1989 only to discover that he was involved in a long-term romance with another journalist, a French woman (ibid.:125), even during their wedding. Marie discovered this soon after in 1990 through a message on an answer phone and was deeply distraught, feeling that their every moment together was a lie, the exact feelings and words which she came to utter when she discovered, or went out of her way to discover, Richard Flaye's infidelities almost twenty years later. Hilsum points out that during the time of the Patrick Bishop fiasco, Marie was 'saved' by her work and her trip to Iraq (ibid.:126). I question the framing of it and will return to it in due course.

In the decade that followed, Marie Colvin kept going from strength to strength in her work as the war correspondent for *The Sunday Times*. She famously covered the first Iraq war and then the Chechnya conflict, which really put her on the map as an accomplished professional. She married again, got pregnant, miscarried a few times, got divorced again and got together with Patrick again which was problematic in itself and ultimately did not work. Hilsum quotes from Marie Colvin's diary entry for 24 December 1999, in which, still in Chechnya, she expresses her sense of loneliness and her doubts about her life, and about Patrick:

> I think he does love me but it's a love where he wants his own life and me to fit into it, hard to describe even to myself, because he doesn't want me around all the time, more knowing I'm there and the comfort of time together. (Ibid: 216)

She did make it home to her mother for the New Year and her sensational escape through the Caucasus Mountains was unprecedented and felt like a sequence out of *Mission Impossible*. She was a woman and she was making it her own.

It is also important to say, and Hilsum stresses it, that Marie found her own voice, which was personal and focused on the individual suffering of the people she would meet and write about. 'The people I meet and my reactions to them – that is part of the story' (ibid.: 221), she wrote, and sounded as if she had read not only the Kaja Silverman work quoted above but also the famous discussions of anthropologists including Clifford Geertz (1988) who would maintain that pretending in any situation to be 'objective' and not including oneself in the story is false (These conversations of course are still ongoing in the academy, in journalism and in the media.) Colvin was committed to her own form of a 'situated knowledge' (Haraway 1988). She believed in collapsing the distance between herself and those she wrote about rather than somehow building it: 'if you go in bare and eat what they eat, drink what they drink, sleep where they sleep, there is less separation' (Hilsum 2018: 221). Many journalists, including her ex-husband Patrick Bishop but also many others, believed that a distance between the reporter and the story was a necessary condition for objective reporting. Academic Sherry Ricchiardi, in an interview piece quoted in Hilsum's book, says, 'That means gaining access to places that have been declared off-limits by one side or other in a conflict. It is here that she becomes vulnerable' (ibid.: 221; Ricchiardi 2001: 46). Colvin's journalism was passionate, subjective, but still rigorous. She told stories of what she saw in the war, focusing on the individual suffering, often of women and children, but she was also reflective about her own position in it. That in itself was a radical feminist gesture whether she wanted it to be or not. That may have also been the reason why she did not leave Homs when there was still time to do so and live to tell another story. In her last email to Richard Flaye from Syria she said: 'It is so hard to witness what is going on here and I only have words' (ibid.: 357).

Lindsey Hilsum here offers an interesting analysis and an observation regarding Colvin's bosses, her editors at *The Sunday Times* who embraced Marie's risk-taking for reasons of their own, in order to get unusual stories, to keep being the best no matter what the risk. The creation of Marie Colvin the female journalist extraordinaire was not just an Antigonian 'don't give up on your desire' pursuit, was not only her own bravery and skill but it was also the creation of the figure which would sell newspapers. There was a convergence of interests here, which suited both Marie Colvin and the newspaper. The representation of the wars she covered was her own although at times her copy was cut back, which she despised and which happened less frequently as she became famous. Her risk-taking was a calculated programme: she wanted to be better than other journalists in order to build her power base. According to Hilsum her friends approached the editors and the senior management of *The Sunday Times* asking them to consider Marie's safety and hold her back, but they felt it was not their responsibility. It was no doubt up to her to create boundaries but she chose not to do that. 'Bearing witness' was undoubtedly one principle but so was the maintaining of her unique position as the war correspondent who got stories nobody else did. And so instead of slowing down, she went on to another war and another, getting herself severely injured by a grenade in Sri Lanka and losing her eye and becoming not so much Medusa but rather the figure conjuring both fear and admiration, a one-eyed pirate.

All Is Fair in Love and War

Marie Colvin met Richard Flaye in 2005 at a party as described in Lindsey's book. At that point I had known Richard quite well for at least five years. He was the live-in partner of a close friend of mine, a fact bracketed completely in Hilsum's book, perhaps because Marie's role in the breakup of that family was problematic. By 2005 various cracks had begun to appear in this previous relationship, and it ended soon after, when my friend somehow logged into Richard's computer to discover evidence of his multiple affairs, including the one with Marie Colvin, and ended the relationship. When, years later, Lindsey Hilsum describes Marie Colvin finding out about Richard Flaye's affairs through using his passwords and hacking into his emails, the story is almost identical to the one in which Marie Colvin was the mistress and not the betrayed woman. Yet even Lindsey Hilsum's unsympathetic account of Richard admits that he announced up front his 'hedonist' life. He warned Marie as to who he was, and she did of course know, as she was one of his affairs before becoming the main story. Given this, I believe it is not helpful, correct or even desirable from the point of view of curating Marie Colvin's legend to suggest that somehow, towards the end of her life, she became a victim of a bad man or indeed, as previously mentioned, I refute any suggestion that her work was in any way a response to her non-standard and, in some respects, problematic personal life. It is important to differentiate between the two: Marie Colvin was a brilliant and determined journalist *and*, arguably, she had an unstable personal life. It is not that 'work saved her' as Hilsum suggests a few times. Work has been a constant theme in Colvin's life and it was the men who, to put it brutally, were at times disposable items in the larger narrative of her life. Worse still, in Hilsum's account Colvin becomes an aging woman who had done everything to create a family for Richard and he, in return, just betrayed her again, as some other men in her life had done.

The legend I would like to contribute to writing to then, as Delehaye would have it, was never a victim. All her life she strove to do things her way, both professionally and personally, at times in ways which were controversial. If anything as the 'other' woman in Richard Flaye's relationship with my friend, she was indeed the dangerous and powerful femme fatale. I can state with the utmost conviction that Marie Colvin remained extremely attractive, powerful and independently minded to the end. I am also convinced that when she got back together with Richard again, it wasn't 'different' or 'sad' or 'a compromise' of some unfortunate kind. I refute this narrative and instead offer that they loved each other and so they wanted to be together however hard it was – and it was extremely hard for Richard too: the long absences, the not knowing if she would come back, the anxieties lasting for weeks and months. He was one of the few men in her life who accepted and loved her as she was and did not try and change her, his own demons notwithstanding. Richard and his kids offered something to Marie Colvin that had so far eluded her: a consistent sense of what a family life might be like, the warmth, the conflicts, the dinners, the parties – and she did respond to it, and very much embraced it, without giving up the core of who she was. That was a gift that to my mind in the end did override everything else in her decision to go back to Richard. I challenge Hilsum's suggestion that Marie was attracted to Richard because he was 'very rich' (ibid.: 292), and this description has always jarred with me when reading this narrative. Wealth is relative but this was no 'prince charming' fairy tale here. Richard Flaye is an Oxford and Harvard educated well-to-do self-made businessman but I doubt that he could be called 'very rich' in comparison to Colvin who herself was pretty wealthy by most people's standards, and certainly financially independent as the star correspondent for the *The Sunday Times*. From my perspective I understood their attraction to each other as an overwhelming sense of finding a soul mate, somebody who would understand each other's demons and tolerate them. As far as I knew she even considered marriage – but there was no chance to take it further.

And if there had been shades of the femme fatale in her life, then I will take it gladly, as I am sure she would, rather than accepting this other narrative of a confused and weakened female, not the potent charismatic beauty any more. This was not the Marie I knew and admired. Yes, she had the PTSD but by the time she went to Syria, she was well enough again and driven by her desire to bear witness. Marie Colvin went back to war because she felt that was her job to carry on, no matter what. The very last thing she said to Richard in an email was indeed 'I love you deeply'. It is interesting to note in passing that in the feature film *A Private War* the part of Richard is minimal, changed beyond any recognition, including altering his name. I suspect as the film would have been 'lawyered' heavily, the producers were advised to make her last lover less important and less recognisable for legal reasons. Once again, this time through omission, her choices are minimised. Once again the complexities of her lived life are marginalised in favour of the narrative simplifications that so often, and for so long, have framed and minimised and sanitised the lives of women unafraid to transgress the bounds of patriarchal structures.

Coda

I was invited to Marie's memorial service in Hammersmith at St Peter's Church and then at the Corinthian Club on the river, the memorial that Lindsey Hilsum mentions in her book too. I was not there with Richard, but Richard was there, and his daughter Ella, so we were hanging out together a little at the reception afterwards. Marie's family looked at me dimly, wondering if I too was one of Richard's girlfriends. For the avoidance of doubt, I have never had any romantic or sexual attachment to Richard Flaye but I do consider him still an excellent friend.

I was driving on the M1 on 22 February 2012 when I heard on the news that Marie Colvin was killed in Syria. I pulled in to the sideway and cried. Somehow I thought she would never die, but she did, damn it. She was not indestructible after all. As the reports poured in, her mother Rosemarie's voice dominated the proceedings, and was heard loud and clear, despite the pain: 'She was totally, totally committed to what she did, and the importance of telling the story and writing it, and getting it to the world. That was her life' (Colvin, in Swain 2012: 529).

The tall and striking Marie Colvin with her pirate-like eye patch whom I bumped into cycling on the river near Hammersmith was funny and warm and never ordinary. I tried not to like her to begin with, as I felt I ought to be angry for her role in the breakup of my friend's and Richard's relationship. That was not possible. Marie Colvin's charisma, her intelligence and, yes, her beauty, were staggering. I remember telling her in 2009 that I was beginning a PhD at Birkbeck. 'Oh man', she said, 'but what about your life in the field? Will you be OK?' And we both had a laugh about me giving something up that she would not consider possible. My friend Richard 'got' her in ways which are exceptional in any relationship and which in the legend I tell override all other issues.

Figure 10.4 Marie Colvin on a river walk in Hammersmith near her home in 2010. Image courtesy of Richard Flaye.

And Marie Colvin? Taken out by the extreme patriarchal government of President Assad she did sacrifice everything after all, however unsaintly she was in other respects. She stayed faithful to her mission, to the end, no matter what. She never succumbed to the fear, she never gave up her power and somehow, through her courage and her transgressions, managed to hold onto her freedom.[3]

Notes

1. Said (1979) quotes from Gramsci and points out that: 'The starting point of critical elaboration is the consciousness of what one really is, and is "loving thyself" as a product of the historical process to date, which has deposited in you an infinity of traces, without leaving an inventory' (ibid.: 25). He goes on to say: 'The only available English translation inexplicably leaves Gramsci's comment at that, whereas in fact Gramsci's Italian text concludes by adding: 'therefore it is imperative at the outset to compile such an inventory' (ibid.: 25). The section about inventory is missing from the English versions of the text.
2. While Irigaray finds Antigone more straightforwardly a feminist figure challenging the patriarchal might, Butler focuses on Antigone in her act of transgressing both gender norms and kinship norms (2003: 6), and proposes that Antigone's act is 'contingency' and not 'an immutable necessity' (ibid.).
3. My sincere thanks to Richard Flaye, for his engagement in this process of reflecting on Marie Colvin's legacy, and for his permission to reproduce a number of images of Marie from his private photography collection.

Works Cited

Bal, Mieke (ed.) (2006) *The Artemisia Files*. Chicago: University of Chicago Press.
Brenner, Marie (2012) 'Marie Colvin's Private War', *Vanity Fair*, 18 July <https://www.vanityfair.com/news/politics/2012/08/marie-colvin-private-war> (last accessed 10 February 2020).
Bronfen, Elisabeth (2004) '*Femme fatale*: Negotiations of Tragic Desire', *New Literary History*, 35 (1), pp. 103–16.
Butler, Judith (1990) *Gender Trouble: Feminism and the Subversion of Identity*. London and New York: Routledge.
Butler, Judith (2003) *Antigone's Claim: Kinship Between Life and Death*. New York: Columbia University Press.
Clinton, Hillary R. (2017) *What Happened*. New York: Simon & Schuster.
Conroy, Paul (2013) *Under the Wire: Marie Colvin's Final Assignment*. New York: Weinstein Books.
Copjec, Joan (ed.) (1993) *Shades of Noir: A Reader*. New York: Verso.

Cowie, Elizabeth (1993) 'Film Noir and Women', in Joan Copjec (ed.), *Shades of Noir: A Reader*. New York: Verso, pp. 121–66.
Cowie, Elizabeth (1997) *Representing the Woman: Cinema and Psychoanalysis*. London: Macmillan.
Doane, Mary Ann (1991) *Femmes Fatales: Feminism, Film Theory, Psychoanalysis*. New York: Routledge.
Delehaye, Hippolyte (1961) [1907] *The Legends of the Saints: An Introduction to Hagiography*, trans. V. M. Crawford. Notre Dame, IN: University of Notre Dame Press.
Farrimond, Katherine (2017) *The Contemporary Femme Fatale: Gender, Genre and American Cinema*. London and New York: Routledge.
Freud, Sigmund (1997) *Writings on Art and Literature*. Stanford, CA: Stanford University Press.
Geertz, Clifford (1988) *Works and Lives: The Anthropologist as Author*. Stanford, CA: Stanford University Press.
Gramsci, Antonio (1982) *Selections from the Prison Books*, trans. Quentin Hoare and Geoffrey Nowell Smith. London: Lawrence & Wishart.
Grant, Catherine (2000) 'Secret Agents: Feminist Theories of Women's Film Authorship' <https://catherinegrant.org/secret_agents/> (last accessed 22 June 2018).
Gray, Emma (2016) 'How "Nasty Woman" Became a Viral Call for Solidarity', *Huffington Post*, 21 October <http://www.huffingtonpost.co.uk/entry/nasty-woman-became-a-call-of-solidarity-for-women-voters_us_5808f6a8e4b02444efa20c92> (last accessed 22 June 2018).
Haraway, Donna (1988) 'Situated Knowledges: The Science Question in Feminism and the Privilege of Partial Perspective', *Feminist Studies*, 14 (3), pp. 575–99.
Harrod, Mary (2018) *Women Do Genre in Film and Television*. London and New York: Routledge.
Hilsum, Lindsey (2018) *In Extremis: The Life of War Correspondent Marie Colvin*. London: Vintage.
Hilsum, Lindsey (2019) 'Marie Colvin's verdict gives meaning to her death', *The Guardian*, 3 February <https://www.theguardian.com/media/2019/feb/03/marie-colvin-murder-verdict--risks-journalists-lindsey-hilsum> (last accessed 10 February 2020).
Honig, Bonnie (2013) *Antigone Interrupted*. Cambridge: Cambridge University Press.
Irigaray, Luce (1985) [1971] *The Speculum of the Other Woman*, trans. G. C. Gill. Ithaca, NY: Cornell University Press.
Irigaray, Luce (1991) 'Questions to Emmanuel Lévinas on the Divinity of Love', in Robert Bernasconi and Simon Critchley (eds), *Re-reading Lévinas*, trans. by M. Whitford. London: Athlone Press, pp. 109–18.
Irigaray, Luce and Whitford, Margaret (eds) (1997) [1991] *The Irigaray Reader*. Oxford: Blackwell.

Johnston, Claire (ed.) (1973) *Notes on Women's Cinema*. London: Society for Education in Film and Television.
Johnston, Elizabeth (2016) 'The original "Nasty Woman"', *The Atlantic*, 6 November <https://www.theatlantic.com/entertainment/archive/2016/11/the-original-nasty-woman-of-classical-myth/506591/> (last accessed 20 October 2017).
Lacan, Jacques (1992) [1959–60] *Seminar VII. The Ethics of Psychoanalysis 1959–1960*, trans. D. Potter. London: Taylor & Francis.
Mérimée, Prosper (1980) *Carmen*. Paris: Bordas.
Mulvey, Laura (1975) 'Visual Pleasure and Narrative Cinema', *Screen*, 16 (3), pp. 6–18.
Muncey, Tessa (2010) *Creating Autoethnographies*. Portland, OR: Sage.
Piotrowska, Agnieszka (2014) *Psychoanalysis and Ethics in Documentary Film*. London: Routledge.
Piotrowska, Agnieszka (2019) *The Nasty Woman and the Neo Femme Fatale in Contemporary Cinema*. London: Routledge.
Piotrowska, Agnieszka (2017) *Black and White: Cinema, Arts and the Politics in Zimbabwe*. London: Routledge.
Piotrowska, Agnieszka (2020) *Creative Practice Research in the Age of Neoliberal Hopelessness*. Edinburgh: Edinburgh University Press.
Ricchiardi, Sherry (2001) 'Highway to the Danger Zone', *American Journalism Review*, 22 (3), pp. 42–9.
Said, Edward (2003) [1979] *Orientalism*. New York: Vintage Books.
Showalter, Elaine (1985) 'Representing Ophelia: Women, Madness, and the Responsibilities of Feminist Criticism', in Patricia A. Parker and Geoffrey H. Hartman (eds), *Shakespeare and the Question of Theory*. London: Methuen, pp. 77–94.
Silverman, Kaja (1988) *The Acoustic Mirror: The Female Voice in Psychoanalysis and Cinema*. Bloomington, IN: Indiana University Press.
Smith, Sidonie (1993) *Subjectivity, Identity and the Body: Women's Autobiographical Practices in the Twentieth Century*. Minneapolis, MN: University of Minnesota Press.
Soler, Colette (2006) *What Lacan Said About Women: A Psychoanalytic Study*, trans. John Holland. New York: Other Press.
Swain, Jon (2012) 'Marie Colvin: The Last Assignment', in *On the Front Line: The Collected Journalism of Marie Colvin*. London: HarperPress, pp. 529–39.
Warner, Marina (2014) *Once Upon a Time: A Short History of Fairy Tale*. Oxford: Oxford University Press.
Young, Iris Marion (1990) 'Abjection and Oppression: Dynamics of Unconscious Racism, Sexism, and Homophobia', in Arleen B. Dallery and Charles E. Scott with P. Holley Roberts (eds), *Crises in Continental Philosophy*. New York: Suny Press, pp. 201–14.
Zajko, Vanda and Leonard, Miriam (eds) (2006) *Laughing with Medusa: Classical Myth and Feminist Thought*. Oxford: Oxford University Press.
Žižek, Slavoj (1989) *The Sublime Object of Ideology*. London: Verso.

Index

absolutists, 42, 65; *see also* conscientious objectors
activism, 156, 159, 162–3, 166
  female, 156
  political, 10, 157
activist filmmakers, 161
Afghanistan, 1, 131, 135, 137–8
agency, 7, 10, 21, 30, 40, 77, 129, 131, 179, 181
  ante mortem, 20
  destructive, 140
  female, 31
  political, 15
agents, 31, 100–1, 176
  secret service, 83
Aleppo, 152–4, 160–4, 167
alignment, 16, 28–9, 138
allies, 8–9, 14, 18–19, 76, 79, 83, 99, 102, 109, 130, 153
altruism, 161, 166
ambiguity, 17, 30, 33
ambivalence, 32, 77
American Sniper, 6, 148
American war literature, 137, 139
analogy, 17, 51, 57, 111
anti-authoritarian, 109, 124
anti-communist, 97, 99
antifascist, 77, 79, 108, 112–13

Antigone, 178–81, 185
anti-Semitic, 87, 94
anti-war, 15, 30, 62, 118, 120, 130
Arab Spring, 152
archetype, 140, 178–9, 181–2
architectures of enmity, 2–3, 7
archives, 30, 43, 56, 72, 113
Arendt, Hannah, 11, 82
audiovisual media, 1, 6
authenticity, 4, 21, 102–3, 146
autobiography, xii, 36
AWOL, 103, 135, 138–41, 145–6, 148

ban, 15, 25–6, 30; *see also* censorship
Basehart, Richard, 101, 104, 108
Bashar al-Assad, 10, 152–7, 160–3, 177
battle, 57, 62–3, 66, 97, 104, 122, 124, 127–9, 132, 139, 143–4
Bauer, Fritz, 75–96
BBC, 20, 55–9, 61–2, 65, 67, 70–1, 74, 82
Bergdahl, Sergeant Bowe, 141–2, 144, 148–9
betrayal, 3, 5, 9, 77, 80, 83–4, 91, 103, 122, 155, 176

bible, the, 64, 125–6, 129, 132
binaries, 15–16, 138–9, 141
biography, 45, 51, 89, 122, 171, 174
Bleasdale, Alan, 58, 60
Blech, Hans Christian, 101, 104
Bolsonaro, Jair, 4
bombardment, 49, 152–54, 160, 162, 164
borders, 2, 4, 7, 146–7, 158, 163
boundaries, 3, 16–17, 25, 37, 44, 46, 55, 97, 135–6, 171, 185
bravery, 111, 138–9, 178, 183, 185
Brexit, 5, 51
British imperialism, 41, 47–50

Cenotaph, 64
censorship, 25–6, 35, 113, 136; *see also* ban
centenary, xi–xii, 37, 70
Channel 4, 57–8, 65, 162, 167
child, xii, 10, 23–5, 35, 39, 104, 106–7, 152–3, 155, 157, 159–64
Christianity, 58, 64, 69, 103, 107, 112, 119, 121–2, 124–7, 129–30, 132
cinema, x, 1–2, 6, 19, 117, 131, 173, 178
  early, 182
  international, 81
  national, 6
  popular, xi, 20
civilian, 16–17, 20, 29, 45, 101, 103, 139, 143–4, 159; *see also* noncombatant
class, x, 7–8, 19, 38, 45, 57, 63, 76, 89, 125, 156

Cold War, 43, 78, 80, 83–6, 93, 97–9, 108, 111, 140
colonialism, 1, 50
Colvin, Marie, 11, 171, 173–4, 176–8, 180–7
combatants, 16–17, 138
commemoration, 14, 31, 37, 39, 48, 54, 57, 61, 63, 70–1
community, 2, 6–7, 46, 76–7, 93, 98, 122, 124–5, 128, 138, 155
conscientious collaborator, 127
conscientious objection, 6, 8–9, 38, 41–6, 48–50, 54–5, 61, 64–6, 70–1, 117, 120–1
consensus, 96
containment, 85, 117, 120–1, 131
contemporaneity, 38–41, 44, 46–7, 50–1
counter-narratives, 1, 55, 70
courage, 54, 56, 65, 79, 81, 128, 136, 139–40, 189
cowardice, 6, 42–3, 54–5, 62, 64–6, 70, 104, 136–41, 145, 147–8
curation, x, 8, 38–40, 51, 186

Daqneesh, Omran, 160, 168
dead bodies, representation of, 17, 33–4, 161–2, 164
death, 10, 12, 14, 20, 24–5, 28–9, 31–2, 55–6, 62–4, 98–9, 105, 160–3, 167, 177, 179–82
Decision before Dawn, 9, 97–8, 100, 102, 106–9
defector, 9
defectors, 9, 99, 112
demilitarisation, 20, 108
democracy, 2, 76, 79–81, 84, 88–9, 93, 109–10, 121, 126, 129

denazification, 76, 90, 97
Der Staat gegen Fritz Bauer, 75, 88, 92
deserters, 6, 9–10, 54–5, 62, 70, 98–9, 102, 105, 135, 138–41, 145–6
destabilisation, 3, 138, 148
Die Akte General / The General, 90, 92, 95
disobedience, 6, 21, 28, 55, 98, 112
documentary film, xi, 55–6, 58, 61, 63, 65, 67, 71–2, 152, 154, 156, 161–3, 166, 173–4
documentary realism, 19
dominant ideas, 3, 55, 70, 172

Eichmann, Adolf, 81–2
emigrant, 77–8
emigrants, 77
enemy, 1–2, 5, 8, 15–17, 21–2, 27–8, 31, 48, 50–1, 80, 98, 111, 114, 118–19, 138
  national, 16, 46
enemy soldiers, 29, 128
erasure, 18, 26
espionage, 5, 106, 110–11
ethics, 40, 111, 166
Europe, xii, 2, 4, 6, 22–3, 51, 92, 109, 111, 152, 154, 156, 158, 160–1, 166–7
execution, 14, 16–19, 25–9, 32, 63–4, 66, 78, 110
exile, 82, 88, 157, 167

faith, 10, 118–19, 121, 124, 126, 132
Falkland Islands, 57–8

family, 42, 63–4, 87–8, 90, 93, 105, 107, 124–6, 128, 146, 152, 155–9, 179, 183, 185–6
fear, 4
female subjectivity, 171, 173–4
femininity, 14, 25, 33, 156, 183
feminism, 33, 178, 180
feminist autobiography, 11, 177
femme fatale, 174, 177–80, 182–3, 186–7
fictionalisation, 14, 18, 92
film, ix–xii, 10, 14–15, 19, 21–2, 26, 28, 30–1, 76–7, 81–94, 96–8, 101–2, 105–12, 117–18, 120–6, 128–33, 143–9, 155–7, 159, 162–5
  anti-war, 15
  mainstream, 10, 82, 133
  postwar, 9
  war, xii, 19, 25, 117
film form, 26, 28
film genre, 84
film history, 25, 31, 35
filmmaker, citizen, 153
filmmakers, 9, 19, 75, 81–2, 148, 152–3, 157, 159, 167, 174, 178
First Word War, x–xi, 6–9, 14–16, 31, 35, 38–9, 43–6, 54–8, 61, 63–6, 70–1, 117, 119, 124–5, 131–2; *see also* Great War, the
First World War Galleries, 38–41, 43–4, 46–9, 52
flashbacks, 68, 102, 124, 127
Flaye, Richard, ix, 172, 175–7, 179, 181, 184–9
foreigner, 16, 98
foreign policy, 4, 149, 160
For Sama, 10, 152–4, 161, 166

framing, 26–7, 154–5, 159, 178, 184
  cultural, 81, 174
Frankfurt Auschwitz Trials (1963–5), 75, 84, 111, 115
freedom, 22, 55, 80, 101, 110, 125, 129, 153–4, 159, 182, 189
Freiwillige Selbstkontrolle der Filmwirtschaft (FSK), 111, 114
fugitive, 14, 21–2, 25, 27, 147

Gandhi, Mahatma, 41, 44
gender, 7–8, 10, 18–20, 89, 135–6, 148, 174
gendered fears, 137, 145
gender norms, 11, 135, 138, 141, 156, 159, 163, 189
generation, 19, 45, 61, 84–5, 87, 89, 91, 129, 139, 174
Geneva Conventions, 17, 101
genre;, ix, 6, 77, 81, 84–6, 120, 122, 136; *see also* film genre
geopolitics, 1, 3, 111
good German archetype, 97, 99, 104–5, 107, 110, 113
government, 4–5, 19, 43, 64, 80, 84, 126, 153, 189
graves, 28, 63–4, 120, 166
Great War
  the, 39, 42, 54–6, 61, 63, 65, 71; *see also* First World War
Great War, The, BBC series, 55–6, 65, 71
guilt, 56, 76, 79, 85, 88, 92, 105, 127, 139

Hacksaw Ridge, 6, 10, 117, 121–2, 124, 128–30, 134
Haig, Field Marshall Sir Douglas, 58, 61–2
Hassan, Raghda, 11, 157–9, 169
hate, 16, 78, 110
Hate film debate (Hetzfilmdebatte), 25
hegemonic masculinity, 133, 135–7, 141, 143–44, 147, 149
heroism, 20, 30, 77, 97, 99, 112, 138, 140–1, 143, 174, 181
heterosexual, 87, 90, 136
High Commission for Germany (HICOG), 108–9, 113–14
high treason, 98–9, 110; *see also* Hochverrat
Hilsum, Lindsey, 174, 176–8, 181–7, 190
historians, 40, 44, 57, 71, 75–6, 174
historical representation, 6, 25, 81–2, 93, 178
historiography, 9, 38–40, 44, 58
history, x–xi, 2, 7–8, 15, 33–4, 39, 41–2, 57, 60, 64–5, 78, 81, 125
  national, 71, 77, 81
  oral, 53, 57, 71, 73
Hitler, Adolf, 78, 89, 98, 103, 108, 110
Hochverrat, 86, 98; *see also* high treason, treason
Hollywood, xi, 99–101, 104–5, 108, 110, 120, 130–2, 135, 141, 173, 180
Holocaust, 81–2, 85, 88, 92–3
home, 39, 42–3, 45–6, 50, 67–9, 94, 97, 109, 126, 128, 155–6, 160, 163

homophobia, 4, 93, 191
homosexuality, 81, 86–7, 89–91, 93, 136, 145
Homs, 152–4, 161, 173, 185
honour, 121–2, 128–9, 139
honour killings, 167
hospital, 31, 66, 102, 124, 146, 160, 162–3, 165
Howe, George, 100
humanitarian, 153, 156, 159, 167
human rights, 153, 155, 168
human shields, 98
hypermasculinity;, 137, 147–8; *see also* masculinity

idealism, 110, 141
ideals, 10, 100–1, 181
identity, 54–5, 58, 71, 76, 81, 83, 92, 118, 132, 146–7
identity formation, 7, 15
ideology, 15, 117, 120, 128, 130
ignorance, 4, 46, 94
immigration;, 2; *see also* migrant, emigrant
imperialism, 20, 40, 47–8, 50
Imperial War Museum, 8, 37–9, 41, 43–4, 47–9, 51, 56, 73
imprisonment, 65, 88, 167; *see also* incarceration
incarceration, 157; *see also* imprisonment
India, 4, 41, 49
indifference, 87, 122
injury, collective, 2
insubordination, 18, 31, 79, 89
intelligence, 5, 21, 33, 90, 100
internationalism, 112
intertitles, 15, 20, 27–8, 30

interwar years, 8, 33, 43–4, 93
introspection, 124, 158
Iraq, 1, 10, 131, 135, 137–8, 142–4, 146–7, 184
Iraq War, 9, 43, 142, 148
Ireland, 21, 47–8, 53
Irish independence, 47–8
Irish republicanism, 8, 38, 41, 47–9, 51, 67
irony, 58, 63, 104
Islamist groups, 161, 167
isolationist, 2, 50
Israel, 1, 81–2, 90
Italy, 69, 139, 183
ITV, 65–7

Japan, 121, 128–9, 132, 140
Al-Jazeera news channel, 156
Jenks, Chris, 3, 7, 10, 16, 37–8, 45, 47, 76–7, 80, 138
Jews, xi, 69, 77, 98, 105, 132
jingoism, 141, 144, 148
Johnson, Boris, 4
journalism, 2, 75, 112, 153–4, 162, 166–7, 173–4, 177, 182–6
judgements, 28, 39–40, 64, 79, 110, 181
jurisdiction, 75, 79
jurisprudence, 98
jurist, 9, 78
jus in bello, 16; *see also* legitimacy
justice, 9, 27, 34, 75, 79, 81, 84, 87–8, 91, 112
juxtaposition, 22, 27, 32, 163–5

al-Kateab, Waad, 10, 156, 162–8
killing, 16–17, 29, 32, 128–9, 132, 144, 146, 153, 158, 173

Knef, Hildegard, 106
knowledge, 48, 71, 83, 124, 171, 173, 176
Korean War, 140
Kurdi, Alan, 160, 167
Kyle, Chris, 148

labels, 6, 11, 137–8, 172
labour, 21, 42, 65, 100
Landesverrat (national treason), 86, 98, 111–12; *see also* traitor
landscape, 57, 126
language, 5, 63
laws, 3–5, 8, 35, 54, 78–81, 89–90, 98, 112, 119, 135
  ethical, 111
  international, 22, 155
  martial, 21, 29, 32, 48
  peacetime, 16
League of Nations, 19, 25
Lebanon, 157–8
legacies, xi–xii, 2, 6, 16, 32, 124, 177
legality, 19, 63, 78–9, 85, 90, 99, 112; *see also* legislation
legend, 173–6, 186, 188
legislation, 5, 19, 167; *see also* legality
legitimacy, 10, 15, 26, 48, 50, 103, 154; *see also* jus in bello
liberation, 101, 112, 156
liminal status, 15, 31
Litvak, Anatole, 9, 101, 104, 106–7, 111
location, 16, 19, 22, 30, 103, 113, 171
London, 56, 65
loneliness, 45, 86, 184

loss, 2, 50, 57, 65, 76, 93, 152, 165
loyalty, 5, 22, 88, 94, 97, 102, 112, 137, 140–1, 143, 145

McAllister, Sean, 11–12, 152, 157–9
McCarthyism, 97, 99, 103
manhood, 67, 137, 139, 141, 143; *see also* masculinity
marriage, 66, 122, 156, 167, 187
martyrdom, 14, 29–30, 32
masculine heroism, 135, 138
masculinity, 10, 42, 129, 135–6, 138–40, 143, 147–8
  soldierly, 10, 136, 143, 145
  traditional, 10, 136–7, 148
masquerade, 83, 139, 161
media, x, 5, 10, 26, 71, 136, 184
  mass, 119
  social, 153
media representations, xii, 162
medic, 103, 105, 120, 122, 127, 162
memorialisation, x, 17–18, 54, 57, 65, 71–2, 78, 187
memory, x, xii, 23, 26, 54, 57–8, 61, 65, 70, 72, 78, 82, 92
  public, x, 19, 71, 96
memory boom, 61, 70
mercy, 22, 63, 119
Middle East, 157
migrants, 4
militarism, 16, 19, 23, 25, 44, 136
military, 10, 17–18, 21, 62–4, 66, 110, 112, 117, 119, 130, 132, 135–41, 144–5, 147, 160–1
military action, 1, 3, 79, 129–30
military conflict, 6–7

military executions, 63
military masculinities, 136–7, 143
Miners' Strike, 57, 59
Modi, Narendra, 4
Monocled Mutineer, The, BBC series, 58–60, 65, 67
morality, 9, 17, 54, 69, 77, 85–9, 91, 97, 119–20, 137, 140
Mossad, 84, 87, 90
motherhood, 64, 66, 122, 124, 126, 146, 152, 159, 162–4, 178–9, 184
motif, 17, 60
motivations, 22, 101, 177
movement
  anti-nuclear, 43
  civil rights, 119
murder, 55, 63, 105, 155
museums, x, 2, 37–40, 43–4, 46–7, 49–50, 75
music, xi, 30, 57, 61
mutiny, 6, 8–9, 54–5, 57–8, 60, 70
myth, 8, 20, 30, 37–8, 49, 61, 126, 129, 173–6

narration, 1, 8, 28, 30, 49, 56, 72, 82, 118, 153, 187
narratives, 7–8, 30, 32, 37, 44, 47, 49–50, 54, 65, 81–3, 173, 176–7, 180
  cultural, 2, 8, 11, 38, 44, 47, 55, 61, 70
nasty woman concept, 171, 174, 177–8, 180, 182
nation, 2, 8–9, 19, 25, 41, 46, 72, 77, 98–9, 118, 120, 146–8, 155
national identity, 2, 6, 18, 38, 40, 43, 49, 71, 97, 135–37, 147–8

nationalism, 2, 4–5, 20, 80, 97, 105, 112, 118–19, 130
National Socialism, 80, 85, 98, 115
Nazi crimes, 78–9, 82–4, 87, 93
Nazism, 50–1, 75–80, 82–3, 85–8, 91–4, 97–8, 100, 103–5, 108, 115, 130
NBC, 138, 150
necrophilia, 17
Netherlands, 14, 25–6
news media, 12, 33, 36, 129, 160–2, 167, 185, 188
new woman, 17, 32
nihilism, 45
non-combatant, 17, 44, 65
norms, 1, 4, 10, 47, 50, 79–80, 131, 135, 139, 172, 174
North American, 152, 154, 156, 160–1, 166–7
nostalgia, 49, 110, 139
novelisation, 15, 19, 21–5
nurse, 8, 14, 17–18, 22, 28, 30–2, 56, 66, 124

objection, 8, 37, 41–2, 80, 103, 117
occupation, 8, 16–17, 20–1, 26, 76, 89, 97, 99
offences, 32, 62, 78–9, 85–6, 111
Office of Strategic Services; *see* OSS
officer, 18, 22, 27–8, 31, 38, 46, 58–9, 63, 66, 125, 127
opposition, 2, 16, 25, 79–80, 111, 161
Orbán, Viktor, 4

Orientalism, 13, 191
OSS (Office of Strategic Services), 100–1, 103–6, 110

Pacific War, 133
pacifism, 6, 8, 10, 42–3, 45, 59, 61, 98, 100, 113, 117–18, 120–32
Palestine, 1, 157–8, 177
parents, 10, 153, 156, 160–6; *see also* family; see also motherhood
Patch, Harry, 61, 71
patriarchal structures, 20, 174, 180, 182–3, 187, 189
patriotism, 19, 29–31, 42, 77, 108–9, 113, 144
peace, 22–3, 43–5, 119, 130, 139
peace movement, 8, 15, 22, 43–4
Peaky Blinders, 67–70
Pelosi, Nancy, 5
Pentagon, 4
People Power: Fighting for Peace exhibition, 43–4, 46
perception, 6, 8, 10, 63, 75, 180–1
perpetrators, 1–2, 20, 24, 37, 76, 83, 85–6
persecution, 94, 99
perspective, 8–10, 33, 61–2, 82–3, 119, 128, 162, 187
philosophy, 44, 101
photography, ix–x, 43, 45, 67, 157, 172, 174
pity, 21–2, 63, 161
plot, 78, 82, 84, 91, 135
poetry, 46, 54, 61, 66, 179
polarisation, 2, 4, 10
police, 57, 69, 84, 89, 153

political allegiance, 5, 7–8, 59, 89, 101, 110
political discourse, 4, 99, 131
political nonconformity, 78, 152
politicians, 3–6, 19, 26, 45, 120
politics, xi, 20, 22–3, 37, 55, 59–60, 80, 104, 163, 171
postcolonial melancholia, 50–2
post traumatic stress disorder (PTSD), 47, 173, 187
postwar, 17, 19, 25, 82, 86, 89, 91, 94, 97
prisoners, 14, 21, 42, 48, 97, 119, 132, 158–9
    political, 157–8
prisoners of war, 100–1, 140
Production Code Administration, 105
propaganda, 1, 6, 25, 27, 42, 119
prosecution, 21, 75, 78, 83–5, 138
protest, 2, 8, 37, 41, 43–6, 145, 152–3, 155–56, 159–60, 162, 166
psychoanalysis, 178
PTSD; *see* post traumatic stress disorder
public opinion, 1, 43, 55, 75–6, 92, 99, 141, 181
punishment, 17, 46, 55, 59, 63, 66, 85, 155–6, 179

Quakerism, 118, 125, 132

racial groups, 19, 57, 118, 136
racism, 4, 118–19
rape, 17, 155–6, 167
realism, 111, 113, 128, 146
rearmament, 99, 113

rebellion, 37, 41, 44, 47–8, 80, 98, 119, 153, 183
reconciliation, 21, 108, 127
reflexivity, 3, 10, 37, 40, 47, 172
regeneration, 75, 118
rehabilitation, 78, 97
religious pacifism, 10, 117–19, 121–2, 124–5, 127, 130–2
remembrance, 54, 57, 61, 64
Remer, Major-General Otto-Ernst, 98
resistance, 16, 21, 25, 38, 44, 46, 76, 78–80, 98–9, 104, 153, 155
revolution, 101, 106, 154–5, 158–9, 163
rhetoric, 3–4, 6, 11, 138, 141
right-wing groups, 59, 99, 141

sacrifice, 17, 20, 54, 56–7, 70, 72, 119, 127, 175, 180–2, 189
Said, Edward, 1, 176
saints, 174–5
Sassoon, Siegfried, 38, 41, 45–6
Second World War, 43, 49, 51, 75–6, 79, 82, 93, 99, 117–19, 129, 139–40
Sergeant York, 10, 117, 121–7, 130–2
sexuality, 7, 67, 87, 89, 91, 93, 180–1, 187
Shot at Dawn, 62–4, 74
situated knowledge, 171, 184, 190
Snowden, Edward, 5
Social Democrats, 77, 84, 88, 93
society, 4, 10, 16, 75, 77, 117, 121, 131, 136–7, 142, 147, 156

soldiers, 8, 10, 17–18, 27, 31–2, 38, 41–2, 45–7, 49, 56–62, 69, 98, 128–9, 135–40, 143–47
solidarity, 18, 43, 50, 94
Somme, 56–8, 62–3, 66, 69
sovereignty, 4, 14, 99
spectatorship, 1–2, 103, 113, 161, 165
Spiegel Affair, 79–80
spies, 16, 32, 36, 54, 103, 110; *see also* espionage
squad, firing, 18, 102
State Department, 113–14
stereotypes, 44, 105, 141, 157
Stop-Loss, 10, 135–6, 142–3, 145–8
style, classical Hollywood, 123, 128, 131
suffering, 2, 45, 67, 104, 160–1, 184–5
suicide, 158, 179
surrender, 48, 106, 121, 128
survival, 3, 20, 63, 65, 99, 118, 129, 183
suspicion, 24, 79, 104, 117
sympathy, 8, 48, 64, 101, 104, 119, 131
Syria, 10–11, 153–6, 158–9, 161, 166, 169, 173, 177, 181, 185, 187–8
Syrian Love Story, A, 11, 152, 154, 157–9
Syrian war, 10, 152–5, 157–64

taboo, 16, 111, 113, 140
television dramas, 31, 65, 70, 181
television news, 154, 161

testimony, 21, 40, 44, 55–6, 61, 71–2, 162
Tommies, 46, 54
traitor, 5–6, 75–8, 80–1, 86, 88, 97–9, 101–2, 106, 108, 113, 141, 145, 155
transgression, 3–11, 16–19, 27, 29–31, 44, 47–50, 54, 69–70, 75–7, 80–1, 119, 135–6, 138, 141–2, 146–8, 154–5, 189
  border, 4
  existential, 6
  figures of, 2–3, 7–8, 10, 15–16, 32, 37–8, 41, 54, 56–7, 62, 64, 69–70, 140–1, 155–6, 173
  historical, 54, 77
  humanitarian, 160
  personal, 152, 166
  political, 10, 81, 155, 157, 159, 162
  social, 4
transgressive acts, 8, 14, 16, 26, 56, 118, 125, 141, 145
trauma, 10, 47, 66, 82, 85, 91–2, 159–60
treachery, 3, 31, 55–6, 76, 98, 110–11
treason, ix, 5–6, 75–86, 89, 91, 98, 100–1, 108–9, 111–12, 138, 141

trial, 14, 16, 18–21, 27, 34, 78, 81–2, 85, 98
Trump, Donald, 4–5, 112, 178
Turkey, 158, 160, 163
Twentieth Century-Fox, 97, 99–100

veterans, 44, 55–6, 61, 68, 71–2, 104, 142
victimhood, 1–2, 24, 61, 64, 76, 80–1, 85, 88, 91–3, 165, 167, 183, 186
victory, 3, 25, 45, 49, 56, 105, 140
Vietnam War, 119, 138, 140, 142

war, ix–xi, 1–3, 6–10, 15–23, 25–6, 31–2, 39, 41–7, 49–50, 53–7, 61–72, 76–9, 87–9, 112–13, 117–21, 123–5, 130–2, 136–42, 144–8, 183–5
war films, 6, 10, 35, 117–20, 122, 127, 129, 131, 136, 142, 146
war hero, 122, 144, 171
war journalism, 11, 173–4, 177, 182, 190
war literature, 139
war poets, 35, 46, 50
western, the, x, 120

EU representative:
Easy Access System Europe
Mustamäe tee 50, 10621 Tallinn, Estonia
Gpsr.requests@easproject.com